Teach Yourself VISUALLY

MacBook®
3rd Edition

MacBook®
3rd Edition

by Guy Hart-Davis

Teach Yourself VISUALLY™ MacBook® 3rd Edition

Published by
John Wiley & Sons, Inc.
10475 Crosspoint Boulevard
Indianapolis, IN 46256

www.wiley.com

Published simultaneously in Canada

Library of Congress Control Number: 2016934101

ISBN: 978-1-119-25267-2

Manufactured in the United States of America

10 9 8 7 6 5 4 3 2

Trademark Acknowledgments

Contact Us

For general information on our other products and services please contact our Customer Care Department within the U.S. at 877-762-2974, outside the U.S. at 317-572-3993 or fax 317-572-4002.

For technical support please visit www.wiley.com/techsupport.

Sales | Contact Wiley at (877) 762-2974 or fax (317) 572-4002.

Credits

Acquisitions Editor
Aaron Black

Project Editor
Lynn Northrup

Technical Editor
Galen Gruman

Copy Editor
Lynn Northrup

Production Editor
Barath Kumar Rajasekaran

Manager, Content Development & Assembly
Mary Beth Wakefield

Vice President, Professional Technology Strategy
Barry Pruett

About the Author

Guy Hart-Davis is the author of *Teach Yourself VISUALLY iPad, 4th Edition; Teach Yourself VISUALLY iPhone 6s; Teach Yourself VISUALLY Android Phones and Tablets, 2nd Edition; Teach Yourself VISUALLY Apple Watch; Teach Yourself VISUALLY Samsung Galaxy S6; Teach Yourself VISUALLY iMac, 3rd Edition; Teach Yourself VISUALLY MacBook Pro, 2nd Edition; Teach Yourself VISUALLY MacBook Air; iMac Portable Genius, 4th Edition;* and *iWork Portable Genius, 2nd Edition*.

Author's Acknowledgments

My thanks go to the many people who turned my manuscript into the highly graphical book you are holding. In particular, I thank Aaron Black for asking me to write the book; Lynn Northrup for keeping me on track and skillfully editing the text; Galen Gruman for reviewing the book for technical accuracy and contributing helpful suggestions; and SPi Global for laying out the book.

How to Use This Book

Who This Book Is For

This book is for the reader who has never used this particular technology or software application. It is also for readers who want to expand their knowledge.

The Conventions in This Book

① Steps

This book uses a step-by-step format to guide you easily through each task. **Numbered steps** are actions you must do; **bulleted steps** clarify a point, step, or optional feature; and **indented steps** give you the result.

② Notes

Notes give additional information — special conditions that may occur during an operation, a situation that you want to avoid, or a cross reference to a related area of the book.

③ Icons and Buttons

Icons and buttons show you exactly what you need to click to perform a step.

④ Tips

Tips offer additional information, including warnings and shortcuts.

⑤ Bold

Bold type shows command names, options, and text or numbers you must type.

⑥ Italics

Italic type introduces and defines a new term.

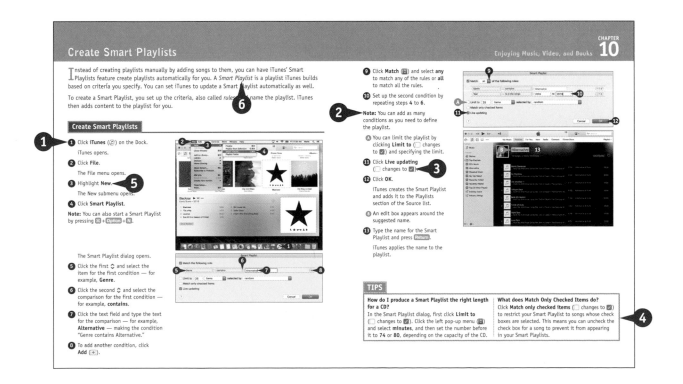

Table of Contents

Table of Contents

Chapter 6　Surfing the Web

Chapter 7　Sending and Receiving E-Mail

Table of Contents

Chapter 10 Enjoying Music, Video, and Books

Chapter 11 Making the Most of Your Photos

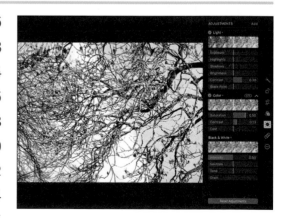

Table of Contents

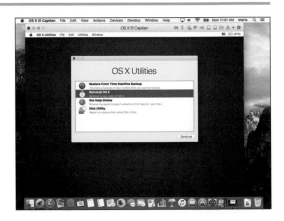

CHAPTER 1

Getting Started with Your MacBook

Apple's MacBook laptops are among the best portable computers you can get. The MacBook models — the powerful MacBook Pro, the lightweight MacBook Air, and the ultraportable 12-inch MacBook — enable you to work or play anywhere that suits you.

Each MacBook comes with OS X, Apple's easy-to-use operating system. This chapter shows you how to set up your MacBook, navigate the OS X interface, and perform essential actions.

Understanding the MacBook Models

MacBook is the family name for Apple's laptop computers. As of this writing, the MacBook family includes the MacBook Pro, the MacBook Air, and the MacBook usually called simply "MacBook" but also known as "12-inch MacBook" to distinguish it from the MacBook Air and MacBook Pro.

Each MacBook has similar core features, such as the display for viewing information and the keyboard and trackpad for entering data and controlling the computer. Beyond that, the MacBook models differ in various ways, from design, size, and weight to screen size, memory and storage capacity, and processor type and speed.

Identify Your MacBook's Main Features

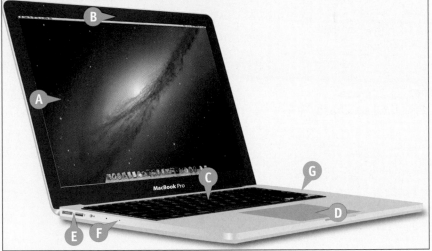

Ⓐ Display

The MacBook's display provides a sharp, bright, and colorful view into all that you do.

Ⓑ Camera

The built-in camera enables you to videoconference, take photos, and more.

Ⓒ Keyboard

Along with the standard letter and number keys, the keyboard provides function keys to control your MacBook. The keyboard has a backlight that illuminates automatically when you are using the MacBook in dim light, enabling you to see what you are doing.

Ⓓ Trackpad

The trackpad enables you to manipulate objects on the screen using finger gestures. The entire trackpad is also the button that you click or double-click to give commands. On some MacBook models, you can also use a pressing movement called *force-touch* or *3D touch* to access commands quickly.

Ⓔ Ports

The ports connect your MacBook to other devices, such as external drives, external displays, iPods, and so on. Different MacBook models have different ports.

Ⓕ Microphones

The microphones enable you to use your MacBook for audio and video calls without needing to connect a headset.

Ⓖ Speakers

The speakers enable you to listen to music or other audio.

Meet Your MacBook's Keyboard

A Brightness

Press **F1** to decrease your screen's brightness or **F2** to increase it.

B Mission Control

Press **F3** to open Mission Control so you can quickly move between working spaces.

C Launchpad

Press **F4** to open or close the Launchpad.

D Keyboard Backlight Brightness

Press **F5** to decrease the brightness of the keyboard backlighting, or press **F6** to increase it.

E Previous/Rewind

Press **F7** to move to the previous item or rewind in iTunes and other applications.

F Play/Pause

Press **F8** to play or pause iTunes and other applications.

G Next/Fast Forward

Press **F9** to move to the next item or fast-forward in iTunes and other applications.

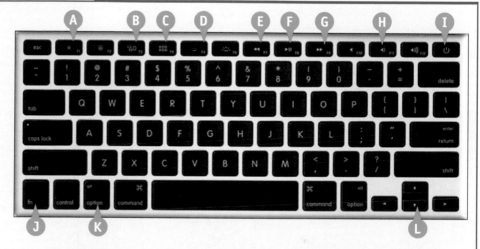

H Volume

Press **F10** to mute your MacBook, **F11** to turn the volume down, and **F12** to turn it up.

I Power Button

Press the Power button to turn on your MacBook; press and hold the Power button to force your MacBook to turn off.

J Alternate Function Key

Hold down the Alternate Function key while pressing a function key to perform the alternate task.

K Modifier Keys

Macs and OS X use four modifier keys that you press to enter capital letters or symbols or to invoke keyboard shortcuts. As usual, you press Shift (**Shift**) to type capital letters or the symbols that appear on the upper part of the keys. You press Command (**⌘**), Option (**Option**), and Control (**Control**) to give keyboard shortcuts.

L Arrow Keys

Press the arrow keys to move around the screen.

continued ▶

Each MacBook model includes two or more ports that enable you to connect other devices to it. For example, a Thunderbolt port enable you to connect external displays or drives to your MacBook, whereas a standard USB port enables you to connect any of a wide range of USB devices.

The selection of ports varies by MacBook family and by MacBook model: the 15-inch MacBook Pro has more ports than the 13-inch MacBook Pro, and the 13-inch MacBook Air has more ports than the 11-inch MacBook Air. The ultra-slim 12-inch MacBook has only two ports: a headphone port for connecting audio output devices and a USB-C port, which combines connectivity with the capability to charge the battery.

Identifying the Ports on Your MacBook

A MagSafe 2 Port

Connect the MacBook's power adapter to this port. The MagSafe 2 connector attaches magnetically, providing a secure connection but detaching easily if force is applied — for example, if someone's foot snags the power cord.

B Thunderbolt 2 Port

Use this high-speed port to connect external displays and Thunderbolt external drives to your MacBook. The port conforms to the Thunderbolt 2 connectivity standard developed by Apple but is backward compatible with the Thunderbolt 1 standard, so you can connect any Thunderbolt 1 or Thunderbolt 2 device to this port.

Thunderbolt uses the same connector size as Mini DisplayPort, a standard for connecting displays to computers.

The Thunderbolt port includes the Mini DisplayPort connections, so you can connect an external display via Thunderbolt.

You can link one Thunderbolt device to another, so you can run multiple devices off a single Thunderbolt port.

C USB Ports

Use these ports to connect USB devices — such as an iPhone, an external drive, or a printer — to your MacBook. The ports support USB 1.1, 2, and 3 versions, enabling you to connect a wide range of devices.

You can connect USB devices directly to the USB ports. If you need to connect multiple devices, connect a USB hub to a USB port on the MacBook, and then connect the devices to the ports on the hub.

D Analog/Digital Audio In/Out

This port looks like a standard analog headphone port, but it works for both analog and digital audio and combines audio output and audio input. For analog audio output, simply connect headphones or analog speakers. For digital audio output, use a TOSLINK cable to connect digital audio equipment, such as surround-sound speakers. For audio input, connect a microphone or other sound input device.

Identifying the Ports on Your MacBook (continued)

E SDXC Card Slot

You can insert SDHC, SDXC, and other types of SD cards here so you can store files or transfer files to or from your MacBook.

SDHC is the abbreviation for Secure Digital High Capacity. The SDHC standard uses the FAT32 file system and supports memory cards up to 32 gigabytes, 32GB.

SDXC is the abbreviation for Secure Digital eXtended Capacity. This is a newer standard that uses a different file system, Extended File Allocation Table or exFAT file, and supports memory cards of up to 2 terabytes, 2TB, which is equivalent to 2048GB. As of this

writing, 512GB is the highest-capacity SDXC card available.

The SDXC card slot accepts regular-size SD cards, which are 32mm × 24mm × 2.1mm. To use a miniSD card or a microSD card, get an adapter.

Standard-size SDXC cards protrude from the SDXC slot. This makes them easy to remove but even easier to damage if you leave them in the slot while transporting your MacBook. If you need to leave an SD card in the

slot, get a microSD card and a low-profile adapter such as those made by Baseqi.

F HDMI

You can connect an HDMI screen or TV to this port to display your MacBook's output on another screen. You can set the external screen or TV either to mirror what is shown on your MacBook's screen or to act as an extension of your MacBook's screen. See the section "Add a Second Display" in Chapter 2 for details.

G USB-C

You connect the MacBook's charger or a standard USB-C cable to this port. The port combines quick charging, data transfer at USB 3's high speeds, and video output.

For video output, you need to use an adapter such as Apple's USB-C Digital Apple TV Multiport

Adapter, which provides an HDMI port, a regular USB port, and a USB-C charging port.

Set Up Your MacBook

If you have just bought your MacBook, you need to set up OS X and create your user account before you can use it. Your user account is where you store your files and settings on the MacBook.

The first user account you create is an administrator account, which can create other accounts later for other users. You may also choose to create a personal account for yourself, leaving the administrator account strictly for administration.

Set Up Your MacBook

1 Position the MacBook on a desk or table and connect it its power supply.

2 Press the power button on your MacBook.

Note: On most MacBook models, the power button is at the upper-right corner of the keyboard.

The Welcome screen appears.

3 Click your country.

A Click **Show All** (☐ changes to ☑) if your country does not appear at first.

4 Click **Continue** (⊘).

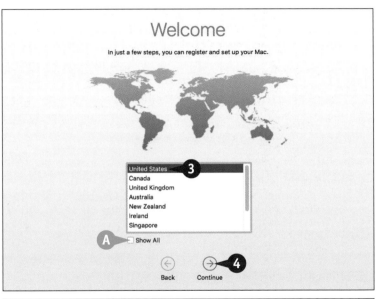

The Select Your Keyboard screen appears.

5 Click your keyboard layout; for example, **U.S.**

B Click **Show All** (☐ changes to ☑) if your keyboard layout does not appear at first.

6 Click **Continue** (⊘).

C You can click **Back** (⊖) at any stage in the setup process if you need to go back and change a choice you made.

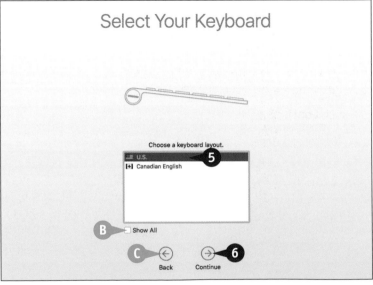

The Transfer Information to This Mac screen appears.

7 Click **Don't transfer any information now** (○ changes to ●).

Note: If you need to transfer data from another Mac or a backup, click **From a Mac, Time Machine backup, or startup disk** (○ changes to ●) and then click **Continue** (→). If you need to transfer data from Windows, click **From a Windows PC** (○ changes to ●) and click **Continue** (→).

8 Click **Continue** (→).

The Enable Location Services screen appears.

9 Click **Enable Location Services on this Mac** (☐ changes to ☑) if you want to use Location Services.

10 Click **Continue** (→).

The Sign In with Your Apple ID screen appears.

11 Click **Sign in with your Apple ID** (○ changes to ●).

12 Type your Apple ID.

13 Type your password.

Ⓓ You can click **Create new Apple ID** to create a new Apple ID.

Note: If you neither have nor want an Apple ID, click **Don't sign in** (○ changes to ●).

14 Click **Continue** (→).

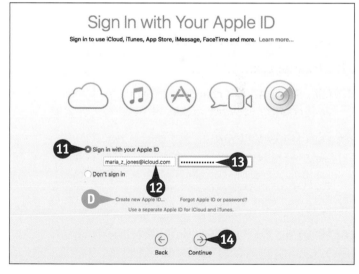

TIPS

Can I use a USB mouse with my MacBook?
Yes. You can use any USB mouse for which OS X has a software driver. To use a USB mouse, connect it to a USB port on your MacBook. If the pointer on the screen moves when you move the mouse, the mouse is working.

What is an Apple ID?
An Apple ID is a free online identity that you use for Apple services such as iCloud, the Mac App Store, and the iTunes Store. To get the most out of your MacBook, you should get an Apple ID.

continued ▶

When creating an account, you can use either your full name or a shortened version. You can edit the username that OS X suggests based on that name. You can choose whether to set a password hint to help yourself remember your password. You can also choose whether to use the iCloud Keychain feature, which enables you to store your passwords and credit-card details securely online. You can then use this information from any Mac, Windows PC, or iOS device with which you use the same Apple ID.

Set Up Your MacBook (continued)

The Terms and Conditions screen appears.

15 Click **Agree** (→).

A confirmation dialog opens.

16 Click **Agree** in the dialog.

The dialog closes.

The Create a Computer Account screen appears.

E Click **Use my iCloud account to log in** (☑ changes to ☐) if you do not want to log in via iCloud.

17 Change the account name that OS X suggests as needed.

18 Click the default picture and choose the picture you want. You can also use your MacBook's camera to take a photo of yourself.

19 Click **Set time zone based on current location** (☐ changes to ☑) to enable OS X to set the time and date automatically.

20 Click **Continue** (→).

The Allow iCloud to Use the Location of This Mac for Find My Mac? dialog opens.

21 Click **Allow** or **Not Now**, as needed.

The first iCloud Keychain screen appears.

22 Click **Set up iCloud Keychain** (○ changes to ◉) if you want to use iCloud Keychain.

23 Click **Continue** (→).

Note: If you clicked **Set Up iCloud Keychain**, type your iCloud security code and click **Continue** (→) on the second iCloud Keychain screen.

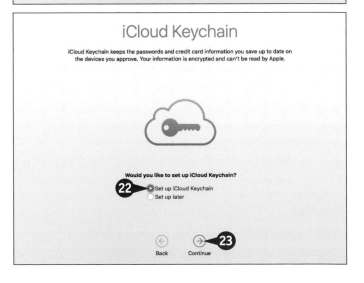

The Diagnostics & Usage screen appears.

24 Click **Send diagnostics & usage data to Apple** (☑ changes to ☐) if you do not want to send this data.

25 Click **Share crash data with app developers** (☑ changes to ☐) if you do not want to share data generated about apps that crash.

26 Click **Continue** (⊝).

The Setting Up Your Mac screen appears while OS X sets up your MacBook.

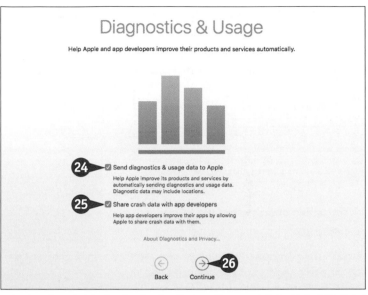

The OS X desktop appears, and you can start using your MacBook as explained in the rest of this book.

TIP

What is iCloud Keychain?

iCloud Keychain is a feature for storing sensitive data securely online so that you can use it on your Mac and your iOS devices. iCloud Keychain can store passwords for Wi-Fi networks, numbers and expiry dates for credit and debit cards, and passwords for websites. With your permission, Macs and iOS devices can access data in iCloud Keychain and use that data automatically for you. For example, the Safari browser can automatically enter your payment details in an online shopping form.

Start Your MacBook and Log In

When you are ready to start a computing session, start your MacBook and log in to OS X with the credentials for the user account you have set up or an administrator has created for you. After you start your MacBook, OS X loads and automatically displays the login screen by default or logs you in automatically. You can then select your username and type your password.

When you log in, OS X displays the desktop with your apps and settings.

Start Your MacBook and Log In

1 Press the power button on your MacBook.

A screen showing the list of users appears.

Note: Your MacBook may not display the list of users and login window. Instead, it may simply log you in automatically or show a different login screen. Chapter 12 shows you how to change this behavior.

Note: You may need to swipe right with two fingers on the trackpad to display your username. Alternatively, start typing the username to display it.

2 Click your username.

The login window appears.

3 Type your password in the Enter Password box.

A If you cannot remember your password, click **Hint** (?).

Ⓑ If your account is set to use your iCloud password, OS X displays a message telling you so. If the account has a local password with a password hint, OS X displays the password hint below the Enter Password box.

④ Type your password.

⑤ Click **Log In** (→).

Note: Instead of clicking **Log In** (→), you can press **Return**.

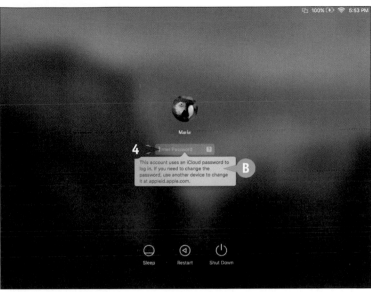

The MacBook displays your desktop, the menu bar, and the Dock. You can now start using the MacBook.

TIPS

Why does my MacBook go straight to the desktop instead of displaying the list of usernames?

Your MacBook is set to log in automatically. Logging in automatically is convenient when you are the only one who uses your MacBook, but it means that anyone who can start your MacBook can use it without providing credentials. Chapter 12 shows you how to turn off automatic login.

Why does my MacBook not show the list of usernames?

Hiding the list of usernames provides extra security and is widely used in companies, but it is usually not necessary for a MacBook used at home. Type your username in the Name field and your password in the Password field, and then click **Log In** (→).

Explore the OS X Desktop

Your MacBook runs the OS X operating system, which is currently in version 10.11, a version called El Capitan. The Macintosh operating system has long been known for being very intuitive and is also pleasing to look at. It was the first major system interface to focus on graphical elements, such as icons. The OS X desktop is the overall window through which you view all that happens on your MacBook, such as looking at the contents of folders, working on documents, and surfing the Web.

OS X Desktop

A Menu Bar

A menu bar usually appears at the top of the screen so that you can access the commands it contains. OS X hides the menu bar in certain situations. The menu bar shows the menus for the active application.

B Drives

The MacBook stores its data, including the software it needs to work, on an internal drive. This drive is a solid-state device, or SSD, rather than an external drive with moving platters, but it is often referred to as an external drive. You can also connect external drives for extra storage.

C SuperDrive

You can connect an external SuperDrive or other compatible optical drive to read from and write to CDs and DVDs.

D Folders

Folders are containers that you use to organize files and other folders stored on your MacBook.

E Files

Files include documents, applications, or other sources of data. There are various kinds of documents, such as text, graphics, songs, or movies.

F Finder Windows

You view the contents of drives, folders, and other objects in Finder windows.

G App and Document Windows

When you use apps, you use the windows that those apps display, for documents, web pages, games, and so on.

Finder Menu Bar and Menus

Ⓐ Apple Menu

This menu is always visible so that you can access special commands, such as Shut Down and Log Out.

Ⓑ Finder Menu

This menu enables you to control the Finder app itself. For example, you can display information about Finder or set preferences to control how it behaves.

Ⓒ File Menu

This menu contains commands you can use to work with files and Finder windows.

Ⓓ Edit Menu

This menu is not as useful in Finder as it is in other applications, but here you can undo what you have done or copy and paste information.

Ⓔ View Menu

This menu enables you to determine how you view the desktop; it is especially useful for choosing Finder window views.

Ⓕ Go Menu

This menu takes you to various places, such as specific folders.

Ⓖ Window Menu

This menu enables you to work with open Finder windows.

Ⓗ Help Menu

This menu provides help with OS X or the other applications.

Ⓘ Configurable Menus

You can configure the menu bar to include specific menus, such as Screen Mirroring, Volume, Wi-Fi, Battery, and many more.

Ⓙ Clock

Here you see the current day and time.

Ⓚ Fast User Switching

This feature enables you to switch user accounts and open the Login window.

Ⓛ Spotlight Menu

This menu enables you to search for information on your MacBook.

continued ▶

The Finder app controls the OS X desktop, and so you see its menu bar whenever you work with this application. When you view the contents of a folder, you do so through a Finder window. There are many ways to view the contents of a Finder window, such as Icon view and List view. The sidebar enables you to quickly navigate the file system and to open files and folders with a single click. The Dock on the desktop and the sidebar in Finder windows enable you to access items quickly and easily.

Finder Windows

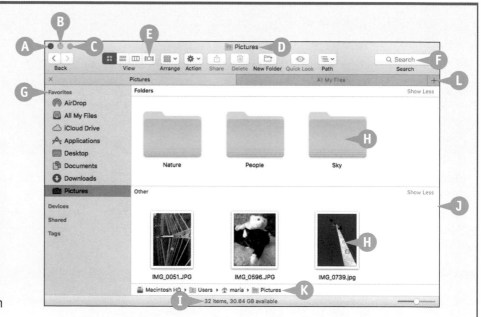

Ⓐ Close Button

Click to close a window.

Ⓑ Minimize Button

Click to shrink a window and move it onto the Dock.

Ⓒ Zoom Button

Click to expand a Finder window to the maximum size needed or possible; click it again to return to the previous size.

Ⓓ Window Title

The name of the location whose contents you see in the window.

Ⓔ Toolbar

Contains tools you use to work with files and folders.

Ⓕ Search Box

Enables you to find files, folders, and other information.

Ⓖ Sidebar

Enables you to quickly access devices, folders, files, and tags, as well as searches you have saved.

Ⓗ Files and Folders

Shows the contents of a location within a window; this example shows the Icon view.

Ⓘ Status Bar

Shows information about the current location, such as the amount of free space when you are viewing the MacBook's drive.

Ⓙ Window Border

Drag a border or a corner to change the size of a window.

Ⓚ Path Bar

Shows the path to the location of the folder displayed in the window.

Ⓛ Tab Bar

Enables you to open multiple tabs containing different Finder locations within the same Finder window and quickly switch among them.

Dock and Sidebar

Ⓐ Favorites

Contains files, folders, searches, and other items that you can open by clicking them.

Ⓑ Devices

Contains your internal drive, any DVD or CD in an external optical drive, external drives, and other devices that your MacBook Pro can access.

Ⓒ Shared

Displays computers and other resources being shared on a network.

Ⓓ Tags

Shows the list of tags you can apply to files and folders to help you identify and sort them easily.

Ⓔ Dock

Shows apps, files, and folders you can access with a single click, along with apps currently running.

Ⓕ Apps

Icons on the left side of the Dock are for apps; each open app has a dark dot under its icon unless you turn off this preference.

Ⓖ Files, Folders, and Minimized Windows

Icons on the right side of the Dock are for files, folders, and minimized windows. The default

Dock includes the Downloads folder for files you download from the Internet along with your Documents folder.

Ⓗ Trash/Eject

OS X puts items you delete in the Trash; to get rid of them, you empty the Trash. When you select an ejectable device, such as a DVD, the Trash icon changes to the Eject icon.

Point and Click with the Trackpad

To tell the MacBook what you want to do, slide your finger across the trackpad to move the on-screen pointer over the object with which you want to work. After you point to an object, you press the trackpad down to click, telling the computer what you want to do with the object. The number of times you click, and the manner in which you click, determine what happens to the object you point at.

Point and Click, Double-Click, or Secondary Click

Point and Click

1 Slide your finger across the trackpad until the pointer points at the appropriate icon.

2 Press the trackpad once to click the trackpad. This is a single click.

The object becomes highlighted, indicating that it is now selected.

Double-Click

1 Slide your finger across the trackpad until the pointer points at the appropriate icon.

2 Click the trackpad twice.

Your selection opens.

Point, Click, and Drag

1 Slide your finger across the trackpad until the pointer points at the appropriate icon.

2 Press down the trackpad and hold it.

The object at which you were pointing becomes attached to the arrow and remains so until you release the trackpad.

③ Drag your finger on the trackpad to move the object.

④ When you get to the object's new position, release the trackpad.

Note: Dragging an item to a different external drive, flash drive, or disk volume copies it there. Changing its location on the same drive moves it instead.

Secondary Click (Control+Click)

① Point to an object on the desktop or even the desktop itself.

Note: To select more than one item at the same time, press and hold ⌘ while you click each item you want to select.

② Press Control +click the trackpad.

A contextual menu appears.

③ Point to the appropriate command on the menu and click the trackpad once to give the command.

TIP

Why do things I click stick to the arrow?
You can configure the trackpad so you can drag things without having to hold down the trackpad. When this setting is on and you click something, it gets attached to the pointer. When you move the pointer, the object moves too. To configure this setting, see the section "Configure the Trackpad or Other Pointing Device" in Chapter 2.

Connect to a Wireless Network

If you have set up a wireless network, you can connect your MacBook to it. Wireless networks are convenient for both homes and businesses because they require no cables and are fast and easy to set up.

Your MacBook includes a wireless network feature that uses some of the wireless network standards called Wi-Fi. You can control wireless networks directly from the Wi-Fi menu at the right end of the menu bar. To connect to a Wi-Fi network, you need to know its name and password.

Connect to a Wireless Network

Note: If you connected your MacBook to a wireless network during setup, you do not need to set up the connection again.

1 Click **Wi-Fi status** (⬭) on the menu bar.

2 Click **Turn Wi-Fi On**.

Note: If the list of wireless networks appears, go to step **4**.

    OS X turns Wi-Fi on.

3 Click **Wi-Fi status** (📶) on the menu bar.

The menu opens and displays a list of the wireless networks your MacBook can detect.

A A lock icon (🔒) indicates that the network is secured with a password or other security mechanism.

B The signal strength icon (📶) indicates the relative strength of the network's signal.

4 Click the network to which you want to connect your MacBook.

20

If the wireless network uses a password, your MacBook prompts you to enter it.

5 Type the password in the Password box.

C If you want to see the characters of the password to help you type it, click **Show password** (☐ changes to ☑).

D If you do not want your MacBook to remember this wireless network for future use, click **Remember this network** (☑ changes to ☐).

6 Click **Join**.

Your MacBook connects to the wireless network, and you can start using network resources.

E The number of arcs on the Wi-Fi status icon (🛜) indicates the strength of the connection, and ranges from one arc to four arcs.

7 To see more details about the wireless network, press **Option** and click the **Wi-Fi status** icon (🛜) on the menu bar.

F The network's details appear, including the physical mode, the wireless channel, and the security type.

TIPS

How do I disconnect from a wireless network?

When you have finished using a wireless network, you can disconnect from it by turning Wi-Fi off. Click **Wi-Fi status** (🛜) on the menu bar and then click **Turn Wi-Fi Off**.

What kind of wireless network do I need for my MacBook?

Wireless networks use several different standards. The latest standard is 802.11ac, which provides the fastest data rates. The best choice for a Mac wireless network is one of Apple's wireless access points, such as an AirPort Extreme or an AirPort Time Capsule; the latter includes backup capabilities.

Give Commands

The easiest ways to give commands in OS X are by using the menus and the toolbar. You can also give commands by pressing keyboard shortcuts.

The menu bar at the top of the window shows the Apple menu ( ) on the left followed by the menus for the active app. Any open window can have a toolbar, usually across its top but sometimes elsewhere in the window.

Give Commands

Give a Command from a Menu

1 On the Dock, click the app you want to activate — Finder ( ) in this example.

Note: You can also click the app's window if you can see it.

2 On the menu bar, click the menu you want to open.

The menu opens.

3 Click the command you want to give.

The app performs the action associated with the command.

Choose Among Groups of Features on a Menu

1 On the Dock, click the app you want to activate — Finder ( ) in this example.

2 On the menu bar, click the menu you want to open.

The app opens the menu.

3 Click the option you want to use.

The app activates the feature you selected.

Give a Command from a Toolbar

1 On the Dock, click the app you want to activate — Finder (⬚) in this example.

2 Click the button on the toolbar, or click a pop-up menu and then click the menu item for the command.

The app performs the action associated with the toolbar button or menu item.

Choose Among Groups of Features on a Toolbar

1 On the Dock, click the app you want to activate — Finder (⬚) in this example.

2 In the group of buttons, click the button you want to choose.

A The app highlights the button you clicked to indicate that the feature is turned on.

B The app removes highlighting from the button that was previously selected.

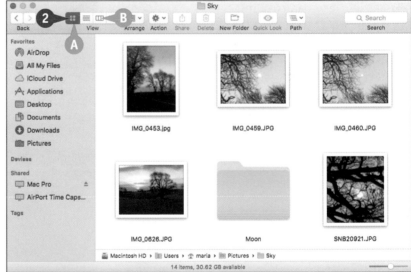

TIP

Is it better to use the menus or the toolbar?

If the toolbar contains the command you need, using the toolbar is usually faster and easier than using the menus. You can customize the toolbar in many apps by opening the **View** menu, choosing **Customize Toolbar**, and then working in the dialog that opens. Use this command, or other similar commands, to place the buttons for your most-used commands just a click away.

Open, Close, and Manage Windows

Most OS X apps use windows to display information so that you can see it and work with it. You can resize most windows to the size you need or expand a window so that it fills the screen. You can move windows and position them so that you can see those windows you require, minimize other windows to icons on the Dock, or hide an app's windows from view.

Open, Close, and Manage Windows

Open a Window

1 Click anywhere on the desktop.

OS X activates Finder and displays the menu bar for it.

Note: Clicking anywhere on the desktop activates Finder because the desktop is a special Finder window. You can also click **Finder** ( ) on the Dock.

2 Click **File**.

The File menu opens.

3 Click **New Finder Window**.

A Finder window opens, showing your files in your default view.

Move, Resize, and Zoom a Window

1 Click the window's title bar and drag the window to where you want it.

2 Click a border or corner of the window and drag until the window is the size and shape you want.

3 Click **Zoom** ( ).

The window zooms to full screen.

4 Move the pointer to the upper-left corner of the screen.

The OS X menu bar and the app's title bar appear.

5 Click **Zoom Back** ( ).

The window zooms back to its previous size.

Close a Window

1 Click **Close** (⬤).

Note: When you move the pointer over the upper-left corner of a window, Close (⬤) changes to Close (⊗), Minimize (⬤) changes to Minimize (⊖), and Zoom (⬤) changes to Zoom (⊘).

The window closes.

Note: You can also close a window by pressing ⌘+W. To close all the windows of the app, press Option + click **Close** (⬤) or press ⌘ + Option +W.

Minimize or Hide a Window

1 Click **Minimize** (⬤).

OS X minimizes the window to an icon on the right side of the Dock.

Note: You can also minimize a window by pressing ⌘+M.

2 Click the icon for the minimized window.

OS X expands the window to its original size and position.

Note: Press and hold Shift while minimizing or restoring a window to see the animation in slow motion.

TIP

How can I find out where a document in a window is located?

To quickly see what folder contains a file or folder, press ⌘+click the window's name in the title bar. The window displays a pop-up menu showing the path of folders to this folder. Click a folder in the path to display that folder in Finder, or click the title bar to hide the pop-up menu again.

Using Notifications

OS X's Notification Center feature keeps you up to date with what is happening in your apps. Notification Center puts all your alerts, from incoming e-mail messages and instant messages to calendar requests and software updates, in a single place where you can easily access and manage them.

You open Notification Center by clicking the icon at the right end of the menu bar. Notification Center opens as a pane on the right side of the screen, and it contains sections you can expand or collapse as needed.

Using Notifications

View a Notification

Ⓐ When you receive a notification, a notification banner appears in the upper-right corner of the screen for a few seconds.

Note: Notification Center can display either banners or alerts. A *banner* appears for a few seconds, and then disappears. An *alert* remains on screen until you dismiss it.

① If you want to see the item that produced the notification, click the banner.

Display Notification Center When Your Desktop Is Visible

① Click **Notification Center** (≔).

Notification Center opens.

② Optionally, click a notification to display the related item in its app.

Ⓑ You can click **Today** to display the Today pane, which shows your calendar events, stock information, weather forecasts, and other data.

③ When you are ready to close Notification Center, click **Notification Center** (≔).

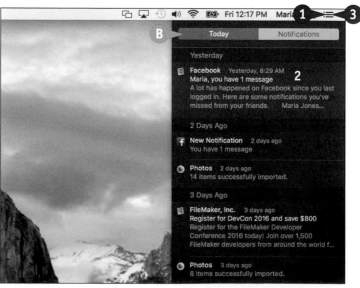

Choose What Types of Notifications to Display and Set Your Do Not Disturb Hours

1 Press **Control** and click **System Preferences** (⚙) on the Dock.

The contextual menu opens.

2 Click **Notifications**.

System Preferences opens and displays the Notifications pane.

3 Click **Do Not Disturb**.

The Do Not Disturb settings appear.

4 Click **From** (☐ changes to ☑) and then set the hours.

5 Choose which calls to accept during Do Not Disturb times.

6 Click an app or feature.

The controls for the app or feature appear.

7 Click **None**, **Banners**, or **Alerts** to set the alert style.

8 Choose other options for the app or feature.

9 Repeat steps **6** to **8** for other apps and features.

10 Click **Notification Center sort order** (🔽) and click **Recents**, **Recents by App**, or **Manually by App**, as needed.

11 Click **Close** (●).

System Preferences closes.

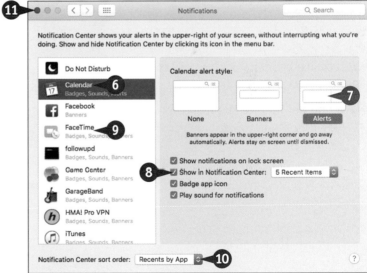

TIP

How do I display Notification Center in a full-screen app?

Move the pointer up to the top of the screen to display the menu bar. You can then click **Notification Center** (☰) toward the right end of the menu bar to display Notification Center.

Put Your MacBook to Sleep and Wake It Up

O S X enables you to put your MacBook to sleep easily and wake it up quickly. So when you are ready for a break but you do not want to end your computing session, put the MacBook to sleep instead of shutting it down.

Sleep keeps all your apps open and lets you start computing again quickly. When you wake your MacBook up, your apps and windows are where you left them, so you can swiftly resume what you were doing.

Put Your MacBook to Sleep and Wake It Up

Put Your MacBook to Sleep

1 Click **Apple** (🍎).

The Apple menu opens.

Note: You can also put your MacBook to sleep by closing its lid.

2 Click **Sleep**.

The MacBook turns its screen off and puts itself to sleep.

Note: You can also put your MacBook to sleep by pressing its power button for a moment.

Wake Your MacBook

1 Click the trackpad or press any key on the keyboard.

Note: If you put the MacBook to sleep by closing its lid, lift the lid instead.

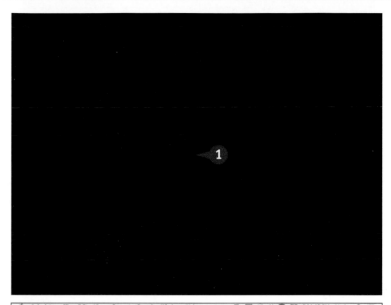

The MacBook wakes up and turns on the screen. All the apps and windows that you were using are open where you left them.

The MacBook reestablishes any network connections that it normally uses and performs regular tasks, such as checking for new e-mail.

TIP

When should I use sleep and when should I shut down my MacBook?
Put your MacBook to sleep when you want to be able to resume using it quickly. Sleep uses only a minimal amount of power. Shut down your MacBook when you plan not to use it for several days or when your MacBook has almost run out of battery power.

Log Out, Shut Down, and Resume

When you have finished using your MacBook for now, end your computing session by logging out. From the login screen, you can log back in when you are ready to use your MacBook again. When you have finished using your MacBook and plan to leave it several days, shut it down.

Whether you log out or shut down your MacBook, you can choose whether to have OS X reopen your apps and documents when you log back on. This helpful feature can help you get back to work — or play — quickly and easily.

Log Out, Shut Down, and Resume

Log Out from Your MacBook

1 Click **Apple** (🍎).

The Apple menu opens.

2 Click **Log Out**.

The MacBook shows a dialog asking if you want to log out.

3 Click **Reopen windows when logging back in** (☐ changes to ☑) if you want to resume your apps and documents.

4 Click **Log Out**.

Note: Instead of clicking **Log Out**, you can wait for 1 minute. After this, the MacBook closes your apps and logs you out automatically. To log out quickly, bypassing the dialog, click **Apple** (🍎), press and hold Option, and then click **Log Out**.

The MacBook displays the window showing the list of users. You or another user can click your name to start logging in.

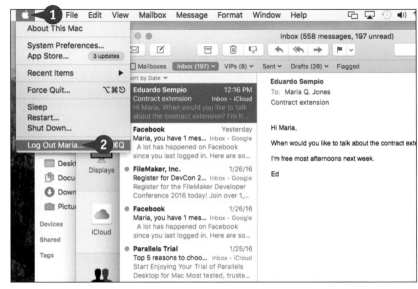

Shut Down Your MacBook

1 Click **Apple** (🍎).

The Apple menu opens.

2 Click **Shut Down**.

A dialog opens asking if you want to shut down.

3 Click **Reopen windows when logging back in** (☐ changes to ☑) if you want to resume your apps and documents.

4 Click **Shut Down**.

Note: Instead of clicking Shut Down, you can wait for 1 minute. After this, the MacBook shuts down automatically. To shut down quickly, bypassing the dialog, click **Apple** (🍎), press and hold Option, and then click **Shut Down**.

The screen goes blank, and the MacBook switches itself off.

TIP

Do I need to save my documents before logging out?

If the apps you are using are designed to use OS X's automatic-saving features, your MacBook automatically saves any unsaved changes to your documents before logging you out. But because not all apps use these features, it is better to save all your documents yourself before you log out. Otherwise, an app may display a dialog prompting you to save unsaved changes, and this dialog may prevent logout or shutdown.

CHAPTER 2

Configuring Your MacBook

You can customize many aspects of OS X to make it work the way you prefer. You can change the desktop background, personalize the Dock icons, and adjust the keyboard and trackpad or other pointing device. You can also run apps or open specific documents each time you log in or set your MacBook to go to sleep automatically when you are not using it.

Change the Desktop Background

OS X enables you to change the desktop background to show the picture you prefer. OS X includes many varied desktop pictures and solid colors, but you can also set any of your own photos as the desktop background. You can tile, stretch, or crop the photo to fill the screen or center it on the screen.

You can also choose between displaying a single picture on the desktop and displaying a series of images that change automatically.

Change the Desktop Background

1 Press **Control**+click the desktop.

The contextual menu opens.

2 Click **Change Desktop Background**.

The Desktop pane in System Preferences appears.

3 Click the category of image you want to see.

Ⓐ Apple contains the built-in desktop backgrounds.

Ⓑ Photos contains your Photos library.

Ⓒ Folders contains your folders.

Ⓓ Click **Add** (**+**) to add a folder.

The images appear in the right-hand pane.

4 Click the image you want to use.

The image appears on the desktop.

5 If you chose a photo or picture of your own, click the pop-up menu (⊙) and click the way to fit the image to the screen. See the tip for details.

6 If you want to set a series of background images, click the category.

7 Click **Change picture** (☐ changes to ✓).

8 Click **Change picture** (⊙) and click the interval — for example, **Every 30 minutes**.

9 Click **Random order** (☐ changes to ✓) if you want the images to appear in random order.

10 Click **Close** (●).

System Preferences closes.

TIP

Which option should I choose for fitting the image to the screen?
In the Desktop & Screen Saver preferences, choose **Fit to Screen** to match the image's height or width — whichever is nearest — to the screen. Choose **Fill Screen** to make an image fill the screen without distortion but cropping off parts that do not fit. Choose **Stretch to Fill Screen** to stretch the image to fit the screen exactly, distorting it as needed. Choose **Center** to display the image at full size in the middle of the desktop. Choose **Tile** to cover the desktop with multiple copies of the image.

Set Up a Screen Saver

OS X enables you to set a screen saver to hide what your screen is showing when you leave your MacBook idle. A *screen saver* is an image, a sequence of images, or a moving pattern that appears on the screen. You can choose what screen saver to use and the length of the period of inactivity before it starts.

OS X comes with a variety of attractive screen savers. You can download other screen savers from websites.

Set Up a Screen Saver

1 Press **Control**+click the desktop.

The contextual menu opens.

2 Click **Change Desktop Background**.

The Desktop pane of Desktop & Screen Saver preferences opens.

3 Click **Screen Saver**.

The Screen Saver pane appears.

4 Click a screen saver in the list on the left.

The screen saver you clicked starts playing in the Preview area.

A You can click **Show with clock** (☐ changes to ☑) to display a clock on the screen saver.

5 Click **Start after** (🔽).

The pop-up menu opens.

6 Click the length of time to wait until the screen saver starts, such as **5 Minutes**.

Note: To turn off the screen saver, select **Never** in the Start After pop-up menu.

7 Position the pointer over the preview.

The Preview button appears.

8 Click **Preview**.

The screen saver preview appears full screen.

9 Click anywhere on the screen saver when you want to stop the preview.

The Screen Saver pane appears.

10 Press ⌘+Q.

System Preferences closes.

TIP

Must I use a screen saver to protect my MacBook's screen from damage?

No. Screen savers originally protected cathode ray tube (CRT) displays from having static images "burned in" to their screens. LCD and LED screens, such as that on your MacBook, do not suffer from this problem, so you need not use a screen saver. Nowadays you can use a screen saver to protect the information on-screen or to provide visual entertainment — or you may prefer to simply put your MacBook to sleep, which also saves battery power.

Configure Energy Saver and Sleep Settings

OS X's Energy Saver feature enables you to configure power settings for when your MacBook is running on battery power and when it is running from the power adapter. Your options include setting your MacBook to turn off the display after a period of inactivity, putting the drive to sleep when possible, dimming the display on battery power, and enabling the Power Nap feature. You can put your MacBook to sleep manually at any time by closing the lid or by clicking **Apple** () and **Sleep**.

Configure Energy Saver and Sleep Settings

① Press Control + click **System Preferences** () on the Dock.

The System Preferences contextual menu opens.

② Click **Energy Saver**.

The Energy Saver pane appears.

③ Click **Battery**.

The Battery tab appears.

④ Click and drag the **Turn display off after** slider to set the period of inactivity before turning off the display.

⑤ Click **Put hard disks to sleep when possible** (changes to ✓) to reduce disk power usage.

⑥ Click **Slightly dim the display while on battery power** (changes to ✓) to reduce power usage by dimming the display.

⑦ Click **Enable Power Nap while on battery power** (changes to ✓) to use the Power Nap feature. See the first tip for details.

⑧ Click **Show battery status in menu bar** (changes to ✓) to display a battery readout in the menu bar. This is usually helpful.

⑨ Click **Power Adapter**.

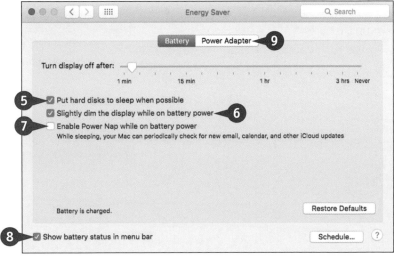

The Power Adapter tab appears.

10 Click and drag the **Turn display off after** slider to set the period of inactivity before turning off the display.

11 Click **Prevent computer from sleeping automatically when the display is off** (☐ changes to ☑) if you need to keep the MacBook awake.

12 Click **Put hard disks to sleep when possible** (☐ changes to ☑) to reduce disk power usage.

13 Click **Wake for Wi-Fi network access** (☐ changes to ☑) to enable waking the MacBook via Wi-Fi.

14 Click **Enable Power Nap while plugged into a power adapter** (☐ changes to ☑) to use the Power Nap feature.

15 Click **Schedule**.

The Schedule dialog opens.

16 On the top row, click **Start up or wake** (☐ changes to ☑) to start or wake your MacBook, set the frequency, and set the time.

17 On the second row, click **Sleep**, **Restart**, or **Shut Down** (☐ changes to ☑) and set the time.

18 Click **OK**.

The Schedule dialog closes.

19 Click **Close** (⬤).

System Preferences closes.

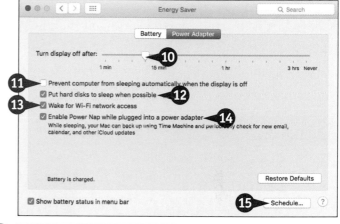

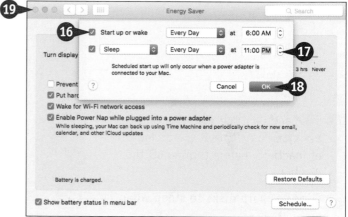

TIPS

What is the Power Nap feature?

Power Nap enables your MacBook to wake periodically during sleep to check for new e-mail messages, calendar items, and other online updates. Power Nap uses a small amount of battery power but is usually very helpful.

Which button do I press to wake my MacBook from sleep?

You can press any key. If you are not certain whether the MacBook is asleep or preparing to run a screen saver, press **Shift**, **Control**, **Option**, or ⌘. These keys do not type a character if the MacBook turns out to be awake instead of asleep. You can also move your finger on the trackpad to wake your MacBook.

Customize the Dock

O S X enables you to customize the Dock so that it contains the icons you find most useful and it appears in your preferred position on the screen. You can add apps, files, or folders to the Dock; reposition the Dock's icons; and remove most of the existing items if you do not need them.

To customize the Dock, you drag items to it, from it, or along it. You can also use the Dock's contextual menu to change the Dock's position, configuration, or behavior.

Customize the Dock

Add an App to the Dock

1 Click **Launchpad** (🚀) on the Dock.

The Launchpad screen appears.

2 Click and drag the app to the left side of the divider line on the Dock.

The app's icon appears on the Dock.

Note: You can also add an app to the Dock by opening the app, pressing `Control` +clicking its icon, highlighting or clicking **Options**, and then clicking **Keep in Dock**.

Add a File or Folder to the Dock

1 Click **Finder** (😀) on the Dock.

2 In the Finder window, navigate to the file or folder you want to add to the Dock.

3 Click and drag the file or folder to the right side of the divider line on the Dock.

The item's icon appears on the Dock.

Remove an Item from the Dock

1 If the app is running, press **Control**+click its Dock icon and click **Quit** on the contextual menu.

2 Press **Control**+click the app's icon on the Dock.

The contextual menu opens.

3 Highlight or click **Options**.

The Options submenu opens.

4 Click **Remove from Dock**.

OS X removes the icon from the Dock.

Note: You can also click an icon and drag it from the Dock toward the desktop. When a Remove pop-up message appears, release the icon.

Configure the Dock

1 Press **Control**+click the Dock divider bar.

A Click **Turn Hiding On** to hide the Dock when the pointer is not over it.

B Click **Turn Magnification Off** to turn off magnification.

C Click **Position on Screen** and then click **Left**, **Bottom**, or **Right** to reposition the Dock.

D Click **Minimize Using** and then click **Genie Effect** or **Scale Effect**.

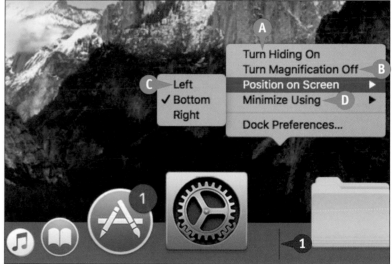

TIP

How else can I customize the Dock?

You can increase or decrease the size of the Dock by clicking the Dock divider bar and dragging it up or down. For more precise control of the Dock, press **Control**+click the Dock divider bar and then click **Dock Preferences** to display the Dock pane in System Preferences. Here you can change the Dock size, turn on and adjust magnification, set the Dock's position, and choose the effect for minimizing windows. You can also choose other options for controlling the Dock's appearance and behavior.

Add or Remove Desktop Spaces

OS X enables you to create multiple desktop spaces on which to arrange your documents and apps. You can switch from space to space quickly to move from app to app. You can tie an app to a particular space so that it always appears in that space or allow it to appear in any space.

When you no longer need a desktop space, you can remove it in just moments. To configure desktop spaces, you use Mission Control.

Add or Remove Desktop Spaces

① Press **F3** or **Control**+**⬆**.

Note: On some keyboards, you press **F9** to invoke Mission Control.

The Mission Control screen appears.

Ⓐ You can click a window to switch quickly to it.

② Move the pointer to the top of the screen.

The bar at the top of the screen grows larger when the pointer is over it.

A panel showing a + sign appears.

Note: If you have positioned the Dock on the right, the + sign appears in the upper-left corner of the screen.

③ Click the + panel.

B Another desktop space appears at the top of the Mission Control screen.

C You can click a window and drag it to the desktop space in which you want it to appear.

4 Click a window you want to display full screen, and then drag it to the bar at the top of the screen.

The app appears as a full-screen item on the row of desktops.

D When you need to close a desktop, move the pointer over it, and then click **Close** (⊗).

5 Click the desktop space or full-screen app you want to display.

The desktop space or app appears.

TIP

How can I assign an app to a particular desktop?
First, use Mission Control to activate the desktop to which you want to assign the app. Then press
`Control` +click or right-click the app's Dock icon, click **Options**, and click **This Desktop**. If you want to use the app on all desktops, click **All Desktops** in the Assign To section of the Options submenu.

Create Hot Corners to Control Screen Display

OS X's Hot Corners feature enables you to trigger actions by moving the pointer to the corners of the screen. You can set up from one to four hot corners. Each hot corner can perform an action such as opening Mission Control, displaying your desktop, or starting the screen saver.

To set up hot corners, you use the Hot Corners dialog. You can open this dialog from the Mission Control pane or the Screen Saver pane in System Preferences.

Create Hot Corners to Control Screen Display

Set Up a Hot Corner

1 Press **Control** + click **System Preferences** (⚙) on the Dock.

The contextual menu opens.

2 Click **Mission Control**.

System Preferences opens and displays the Mission Control pane.

3 Click **Hot Corners**.

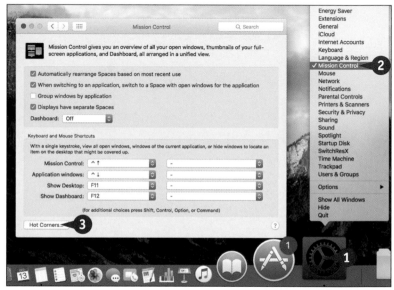

The Hot Corners dialog opens.

4 Click the pop-up menu (⟳) for the hot corner you want to set.

The pop-up menu opens.

5 Click the action you want to assign to the corner.

6 Choose other hot corner actions as needed.

Note: You can set up multiple hot corners for the same feature.

7 Click **OK**.

The Hot Corners dialog closes.

8 Press `Control` + click **System Preferences** (⚙) on the Dock.

The contextual menu opens.

9 Click **Quit**.

System Preferences closes.

Use a Hot Corner to Run Mission Control

1 Move the pointer to the hot corner you allocated to Mission Control.

The Mission Control screen appears.

2 Click the window you want to display.

Are there other ways I can run Mission Control?

You can also run Mission Control by using a gesture, a trackpad click, or a button on a mouse you have connected to your MacBook. In the Keyboard and Mouse Shortcuts section in Mission Control preferences, click **Mission Control** (◌) and select the gesture or mouse button. Press and hold ⌘, `Option`, `Control`, `Shift`, or a combination of the four keys to add them to the keystroke. Use the same technique for the Application Windows pop-up menu, the Show Desktop pop-up menu, and the Show Dashboard pop-up menu.

Make the Screen Easier to See

OS X's Accessibility features include several options for making the contents of your MacBook's screen easier to see. You can invert the colors, use grayscale instead of colors, enhance the contrast, and increase the cursor size. You can also turn on the Zoom feature to enable yourself to zoom in quickly up to the limit you set. To configure these options, you open System Preferences and work in the Accessibility pane.

Make the Screen Easier to See

1 Press `Control`+click **System Preferences** (⚙) on the Dock.

The System Preferences contextual menu opens.

2 Click **Accessibility**.

The Accessibility pane appears.

3 Click **Zoom**.

The Zoom options appear.

4 Click **Use keyboard shortcuts to zoom** (☐ changes to ☑).

5 Click **Zoom follows the keyboard focus** (☐ changes to ☑) to make the zoomed area follow the keyboard's focus.

6 Click **Zoom Style** and select **Fullscreen** or **Picture-in-picture**, as appropriate.

7 Click **More Options**.

The More Options dialog opens.

8 Click and drag the **Maximum Zoom** slider to set the maximum zoom.

9 Click and drag the **Minimum Zoom** slider to set the minimum zoom.

10 Click **Show preview rectangle when zoomed out** (☐ changes to ☑) if you want to display a preview rectangle.

11 In the When Zoomed in, the Screen Image Moves area, click the option button for the zoom motion you want (○ changes to ◉).

12 Click **OK**.

The More Options dialog closes.

13 Click **Display**.

The Display options appear.

14 Click **Invert colors** (☐ changes to ☑) if you want to invert the video colors.

15 Click **Increase contrast** (☐ changes to ☑) if you want to increase screen contrast.

16 Click **Reduce transparency** (☐ changes to ☑) if you want to make the interface less transparent.

17 Click **Use grayscale** (☐ changes to ☑) if you prefer grayscale.

18 Click **Differentiate without color** (☐ changes to ☑) to increase contrast without changing colors.

19 Click and drag the **Display contrast** slider to increase the contrast.

20 Click and drag the **Cursor size** slider to make the cursor bigger.

21 Click **Shake mouse pointer to locate** (☐ changes to ☑) to enable locating the pointer by shaking the mouse.

22 Click **Close** (●).

System Preferences closes.

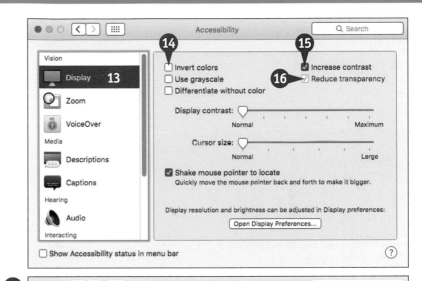

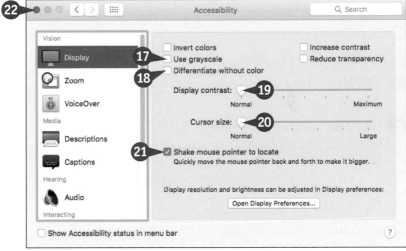

TIP

What is the quickest way to turn on the Universal Access features for seeing the screen?
Use keyboard shortcuts. Press `Option`+`⌘`+`8` to toggle zoom on or off. With zoom turned on, press `Option`+`Control`+`=` to zoom in by increments. Press `Option`+`⌘`+`-` to zoom out by increments. If you enable the Smooth Images feature by clicking **Smooth images** (☐ changes to ☑) in the Zoom options, you can press `Option`+`⌘`+`\` to toggle Smooth Images on or off.

Configure the Keyboard

OS X enables you to customize the settings for your keyboard. You can change the repeat rate and the delay until repeating starts; you can create text shortcuts; and you can turn on automatic spell checking.

If you have difficulty pressing the keys, you can turn on Sticky Keys or Slow Keys. Sticky Keys enables you to set a modifier key, such as ⌘, without having to hold it down. Slow Keys increases the delay between you pressing a key and OS X registering the keystroke.

Configure the Keyboard

① Press **Control**+click **System Preferences** (⚙) on the Dock.

The contextual menu opens.

② Click **Keyboard**.

System Preferences opens and displays the Keyboard pane.

③ Click and drag the **Key Repeat** slider to control how quickly a key repeats.

④ Click and drag the **Delay Until Repeat** slider to set the repeat delay.

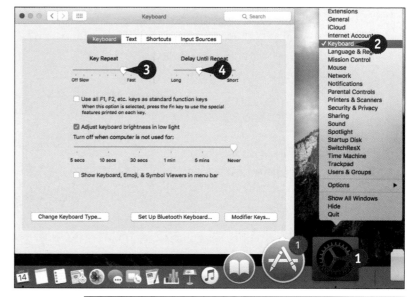

⑤ Click **Use all F1, F2, etc. keys as standard function keys** (☐ changes to ☑) if you want to use the dedicated keys as regular function keys.

⑥ Click **Adjust keyboard brightness in low light** (☐ changes to ☑) to have your MacBook adjust the keyboard brightness automatically.

⑦ Click and drag the **Turn off when computer is not used for** slider to set a time-out for the keyboard lighting.

⑧ Click **Text**.

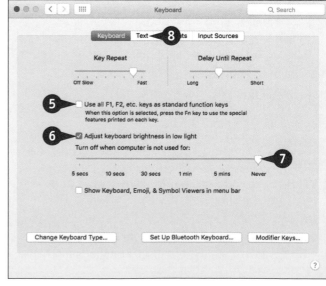

The Text pane appears.

9 Click **Add** (+).

10 Type the text that will trigger the replacement.

11 Type the replacement text.

Note: OS X and iOS make your text shortcuts available to all your Macs and iOS devices using the same Apple ID.

12 Click **Correct spelling automatically** (☐ changes to ✓) to use automatic spell checking.

13 Click **Use smart quotes and dashes** (☐ changes to ✓) if you want OS X to replace regular quotes and dashes with smart quotes and dashes.

14 Press Control+click **System Preferences** (⚙) on the Dock.

The contextual menu opens.

15 Click **Accessibility**.

The Accessibility pane appears.

16 Click **Keyboard**.

17 Click **Enable Sticky Keys** (☐ changes to ✓) if you want to press modifier keys separately from the keys they modify.

18 Click **Enable Slow Keys** if you want to slow down OS X's registration of keystrokes.

Ⓐ You can click **Options** to configure Sticky Keys or Slow Keys.

19 Click **Close** (●).

System Preferences closes.

TIP

What is the purpose of the Shortcuts pane and the Input Sources pane in Keyboard preferences?
You use the Shortcuts pane to configure keyboard shortcuts for controlling OS X and apps directly from the keyboard. For example, you can set a keyboard shortcut to show Notification Center or to switch to a particular desktop.

You use the Input Sources pane to load the keyboard layouts you want to use. For example, if you use the Dvorak keyboard layout instead of the U.S. keyboard layout, you can add the Dvorak layout and remove the U.S. layout. Or you can have both, and switch between them as desired.

Configure the Trackpad or Other Pointing Device

OS X automatically configures your MacBook's trackpad with default settings. You can customize the settings to make the trackpad work the way you prefer. For example, you can select which gestures to use.

You can adjust the speed at which OS X tracks the movement you input with your trackpad. If you find the trackpad awkward, you can also connect a mouse or turn on the Mouse Keys feature, which enables you to control the pointer from the keyboard.

Configure the Trackpad or Other Pointing Device

1 Press `Control` + click **System Preferences** (⚙) on the Dock.

The contextual menu opens.

2 Click **Trackpad**.

System Preferences opens and displays the Trackpad pane.

3 Click each feature you want to use (☐ changes to ☑).

Ⓐ You can click a pop-up menu (⌄) to choose options for a feature.

4 Click and drag the **Tracking speed** slider to adjust the tracking speed.

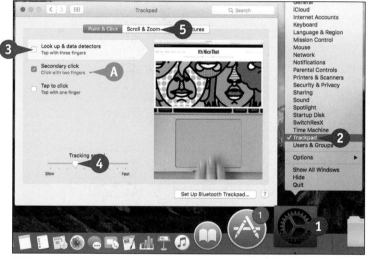

5 Click **Scroll & Zoom**.

The Scroll & Zoom pane appears.

6 Click **Scroll direction: natural** (☐ changes to ☑) to have scrolling follow your finger movements.

7 Click **Zoom in or out** (☐ changes to ☑) to zoom by pinching in or out.

8 Click **Smart zoom** (☐ changes to ☑) to zoom by double-tapping with two fingers.

9 Click **Rotate** (☐ changes to ☑) to rotate objects by placing two fingers and rotating them.

10 Click **More Gestures**.

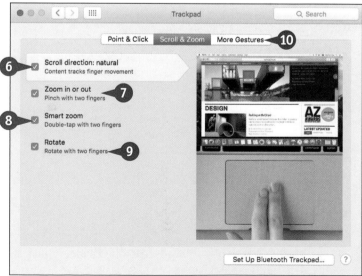

The More Gestures pane appears.

11 Click each feature you want to use (☐ changes to ☑).

B You can click a pop-up menu (∨) to choose options for a feature.

12 Click **Show All** (⊞).

The System Preferences pane appears.

13 Click **Accessibility** (♿).

The Accessibility pane appears.

14 Click **Mouse & Trackpad**.

C You can click **Enable Mouse Keys** (☐ changes to ☑) to turn on Mouse Keys. With Mouse Keys on, you press ⑦, ⑧, ⑨, Ⓤ, Ⓘ, Ⓞ, Ⓙ, Ⓚ, and Ⓛ to move the pointer.

15 Click and drag the **Double-click speed** slider to adjust the double-click speed.

D You can click **Ignore built-in trackpad when mouse or wireless trackpad is present** (☑ changes to ☐) to deactivate the trackpad.

16 Click **Close** (⬤).

System Preferences closes.

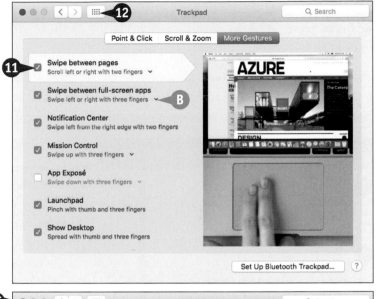

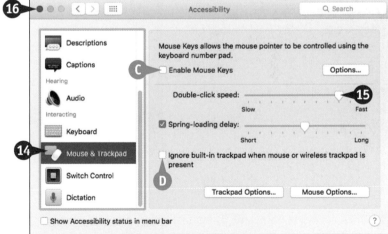

TIPS

How do I configure a mouse attached to my MacBook?

Press Control+click **System Preferences** (⚙) on the Dock, and then click **Mouse** on the contextual menu. The options in the Mouse preferences pane vary depending on the mouse model, but you can always adjust the tracking speed and the double-click speed. You can also usually choose which mouse button to use as the primary button.

What does the Spring-Loading Delay setting do in the Mouse & Trackpad pane in Accessibility preferences?

Spring-Loading Delay controls how long OS X waits before opening a folder to which you have dragged files in the Finder. The delay enables you either to drop the files on the folder without opening it or open the folder so you can navigate within it.

Configure iCloud Settings

Apple's iCloud service adds powerful online sync features to your MacBook. With iCloud, you can sync a wide variety of information via the Internet. You can also use the Find My Mac feature to locate your MacBook if it goes missing.

To use iCloud, you set your user account to use your Apple ID, and then choose which features to use. If you added your iCloud account when first setting up your MacBook, iCloud is already configured, but you may want to select different settings for it.

Set Up iCloud and iCloud Keychain

1 Press **Control** +click **System Preferences** (⚙) on the Dock.

The contextual menu opens.

2 Click **iCloud**.

System Preferences opens and displays the iCloud pane.

Note: If the Sign In with Your Apple ID prompt appears, type your Apple ID and password, and then click **Sign In**.

3 Click each feature you want to use (☐ changes to ☑).

4 Click **Options** to the right of iCloud Drive.

The Options dialog for iCloud Drive opens.

5 Click each app you want to enable to store documents and data in iCloud (☐ changes to ☑).

6 Click **Done**.

The Options dialog for iCloud Drive closes.

7 Click **Options** to the right of Photos.

The Options dialog for Photos opens.

8 Click **iCloud Photo Library** (☐ changes to ☑) if you want to store all your photos and videos in iCloud.

9 Click **My Photo Stream** (☐ changes to ☑) to store your recent photos in iCloud.

10 Click **iCloud Photo Sharing** (☐ changes to ☑) to enable sharing albums with other people via iCloud and viewing their shared albums.

11 Click **Done**.

The Options dialog for Photos closes.

12 Click **Manage**.

The Manage Storage dialog opens.

13 In the left pane, click the item you want to manage. This example uses **Backups**.

The right pane shows the details for the item you clicked.

14 Use the management features as needed. For example, you can click a backup and then click **Delete** to delete it.

15 Click **Done**.

The Manage Storage dialog closes.

16 Click **Close** (●).

System Preferences closes.

TIP

What does the Account Details button in iCloud preferences do?

Click **Account Details** to open the Account Details dialog. You can set your name in the General pane; enter e-mail addresses and choose e-mail preferences in the Contact pane; configure two-factor authentication in the Security pane; manage your devices in the Devices pane; and manage your payment methods in the Payment pane.

Add a Second Display

OS X enables you to add an external display to your MacBook to give yourself more space for your apps. For a MacBook Air or MacBook Pro, the easiest type of display to connect is a Thunderbolt display, but you can also connect other types of displays by using suitable converter cables. For a 2015 MacBook, the easiest type of display is HDMI.

After connecting the external display using a suitable cable, you use the Displays pane in System Preferences to set the resolution and specify the arrangement of the displays.

Add a Second Display

① Connect the display to your MacBook.

Note: To connect an external display to the 2015 MacBook, you need Apple's USB-C Digital AV Multiport Adapter or a functional equivalent. This adapter provides an HDMI port for connecting the external display.

② Connect the display to power and turn it on.

③ Click **Apple** ().

The Apple menu opens.

④ Click **System Preferences**.

The System Preferences window opens.

⑤ Click **Displays** (🖥).

Note: Your MacBook may automatically open the Displays pane of System Preferences after you connect the display and turn it on.

The Displays pane opens on each display.

6 In the Displays pane for the external display, click **Display**.

7 Click **Default for display** (○ changes to ◉) to apply the display's best resolution.

Ⓐ You can click **Scaled** (○ changes to ◉) and then click a different resolution.

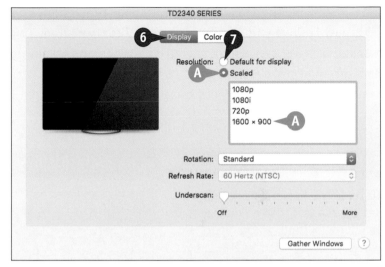

8 In the Displays pane for the MacBook's display, click **Arrangement**.

The Arrangement pane appears.

9 Click and drag either display thumbnail to match the displays' physical locations.

10 To move the menu bar and Dock, click and drag the menu bar from the icon for the MacBook's display to the icon for the external display.

11 Click **Close** (●).

System Preferences closes.

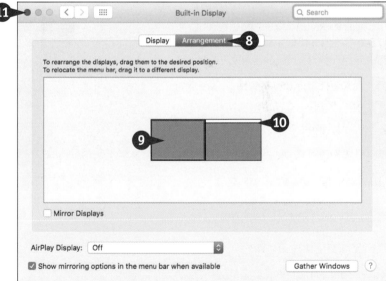

TIPS

Can I add two external displays?

This depends on your MacBook's specification and the monitor types. Most MacBook Air and MacBook Pro models released from 2011 onward support two Thunderbolt displays.

Can I use my iMac as a display for my MacBook?

If your iMac supports Target Display mode, as most recent iMac models do, you can use it as a display for a MacBook Air or a MacBook Pro. With the iMac running, connect a male-to-male Mini DisplayPort cable to each Mac's Thunderbolt port or Mini DisplayPort. The iMac enters Target Display mode automatically, and the MacBook's screen appears. You can press ⌘+F2 to toggle between Target Display mode and the iMac's own output.

Using an Apple TV and HDTV as an Extra Display

With a second-generation or later Apple TV, you can wirelessly broadcast your MacBook's display on the device to which the Apple TV is connected. This is great for watching movies or videos on a big-screen TV, enjoying a shared web-browsing session, or giving presentations from your MacBook to a group of people. To broadcast to an Apple TV, your MacBook uses AirPlay. This technology enables Macs and iOS devices to send a signal to an Apple TV for it to display on a television.

Using an Apple TV and HDTV as an Extra Display

Note: If the Apple TV is not already set up, connect it to a power outlet, to your television, and to your wireless network. Enable AirPlay by opening the Apple TV's Settings screen, selecting **AirPlay**, and setting AirPlay to On.

1 Click **Wi-Fi** (🛜) on the menu bar.

The Wi-Fi menu opens.

2 Click the network to which Apple TV is connected.

Note: Your MacBook and the Apple TV must be on the same network for AirPlay to work.

3 Click **AirPlay** (🖥) on the menu bar.

The AirPlay menu opens.

4 Click **Open Displays Preferences**.

The Displays preference pane in the System Preferences app opens.

5 Click **AirPlay Display** (◉).

The AirPlay Display pop-up menu opens.

6 Click the Apple TV.

Your MacBook's desktop appears on the television to which the Apple TV is connected. By default, the Apple TV mirrors the MacBook's screen, showing the same image.

7 Click **Show mirroring options in the menu bar when available** (☐ changes to ☑).

8 Click **Close** (●).

System Preferences closes.

9 Click **AirPlay** (🖥) on the menu bar.

The AirPlay menu opens.

10 Click **Use As Separate Display** if you want to use the HDTV as a separate display.

11 When you finish using the Apple TV, click **AirPlay** (🖥) on the menu bar.

The AirPlay menu opens.

12 Click **Turn AirPlay Off**.

Your MacBook stops displaying content via the Apple TV.

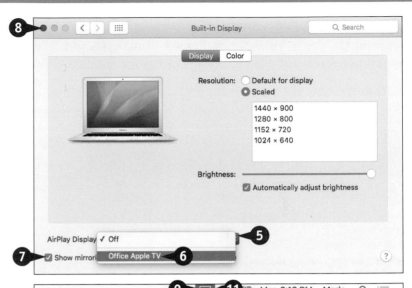

TIP

Why do I not see any AirPlay devices available on my MacBook?
First, check the network configuration of each device to make sure all devices are on the same network. Second, the network you are using may not support the protocols AirPlay uses; in some public areas, networks are designed to prevent streaming of content. If you cannot use a different network, see if the available one can be reconfigured to support AirPlay.

Set Up Your Social Networking Accounts

OS X includes built-in support for the major social networks, including Facebook, LinkedIn, Twitter, and Flickr. OS X makes it easy to post updates, photos, and videos to your accounts on these social networks. For example, you can quickly create a Facebook post or share a photo to Twitter.

Before you can use a particular social network, you must set up the social networking account in your user account. To do this, you use System Preferences.

Set Up Your Social Networking Accounts

① Press Control + click **System Preferences** (⚙) on the Dock.

The contextual menu opens.

② Click **Internet Accounts**.

System Preferences opens and displays the Internet Accounts pane.

③ In the right pane, click the account type you want to add. This example uses **Facebook**.

Ⓐ If an account is selected in the left pane, click **Add** (+) to display the list of account types.

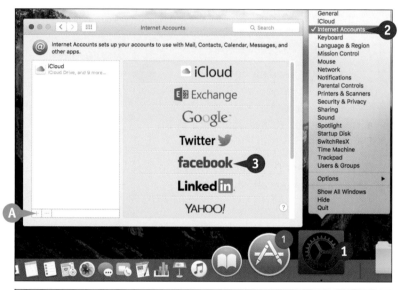

A dialog for entering the account information opens. This example shows the Facebook dialog.

④ Type your e-mail address, phone number, or username.

⑤ Type your password.

⑥ Click **Next**.

A dialog opens showing further information.

7 Click **Sign In**.

System Preferences signs you into the social networking service.

B The account appears in the left pane of the Internet Accounts pane.

8 Click **Contacts** (☐ changes to ☑) to allow Facebook to use your data in the Contacts app.

9 Click **Calendars** (☐ changes to ☑) to allow Facebook to add events to the Calendar app.

10 Click **Notifications** (☐ changes to ☑) to allow Facebook to raise notifications.

11 Click **Share Menu** (☐ changes to ☑) to make Facebook appear on the Share menu.

12 Click **Close** (⬤).

The System Preferences window closes.

TIP

What does the Details button for an Internet account do?
Clicking the Details button opens the Details dialog for the selected Internet account. This dialog box enables you to change key details about the account. For example, for a Facebook account, you can specify how to display your name, and you can change the description that the Internet Accounts pane displays for the account.

Connect External Devices

To extend your MacBook's capabilities, you can connect a wide variety of external devices. This section covers connecting speakers for audio output, connecting printers for creating hard-copy output from digital files, and connecting external drives for extra storage.

Connect Speakers

Each MacBook model has built-in speakers, but you can connect external speakers when you need greater volume. The easiest way to connect speakers is via the 3.5mm headphone jack that each MacBook model includes. On some models, the headphone jack can output only an analog signal. On other models, the headphone jack can output either an analog signal or a digital signal, and switch automatically between analog and digital depending on the type of cable you connect.

You can also connect speakers via a USB port. For the 2015 MacBook, you need Apple's USB-C Digital AV Multiport Adapter or a similar adapter to provide a regular USB port instead of the USB-C port.

If you prefer not to connect your MacBook to speakers via a cable, you can use AirPlay or Bluetooth instead. For AirPlay, you need either speakers that are AirPlay-capable or speakers connected either to an AirPort Express wireless access point or to an Apple TV. For Bluetooth, you need either compatible Bluetooth speakers or a compatible Bluetooth audio receiver.

Whichever means of connection you use, you can use the Output pane in Sound preferences to specify which audio device to use. To give yourself easy control of audio inputs and outputs as well as the volume, click **Show volume in menu bar** (☐ changes to ☑).

You can then press Option +click **Volume** (◀◎) to display a menu for selecting sound output and input options quickly. For example, you can click a device in the Output Device list on the menu to direct the sound output to that device. You can also click **Sound Preferences** at the bottom of the menu to display the Sound pane in System Preferences.

Connect a Printer

To print from your MacBook, you need to connect a printer and install a *driver*, the software for the printer. OS X includes many printer drivers, so you may be able to connect your printer and simply start printing. But if your printer is a new model, you may need to locate and install the driver for it.

You can connect a printer directly to your MacBook by using a USB cable. For the 2015 MacBook, you need Apple's USB-C Digital AV Multiport Adapter or a similar adapter to provide a regular USB port.

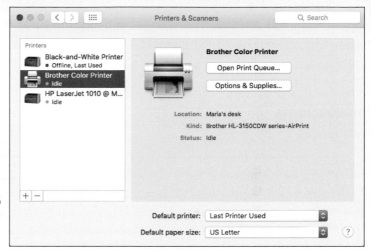

After connecting the printer to the MacBook and to power, and powering on the printer, press `Control`+click **System Preferences** (⚙) on the Dock and then click **Printers & Scanners** on the contextual menu to display the Printers & Scanners pane in System Preferences. See if the printer appears in the Printers list in the left pane. If not, click **Add** (➕) and use the Add dialog to add the printer.

Connect an External Drive

To give yourself more disk space, you can connect an external drive to your MacBook. For the MacBook Air or MacBook Pro, you can use either a Thunderbolt drive or a USB drive — preferably USB 3, because USB 3 is much faster than USB 2. A Thunderbolt drive gives better performance than USB 3, but usually costs more. For the 2015 MacBook, you can use only a USB drive, and you need Apple's USB-C Digital AV Multiport Adapter or a similar adapter to provide a regular USB port.

For best results, choose a drive that is designed for use with Macs. Normally, after connecting a drive, you will find that it appears in the Devices section of the sidebar in Finder windows; if so, you can simply start using the drive. But if you need to store large files on the drive, you may want to reformat the drive using the OS X Extended (Journaled) file system. You can do this by using Disk Utility, which you can launch by clicking **Launchpad** (🚀) on the Dock, typing **disk**, and then clicking **Disk Utility** (💾).

Explore Other Important Settings

OS X is highly configurable, and the System Preferences app includes many settings beyond those you have met so far in this chapter. This section introduces you to four other categories of settings you may want to explore in order to get the most out of your MacBook: Language & Region, Extensions, Startup Disk, and Dictation & Speech.

To choose these settings, first display the System Preferences window by either clicking **System Preferences** (⚙) on the Dock or clicking **Apple** () on the menu bar and then clicking **System Preferences** on the menu.

Choosing Language & Region Settings

Click **Language & Region** (🌐) to display the Language & Region preferences pane. Use the controls in the Preferred Languages pane to specify the languages you want to use, and then use the controls on the right side to specify the region, the first day of the week, the calendar type, and whether to use 24-hour time.

Click **Advanced** to open the Advanced dialog box. Here, you can choose a wider variety of language and region settings. For example, you can click the **Dates** tab at the top and configure custom date formats as needed, or click the **Times** tab and set up exactly the time formats your company or organization prefers.

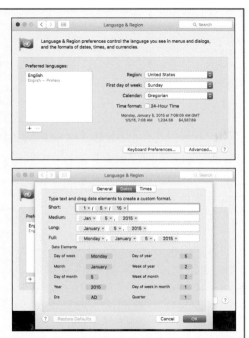

Choosing Extensions Settings

Click **Extensions** (🧩) to display the Extensions preferences pane, which enables you to manage extensions, add-on components that provide additional functionality to OS X.

In the left pane, click the category of extensions you want to configure. For example, click **Share Menu** in the left pane to display the Select Extensions for Sharing with Others list in the right pane, and then select (☑) or clear (☐) the check boxes to specify which items you want to have on the Share menu. Then click **Today** in the left pane to display the Select Widgets for the Today View in Notification Center list, and then select (☑) or clear (☐) the check boxes to specify which items to include in the Today view.

Choosing Startup Disk Settings

Click **Startup Disk** (🖴) to display the Startup Disk preferences pane. Here, you can choose which disk to use for starting your MacBook. This functionality is useful for troubleshooting your MacBook and repairing its operating system — see Chapter 13 for more information — but it also enables you to switch among multiple operating systems installed on your MacBook. For example, if you configure your MacBook to run Windows as well as OS X, you can use the Startup Disk pane to choose which operating system to start.

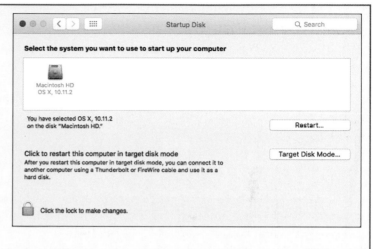

Choosing Dictation & Speech Settings

Click **Dictation & Speech** (🎤) to display the Dictation & Speech preferences pane.

Click the **Dictation** tab at the top to configure settings for dictation. On the Dictation line, click **On** (◯ changes to ◉) to enable dictation, and then click **Use Enhanced Dictation** (☐ changes to ☑), which enables you to dictate text when your MacBook is offline and to dictate text continuously instead of having to pause during dictation.

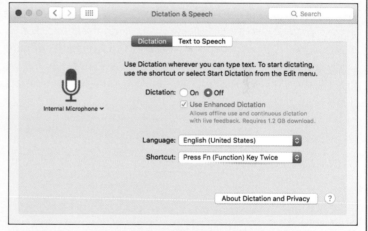

Click the **Text to Speech** tab at the top to configure text-to-speech settings — having your MacBook speak selected text and notifications to you. Click **System Voice** (◉) to choose among different system voices; click **Customize** to download other voices, including novelty voices; and then click and drag the **Speaking Rate** slider to set the speaking speed.

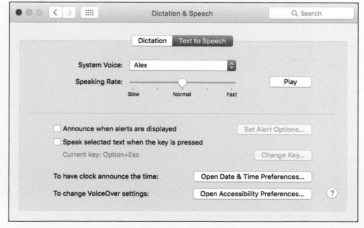

CHAPTER 3

Sharing Your MacBook with Others

OS X makes it easy to share your MacBook with other people. Each user needs a separate user account for documents, e-mail, and settings.

Create a User Account

A user account is a group of settings that controls what a user can do in OS X. By creating a separate user account for each person who uses your MacBook regularly, you can enable users to have their own folders for documents and to use the settings they prefer. You can also use the Parental Controls feature to apply limitations to the actions a user can take.

When initially setting up your MacBook, you create an administrator account that you can use to configure OS X. You can also create a non-administrator account for yourself for day-to-day use.

Create a User Account

1 Press **Control** + click **System Preferences** (⚙) on the Dock.

The contextual menu opens.

2 Click **Users & Groups**.

Note: You must use administrator credentials to create another account. The easiest way to do this is to use an administrator account; you can also provide an administrator name and password from another account. To check whether you are an administrator, see if your account shows Admin in the Users & Groups pane.

The System Preferences window opens.

The Users & Groups pane appears.

3 Click the **lock** icon (🔒) to unlock System Preferences.

System Preferences displays a dialog asking you to type your password or an administrator name and password.

4 Type your password in the Password field.

5 Click **Unlock**.

System Preferences unlocks the preferences (🔒 changes to 🔓).

6 Click **Add** (➕).

The New Account dialog opens.

7 Click **New Account** (🔷) and then click **Standard**.

8 Type the user's full name, such as Kay or Kay Jones, and account name, such as kay.

9 Click **Use iCloud password** (◯ changes to ⦿) to make the user log in using her existing iCloud password.

10 Type the user's iCloud e-mail address in the box.

11 Click **Create User**.

The New Account dialog closes.

A The new account appears in the Other Users list.

12 Click **System Preferences**.

The System Preferences menu opens.

13 Click **Quit System Preferences**.

The System Preferences app closes.

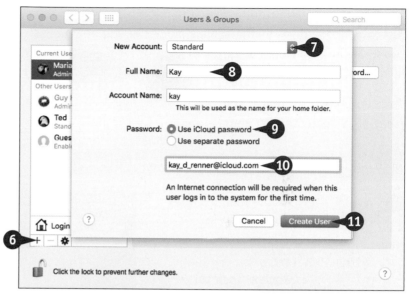

TIP

Should I click Use iCloud Password or Use Separate Password?

If the person has an iCloud account, click **Use iCloud password** (◯ changes to ⦿). The person then logs into the user account using her iCloud password and is prompted to set up iCloud for her account.

If the person does not have an iCloud account, click **Use separate password** (◯ changes to ⦿). In the boxes that appear for setting a password and a password hint, you can either type a password or click **Password Assistant** (🔑) to open the Password Assistant, which suggests hard-to-break passwords. Either way, the user should set a new password immediately after signing in for the first time.

Configure Your MacBook for Multiple Users

OS X includes a feature called *Fast User Switching* that enables multiple users to remain logged in to your MacBook at the same time. After you enable Fast User Switching, another user can log in either directly from your OS X session or from the login screen. Your OS X session keeps running in the background, ready for you to resume it.

You can enable the Guest User account to give a visitor temporary use of your MacBook without creating a dedicated account.

Configure Your MacBook for Multiple Users

1 Press **Control**+click **System Preferences** (⚙) on the Dock.

Note: You can click **Apple** (🍎) and then click **System Preferences** to open the System Preferences window. Then click **Users & Groups** (👥) to display the Users & Groups pane.

The contextual menu opens.

2 Click **Users & Groups**.

The System Preferences app opens and displays the Users & Groups pane at the front.

3 Click the **lock** icon (🔒).

System Preferences displays a dialog asking you to type your password.

Note: If you are using a standard account or managed account, the dialog prompts you to provide administrator credentials.

4 Type your password or credentials.

5 Click **Unlock**.

System Preferences unlocks the preferences (🔒 changes to 🔓).

6 Click **Login Options**.

The Login Options pane appears.

7 Click **Automatic login** (⬦) and click **Off** to ensure that whoever logs in must use his own user account.

8 Click **Show fast user switching menu as** (☐ changes to ☑).

9 Click **Show fast user switching menu as** (⬦).

Ⓐ Guest User is a special account you can use to enable someone to use your MacBook temporarily without creating a dedicated account.

10 Click **Full Name** to show usernames, click **Account Name** to show account names, or click **Icon** to show icons.

Fast User Switching is now enabled.

11 Click **Close** (●).

The System Preferences window closes.

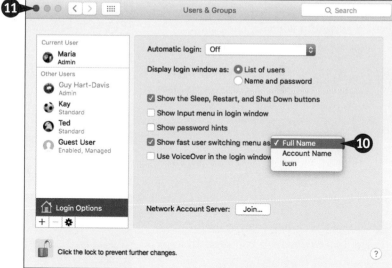

Note: Fast User Switching uses more memory and resources, so it can make your MacBook run more slowly. If your MacBook runs too slowly, try turning Fast User Switching off. For some MacBook models, you may also be able to add RAM to improve performance.

TIP

How do I set up the Guest User feature?
In the left pane in Users & Groups preferences, click **Guest User** to display the Guest User pane. Click **Allow guests to log in to this computer** (☐ changes to ☑). Click **Allow guest users to connect to shared folders** (☑ changes to ☐). You can then click **Enable parental controls** (☐ changes to ☑), click **Open Parental Controls**, and apply parental controls as explained later in this chapter.

Share Your MacBook with Fast User Switching

With Fast User Switching enabled, multiple users can remain logged in to OS X on your MacBook. Only one user can use the keyboard, trackpad, and screen at any given time, but each other user's computing session keeps running in the background, with all her applications still open.

OS X automatically stops multimedia playing when you switch users. For example, if another user is still playing music in iTunes when you switch to your user account, iTunes stops playing the music.

Share Your MacBook with Fast User Switching

Log In to the MacBook

Ⓐ You can click the scroll buttons, ◀ and ▶, to scroll the list left or right, respectively. Alternatively, move the pointer over the list and swipe left or right with two fingers on the trackpad.

① On the login window, click your username.

Ⓑ If you have enabled the Guest User account, a guest can click **Guest User** to log in.

OS X prompts you for your password.

Ⓒ You can click **Back** (◀) to return to the login window if you need to log in using a different account.

② Type your password.

③ Click **Log In** (→).

Your desktop appears.

Display the Login Window

1 When you are ready to stop using the MacBook, but do not want to log out, click your name, account name, or icon on the menu bar.

The Fast User Switching menu opens.

2 Click **Login Window**.

The login window appears.

D Your username shows a check mark icon ( ), indicating that you have a session open.

Any of the MacBook's users can log in by clicking his username.

TIP

How can I log another user out so that I can shut down?

From the Fast User Switching menu, you can see what other users are logged in to the MacBook. If possible, ask each user to log in and then log out before you shut down. If you must shut down the MacBook, and you are an administrator, click **Shut Down** ( ) in the login window. OS X warns you that there are logged-in users. Type your name and password, and click **Shut Down**.

Turn On Parental Controls for an Account

OS X's parental controls enable you, as an administrator, to limit the actions that a particular user can take on the MacBook. For example, you can prevent a user from running certain apps, allow her to chat only with specific people, or prevent her from using the MacBook at night.

You can apply parental controls to any standard account. You can then choose the specific settings the account needs. Later, you can review logs of the actions the user has taken.

Turn On Parental Controls for an Account

1 Press **Control** +click **System Preferences** ( ) on the Dock.

Note: Alternatively, you can click **Apple** ( ), click **System Preferences** to open the System Preferences window, and then click **Users & Groups** ( ) to display the Users & Groups pane.

The contextual menu opens.

2 Click **Users & Groups**.

The System Preferences app opens the Users & Groups pane at the front.

3 Click the **lock** icon ( ).

System Preferences displays a dialog asking you to type your password.

Note: If you are using a standard account or managed account, the dialog prompts you to provide administrator credentials.

4 Type your password or an administrator's credentials.

5 Click **Unlock**.

System Preferences unlocks the preferences (🔒 changes to 🔓).

6 Click the account to which you want to apply parental controls.

The settings for the account appear.

7 Click **Enable parental controls** (☐ changes to ☑).

Note: When you click the Enable Parental Controls check box, the user type under the username in the list of users changes from Standard to Managed.

8 Click **Open Parental Controls**.

The Parental Controls pane opens.

You can now choose parental control settings, as explained in the next five sections.

Can I apply parental controls to any user account?
You can apply parental controls to any standard user account. To apply parental controls to an account, you must use an administrator account or provide administrator credentials. You cannot apply parental controls to an administrator account, but you can downgrade an administrator account to a standard account, and then apply the controls to the standard account. Your MacBook must always have at least one administrator account to manage the other user accounts.

Control What Apps a User Can Run

OS X's parental controls enable an administrator to limit the apps a managed user can run. For example, you can control which apps are available to a user. If you do not allow the user to play certain games, you can make those games unavailable. You can also disallow use of the MacBook's camera.

You can limit a user's contacts for e-mail using the Mail app. In Game Center, you can control whether the user can join multiplayer games and add friends.

Control What Apps a User Can Run

1 In the Parental Controls preferences pane in System Preferences, click the user account you want to change.

2 Click the **Apps** tab.

The Apps pane appears.

3 Click **Allow use of camera** (☑ changes to ☐) if you want to disallow use of the MacBook's camera.

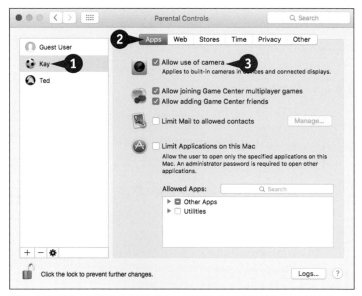

4 Click **Allow joining Game Center multiplayer games** (☑ changes to ☐) to prevent the user from joining multiplayer games.

5 Click **Allow adding Game Center friends** (☑ changes to ☐) to prevent the user from adding friends in Game Center.

6 Click **Limit Mail to allowed contacts** (☐ changes to ☑) to allow e-mail to only the addresses you specify.

7 Click **Manage**.

The Manage Allowed Contacts dialog opens.

8 Click **Send requests to** (☐ changes to ☑).

9 Type your address.

10 Click **Add** (**+**).

A text box opens.

11 Start typing the contact's name.

12 Click the matching contact.

13 When you finish managing the list, click **Done**.

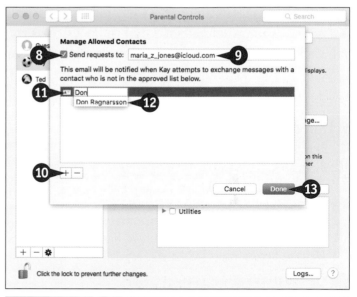

The Manage Allowed Contacts dialog closes.

14 Click **Limit Applications on this Mac** (☐ changes to ☑).

15 In the Allowed Apps list, select the check box (☑) for each app you will allow the user to use. Clear the check box (☐) for each app you will not allow.

Ⓐ You can click **Search** (🔍) and start typing an app's name to locate the app quickly.

TIP

Why would I disallow use of the MacBook's camera?

You might disallow use of the MacBook's camera to ensure that the user cannot use video chat or take *selfies* — self-portraits — with the MacBook.

Disallowing use of the camera may also give some protection against rogue apps that use the camera without the user's agreement — for example, to spy on the user.

Limit Website Access for a User

OS X's parental controls enable an administrator to limit the websites a managed user can access. You can either set Safari to limit access to adult websites or allow a user access to only the websites on an approved list. This limiting of access works only for Safari, not for any other browsers, so you should use the Apps parental controls to make Safari the only web browser the user can run. You should also prevent the user from installing apps.

Limit Website Access for a User

Display the Web Pane and Specify Allowed and Blocked Sites

1. In the Parental Controls preferences pane in System Preferences, click the user account for which you want to limit website access.

2. Click **Web**.

    The Web pane appears.

3. In the Browser Restrictions area, click **Try to limit access to adult websites** (○ changes to ●) if you need to prevent the user from accessing adult websites.

4. Click **Customize**.

    The Customize dialog opens.

5. Click **Add** (+).

    A new entry appears in the Never Allow These Websites box.

6. Type or paste the web address to disallow and press [Return].

    Ⓐ You can also add permitted addresses to the Always Allow These Websites field.

7. When you finish adding addresses, click **OK**.

    The Customize dialog closes.

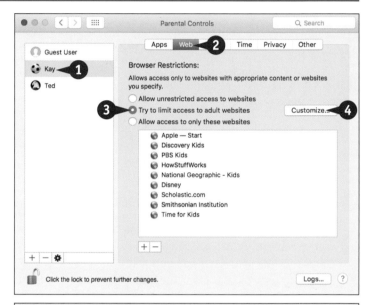

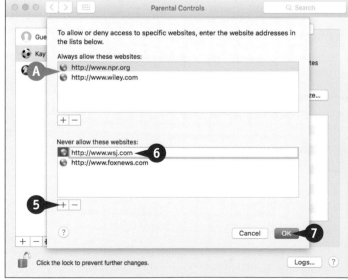

Allow Access to Only Specific Websites

1 To allow only certain websites, click **Allow access to only these websites** (○ changes to ●).

2 To add a site, click **Add** (+).

The Add pop-up menu opens.

3 Click **Add Bookmark**.

Note: You can click Add Folder on the Add pop-up menu to create a folder. You can then drag permitted websites into the folder to organize them.

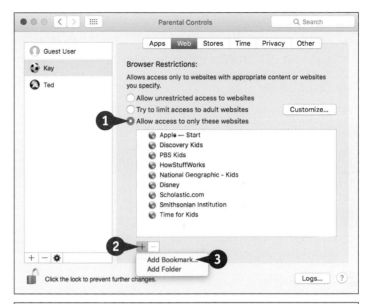

A dialog opens for adding a website.

4 In the Website Title box, type a descriptive name for the website.

5 In the Address box, type or paste the website address.

6 Click **OK**.

The website you added appears in the list.

B To remove a site, click it and then click **Remove** (—).

Note: When you permit a user to visit only certain websites, those sites appear on the Bookmarks bar in Safari.

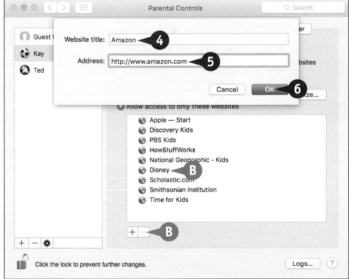

TIP

How effective is the blocking of adult websites?

The blocking of adult websites is only partly effective. OS X can block sites that identify themselves as adult sites using standard rating criteria, but many adult sites either do not use ratings or do not rate their content accurately. Because of this, do not rely on OS X to block all adult material. It is much more effective to choose **Allow access to only these websites** and provide a list of permitted sites. You can add to the list by vetting and approving extra sites when the user needs to access them.

Set Store Restrictions and Time Limits

OS X's parental controls enable an administrator to disable a managed user's access to the iTunes Store and the iBooks Store. As an administrator, you can also restrict explicit music and books, and you can set ratings limits for movies, TV shows, and apps.

You can also set time limits for a managed user's access to the MacBook. You can set the permitted number of hours for weekdays, set permitted hours for weekends, and specify "bedtime" hours for school nights and for weekend nights.

Set Store Restrictions and Time Limits for a User

Set Store Restrictions

1 In the Parental Controls preferences pane in System Preferences, click the user account for which you want to set store restrictions.

2 Click **Stores**.

The Stores pane appears.

3 Click **iTunes Store** (☐ changes to ☑) to disable the iTunes Store and iTunes U.

4 Click **iTunes U** (☐ changes to ☑) to disable iTunes U only.

5 Click **iBooks Store** (☐ changes to ☑) to disable the iBooks Store.

6 Click **Music with explicit content** (☐ changes to ☑) to restrict music with explicit lyrics or titles.

7 Click **Movies to** (☐ changes to ☑) to restrict movies to the level you choose in the pop-up menu.

8 Click **TV shows to** (☐ changes to ☑) to restrict TV shows to the level you choose in the pop-up menu.

9 Click **Apps to** (☐ changes to ☑) to restrict apps to the level you choose in the pop-up menu.

10 Click **Books with explicit sexual content** (☐ changes to ☑) to restrict explicit books.

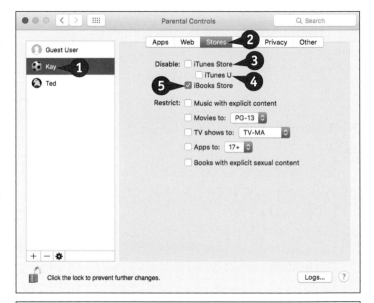

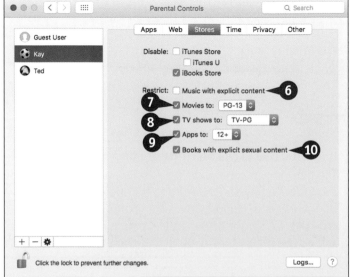

Set Time Limits

1 In the Parental Controls preferences pane in System Preferences, click the user account for which you want to set time limits.

2 Click **Time**.

The Time pane appears.

3 To set a weekday time limit, click **Limit weekday use to** (☐ changes to ☑).

4 Click and drag the slider to set the limit.

5 To set a weekend time limit, click **Limit weekend use to** (☐ changes to ☑).

6 Click and drag the slider to set the limit.

7 To set a block of time when the MacBook is not available on school nights, click **School nights** (☐ changes to ☑).

8 Set the start and end times for school nights.

9 To set a block of time when the MacBook is not available on weekend nights, click **Weekend** (☐ changes to ☑).

10 Set the start and end times for weekend nights.

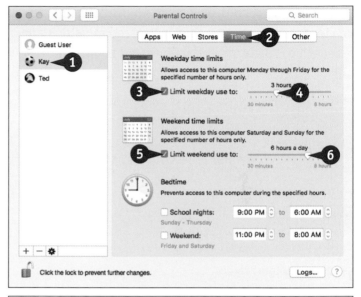

TIPS

How can I allow a managed user access to the MacBook at other times?

Parental controls make no exception for holidays and vacations, but an administrator can override parental controls. For example, when OS X displays the Your Computer Time Is Almost Up dialog, you can enter your administrator name and password to authorize an extra period of time, from 15 minutes to the rest of the day.

How can I allow a managed user to use the MacBook only during the evening?

You can use the Bedtime feature to block any time. For example, set School Nights as 9:00 PM to 6:00 PM to permit the user to use the MacBook from 6–9 PM.

Choose Privacy Restrictions for a User

OS X's parental controls enable you, as an administrator, to choose settings to protect a managed user's privacy. You can choose which apps can request access to potentially sensitive information, such as the MacBook's location, and files, such as contacts and photos. You can also control which services the user and his apps can change and which they cannot change.

Choose Privacy Restrictions for a User

1 In the Parental Controls preferences pane in System Preferences, click the user account for which you want to choose privacy settings.

2 Click **Privacy**.

The Privacy pane appears.

3 Click **Manage Privacy**.

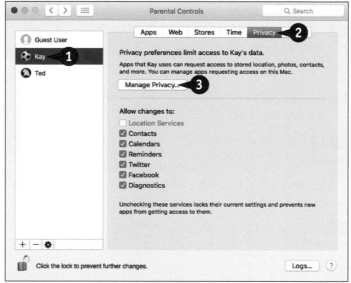

The Privacy pane in Security & Privacy preferences appears.

4 Click **Location Services**.

The Location Services preferences appear.

5 Click **Enable Location Services** to enable (☑) or disable (☐) the feature.

6 If you enable Location Services, click each app in the list to enable (☑) or disable (☐) its use of Location Services.

7 Click **Contacts** and choose which apps can access contacts.

8 Click **Calendars** and choose which apps can access calendars.

9 Click **Reminders** and choose which apps can access reminders.

10 Click **Accessibility** and choose which apps can control your MacBook.

11 Click **Diagnostics & Usage**.

12 Click **Send diagnostic & usage data to Apple** to enable (✓) or disable (☐) sharing diagnostic and usage data.

13 Click **Share crash data with app developers** to enable (✓) or disable (☐) sharing apps' crash data with their developers.

14 Click **Back** (<).

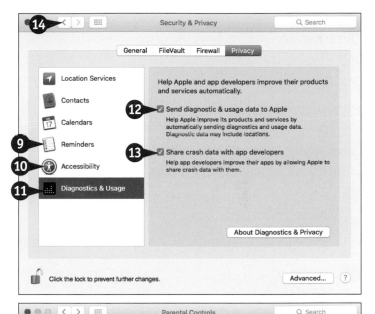

The Privacy pane in Parental Controls preferences appears again.

15 In the Allow Changes To list, click to clear the check box (☐) for each app or service that you want to prevent the user from changing.

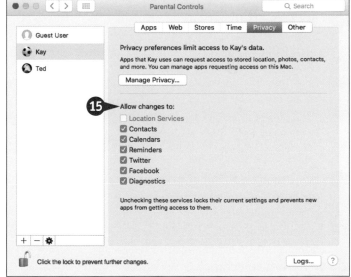

TIP

Should I share diagnostic, usage, and crash data?

Normally, it is helpful to share your diagnostic data and usage data with Apple, and your crash data with the developers of the apps that crash. Apple makes the shared data anonymous, so it is not tied to your name, e-mail address, or Apple ID.

The data you and others share may help Apple's programmers and independent developers to fix problems with OS X and apps that run on it. The community of Mac users benefits as a result, which should result in a better Mac computing experience for all, including you.

Apply Other Restrictions to a User

The Other pane in Parental Control preferences enables an administrator to apply six other types of restrictions.

First, you can disable the Dictation feature. Second, you can prevent the user from changing printer and scanner settings. Third, you can prevent the user from burning CDs and DVDs with the Finder. Fourth, you can hide explicit language in the Dictionary app. Fifth, you can prevent the user from modifying the Dock. Sixth, you can turn on Simple Finder for any user who finds the OS X interface too complex.

Apply Other Restrictions to a User

1 In the Parental Controls preferences pane in System Preferences, click the user account for which you want to choose other restrictions.

2 Click **Other**.

The Other pane appears.

3 Click **Turn off Dictation** (☐ changes to ✓) if you want to prevent the user from enabling Dictation.

4 Click **Disable editing of printers and scanners** (☐ changes to ✓) if you want to prevent the user from changing settings for printers and scanners, adding printers or scanners, or removing printers or scanners.

Note: Adding a printer or scanner means setting it up in the Printers & Scanners pane in System Preferences, not physically connecting it. Similarly, removing a printer or scanner means removing its configuration details rather than disconnecting it.

5 Click **Block CD and DVD burning in the Finder** (☐ changes to ✅) if you want to prevent the user from burning CDs using the Finder.

6 Click **Restrict explicit language in Dictionary** (☐ changes to ✅) if you want to suppress potentially offensive words in the Dictionary app.

7 Click **Prevent the Dock from being modified** (☐ changes to ✅) if you want to prevent the user from changing the Dock layout.

8 Click **Use Simple Finder** (☐ changes to ✅) if you want to turn on the Simple Finder feature.

9 Click the **lock** icon (🔓).

System Preferences locks the Parental Controls feature, and the main Parental Controls pane appears.

A Click the **lock** icon (🔒) if you need to make further changes.

B After unlocking the Parental Controls feature, you can click **Manage parental controls from another computer** (☐ changes to ✅) to enable yourself to manage the Parental Controls feature on this MacBook from another Mac.

10 When you finish working with parental controls, click **Close** (⬤).

The System Preferences window closes.

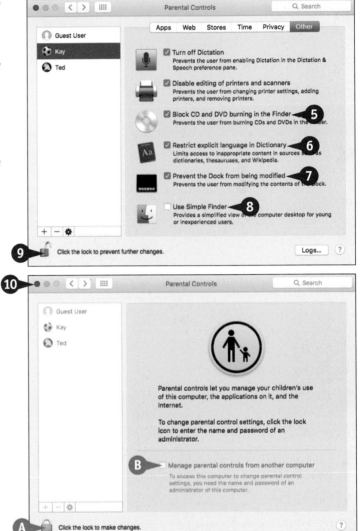

TIP

What is Simple Finder and who should use it?

Simple Finder is a simplified version of the Finder designed for use by younger, older, or less-experienced computer users. Simple Finder provides a more streamlined look with fewer choices, making it easier to find applications and folders, and prevents the user from changing important settings. Some users benefit from using Simple Finder in the long term, whereas for others it is a step toward using the regular Finder after more computing experience. When a user needs to take actions beyond the bounds of Simple Finder, an administrator can give temporary permission by entering an administrative password.

Review a User's Actions

After you, as an administrator, enable parental controls for a managed user, OS X logs the actions the user takes with the controlled apps and features. You can review the logs of a user's actions to see what the user has done and what he has tried to do. Using this information, you can decide whether to tighten or loosen the parental controls. You can review the parental control logs either from your MacBook or from another Mac.

Review a User's Actions

1 In the Parental Controls preferences pane in System Preferences, click the user account for which you want to review actions.

2 Click **Logs**.

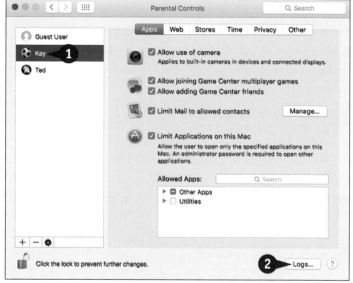

The Logs dialog opens.

3 Click **Show activity for** (⬍) and then click the length of time you want to review, such as **Today** or **One Week**.

4 Click the button for the log you want to review. For example, click **Applications**.

The Applications log appears.

5 Click **Expand** (▶) to expand a collapsed category, or click **Collapse** (▼) to collapse an expanded category.

6 Click an app.

Ⓐ The app's section in the pie chart moves outward.

Ⓑ You can click **Restrict** to restrict use of the app.

Ⓒ You can click **Open** to open the app — for example, to see what it does.

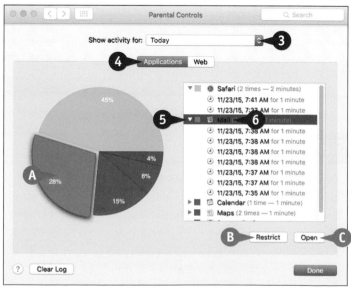

84

7 Click the button for another log. For example, click **Web**.

The Web log appears.

D The pie chart shows colored slices representing the websites.

8 Click **Expand** (▶) to expand a collapsed category, or click **Collapse** (▼) to collapse an expanded category.

9 Click a website.

E You can click **Restrict** to block the website.

F You can click **Open** to open the website in Safari.

10 When you finish reviewing a log, click **Clear Log**.

A dialog opens to confirm you want to clear the log.

11 Click **Continue**.

System Preferences clears the log.

12 When you finish reviewing all the logs, click **Done**.

The Logs dialog closes.

How do I allow a user to access a blocked website?

If the website appears on the list in the Web pane of the Logs dialog, click the website and then click **Allow**. For a blocked website, the Allow button appears in place of the Restrict button.

If the website does not appear in the Logs dialog, use the Web pane in Parental Control preferences instead. If you have selected **Try to limit access to adult websites** (◉), click **Customize** and then click **Add** (╋) to start adding the site. If you have selected **Allow access to only these websites** (◉), click **Add** (╋) below the list to start adding the site.

CHAPTER 4

Running Apps

OS X includes many apps, such as the TextEdit word processor, the Preview viewer for PDF files and images, and the iTunes player for music and videos. You can install other apps as needed. Whichever apps you run, you can switch among them easily, quit them when you finish using them, and force them to quit if they crash.

Open an App and Quit It

OS X enables you to open your MacBook's apps in several ways. The Dock is the quickest way to launch apps you use frequently. Launchpad is a handy way to see all the apps installed in your MacBook's Applications folder and its subfolders. You can also launch an app from the Applications folder, but typically you do not need to do so.

When you finish using an app, you quit it by giving a Quit command. You can quit an app either from the menu bar or by using a keyboard shortcut.

Open an App and Quit It

Open an App from the Dock

1 Click the app's icon on the Dock.

Note: If you do not recognize an app's icon, position the pointer over it to display the app's name.

A The app opens.

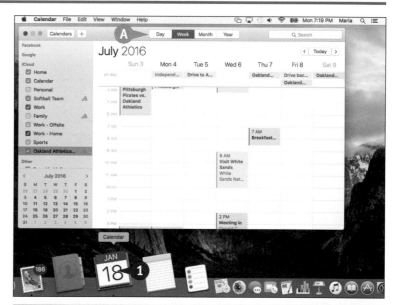

Open an App from Launchpad

1 Click **Launchpad** (🚀) on the Dock.

The Launchpad screen appears.

To scroll to another screen, swipe left or right with two fingers on the trackpad.

B You can also click a dot to move to another screen.

2 Click the app.

The app opens.

Note: To launch an app you have used recently, click **Apple** (🍎), highlight **Recent Items**, and then click the app in the Applications list.

Open an App from the Applications Folder

1 Click **Finder** (🙂) on the Dock.

A Finder window opens.

2 Click **Applications** in the left column.

An icon appears for each app.

3 Double-click the app you want to run.

The app opens.

Note: You can also open an app by clicking **Spotlight** (Q), starting to type the app's name, and then clicking the appropriate search result.

Quit an App

1 Click the app's menu, the menu with the app's name — for example, **Chess.**

The menu appears.

2 Click the Quit command from the menu that has the app's name — for example, **Quit Chess**.

Note: You can also quit the active app by pressing ⌘+Q.

Note: You can quit some single-window apps, such as System Preferences and Dictionary, by clicking **Close** (●). But for most apps, clicking **Close** (●) closes the window but leaves the app running.

TIPS

How do I add an app to the Dock?

Open the app as usual — for example, by using Launchpad. Press Control+click its Dock icon, highlight **Options** on the contextual menu, and then click **Keep in Dock**. You can also click an app in Launchpad or the Applications folder and drag it to the Dock.

What happens if a document in the app I quit contains unsaved changes?

Some apps automatically save your changes when you quit the app. Other apps display a dialog asking if you want to save the changes. Click **Save** to save the changes or **Don't Save** to discard the changes.

Install an App from the App Store

Your MacBook comes with many useful apps already installed, such as Safari for browsing the Web, Mail for reading and sending e-mail, and iTunes for enjoying music and video.

To get your work or play done, you may need to install other apps on your MacBook. You can install apps in three ways: by downloading them from Apple's App Store, by downloading them from other websites and then installing them, or by installing them from a CD or DVD.

Install an App from the App Store

① Click **App Store** (⬡) on the Dock.

Ⓐ The App Store window opens.

The Featured screen includes sections such as Best New Apps and Best Games.

② Click **Top Charts.**

The Top Charts screen appears, showing a Top Paid section, a Top Free section, and a Top Grossing section.

Ⓑ You can also click **Categories** to browse apps by categories, such as Business and Entertainment.

③ Click the app you want to view.

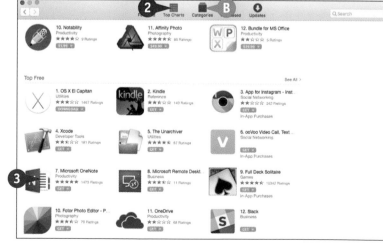

The app's screen appears.

④ Click the app's price button, and then click the **Buy App** button that replaces the price button. For a free app, click **Get** and then click **Install App**.

The Sign In to Download from the App Store dialog appears.

⑤ Type your Apple ID.

⑥ Type your password.

⑦ Click **Sign In**.

Note: If a dialog opens confirming the purchase, click **Buy**.

The download begins.

⑧ Click **Launchpad** (🚀).

The Launchpad screen appears.

Ⓒ A blue dot indicates a new app installed from the App Store or a recently updated app.

⑨ Click the app's icon.

The app opens.

How do I update apps downloaded from the App Store?
Click **App Store** (🅰) on the Dock or on the Launchpad screen, or click **Apple** () and then click **App Store**, to open the App Store app. Click **Updates** on the app's toolbar to display the Updates screen. If any updates appear, click to download and install them. App Store checks for app updates as well as operating system updates.

Install an App from a Disc or the Internet

If an app is not available on Apple's App Store, you can acquire it either on a CD or DVD or as a file that you download. To install an app from a downloaded file, you open the file. To install an app from a CD or DVD, you must either connect an optical drive to your MacBook or use the Remote Disc feature to access an optical drive on another Mac.

Before installing an app in these ways, you may need to change the Gatekeeper setting in Security & Privacy preferences.

Install an App from a Disc or the Internet

Install an App

1 Open the disc or file that contains the app.

If the app is on a CD or DVD, connect an optical drive to your MacBook, and insert the disc in it.

If the app is in a file, double-click the file.

A Finder window opens showing the contents of the disc or file.

2 If there is a file containing installation instructions, follow the instructions. Otherwise, double-click the Installer icon. If there is no installer, see the first tip in this section.

A Some apps let you choose between a standard install and a custom install.

3 Click **Install**.

A dialog opens prompting you to type your password.

Note: To install most apps, you must have an administrator account or provide an administrator's name and password.

4 Type your password.

5 Click **Install Software**.

The installation continues. When it completes, Installer displays a screen telling you that the installation succeeded.

6 Click **Close**.

Installer closes.

Note: If OS X prevents you from installing the app, click **Apple** (🍎) and then click **System Preferences**. Click **Security & Privacy**, and then click **General**. Click **Mac App Store and identified developers** (⬜ changes to ⚫).

Run the App You Installed

Note: If Installer has added an icon for the app to the Dock, click that icon to run the app.

1 Click **Launchpad** (🚀) on the Dock.

Ⓡ Click the dot to display another Launchpad screen if necessary.

2 Click the app's icon.

The app opens.

TIPS

How do I install an app that has no installer or installation instructions?

If the app does not have an installer or specific installation instructions, click the icon in the Finder window for the app's disc or file, and then drag the app's icon to the Applications folder in the sidebar.

How do I use Remote Disc?

Click **Finder** (🙂) on the Dock to open a Finder window. Position the pointer over Devices in the sidebar and click **Show** to display the Devices list. Click **Remote Disc**, and then click the appropriate optical drive.

Run an App Full Screen

OS X enables you to run an app full screen instead of in a window. Running an app full screen helps you focus on that app, removing the distraction of other open apps.

You can instantly switch the active app to full-screen display. When you need to use another app, you can switch to that app full screen as well — and then switch back to the previous app. When you finish using full-screen display, you can switch back to displaying the app in a window.

Switch the Active App to Full Screen

1 Click **Zoom** (●).

Note: In many apps, you can also switch to full screen by clicking **View** on the menu bar and selecting **Enter Full Screen** or pressing Control + ⌘ + F.

The app expands to take up the full screen.

Switch to Another App

1 Swipe left or right with three fingers on the trackpad.

Note: You can also switch apps by using Application Switcher or Mission Control.

The next app or previous app appears.

2 Swipe in the opposite direction.

The app you were using before you switched appears.

Return from Full-Screen Display to a Window

1 Move the pointer to the upper-left corner of the screen.

The menu bar and the app's title bar appears.

2 Click **Zoom Back** ( ).

The app appears in a window again.

Note: Alternatively, move the pointer to the top of the screen, click **View**, and then click **Exit Full Screen** on the View menu.

TIPS

How do I display the Dock in full-screen view?
Move the pointer to the bottom of the screen; the Dock slides into view. If you have positioned the Dock at the left side or right side of the screen, move the pointer to that side to display the Dock.

Can I exit full-screen display by using the keyboard?
Yes. Press **Esc** once or twice to return from full-screen view to windowed view. In many apps, you can also press **⌘**+**Control**+**F** to exit full-screen display.

Run Apps at Login

OS X enables you to set apps to open automatically each time you log in to your MacBook. By opening your most-used apps automatically, you can save time getting started with your work or play. Opening apps at login does make the login process take longer, so it is best to run only those apps you always use. You can configure an app to open automatically either from the Dock or by using the Login Items pane in Users & Groups preferences.

Run Apps at Login

Use the Dock to Set an App to Run at Login

1 If the app does not have a Dock icon, click **Launchpad** (🚀) on the Dock and then click the app.

The app's icon appears on the Dock.

2 Press **Control**+click the app's Dock icon.

The contextual menu opens.

3 Click **Options**.

Note: You can also highlight **Options** without clicking.

The Options submenu opens.

4 Click **Open at Login**.

A check mark appears next to Open at Login.

Use System Preferences to Set an App to Run at Login

1 Press **Control**+click **System Preferences** (⚙) on the Dock.

The contextual menu opens.

2 Click **Users & Groups**.

The Users & Groups pane appears, showing your user account.

3 Click **Login Items**.

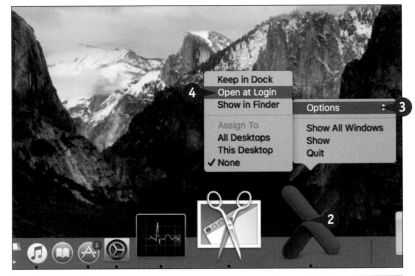

The Login Items pane appears.

Note: If you need to run an app in the background, click **Hide** (☐ changes to ☑) next to the app.

④ Click **Add** (➕).

A dialog opens showing a list of the apps in the Applications folder.

Note: You can also add documents to the list for automatic opening. To do so, navigate to the document, click it, and then click **Add**. OS X opens the document in its default app at login.

⑤ Click the app you want to run automatically at login.

Note: To select multiple apps, click the first, and then press ⌘+click each of the others.

⑥ Click **Add**.

The dialog closes.

The app appears in the list.

⑦ Click **Close** (🔴).

System Preferences closes.

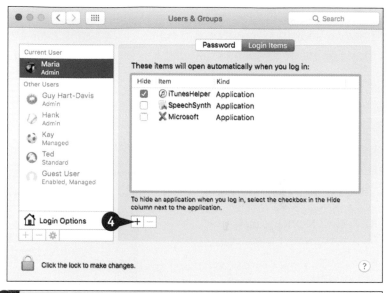

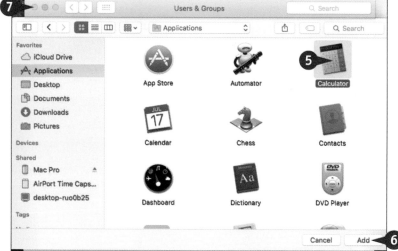

TIP

How else can I add an app to the Login Items pane?
Instead of clicking **Add** (➕) and using the dialog to pick the apps, you can click and drag the apps from a Finder window. Click **Finder** (🙂) on the Dock to open a Finder window, and then click **Applications** in the sidebar. Click the app you want, and then drag it across to the Login Items pane of Users & Groups preferences.

Using Split View

OS X includes Split View, which enables you to divide the screen between two apps. When you need to view two apps simultaneously, using Split View can save time and effort over resizing and positioning app windows manually.

Depending on the apps you choose and the screen resolution on your MacBook, the split in Split View may not be equal. As of this writing, only some apps work in Split View, but OS X clearly identifies windows that are not available in Split View.

Using Split View

1 Click and hold **Zoom** (●) in the window of the first app you want to use in Split View.

OS X switches to the screen for setting up Split View.

2 Drag the app window to the left side or the right side of the screen, as needed.

Note: If you want to position the first app on the blue-shaded side of the screen, you can simply release **Zoom** (●) at this point.

OS X snaps the window to the side of the screen and resizes the window to occupy that section of the screen.

Any apps available for use in Split View appear on the opposite side of the screen.

Note: The message *No Available Windows* appears if none of the other open app windows are available in Split View.

③ Click the app you want to position on the other section of the screen.

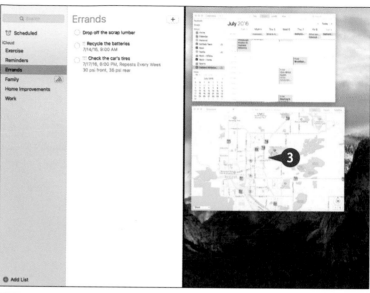

OS X snaps the window to the side of the screen and resizes the window to occupy the other section of the screen.

You can then work in the app windows as normal.

Ⓐ You can resize the windows by clicking and dragging the separator bar between them.

Note: When you are ready to finish using Split View, move the pointer to the upper-left corner of a window. When the title bar for the window appears, click **Zoom Back** (⦿).

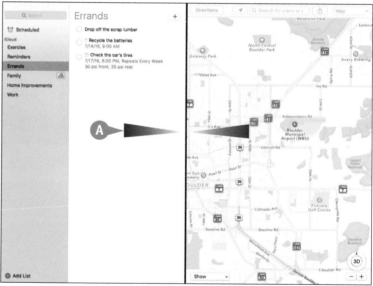

TIPS

How do I move an app to the other side in Split View?

Move the pointer to the top of the app's window. When the title bar appears, click it and drag it to the other side of the screen. OS X switches the two windows.

Are there other ways to switch to Split View?

If you are using an app full screen, swipe up with three fingers on the trackpad to open Mission Control. You can then drag a window onto the full-screen app's thumbnail in the Spaces bar at the top of the screen. OS X switches the apps to Split View.

Switch Quickly Among Apps

OS X enables you to switch quickly among your open apps by using either the trackpad or the keyboard.

If you have several apps displayed on-screen, you may be able to switch by clicking the window for the app you want to use. If the app is not visible, you can click the app's icon on the Dock. If the app has multiple windows, you can then select the window you need.

Switch Quickly Among Apps

Switch Apps Using the Trackpad

1 If you can see a window for the app to which you want to switch, click anywhere in that window.

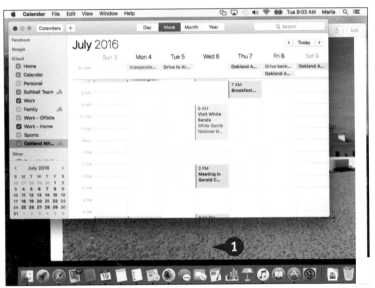

2 If you cannot see a window to which you want to switch, click the app's icon on the Dock.

All the windows for that app appear in front of the other apps' windows.

3 Click **Window** on the menu bar.

The Window menu opens.

4 Click the window you want to bring to the front.

Note: To bring a specific window to the front, press Control + click the app's icon on the Dock to display the contextual menu, and then click the window you want to see. You can also click and hold the app icon on the Dock to display the contextual menu.

Switch Among Apps Using the Keyboard

1 Press and hold ⌘ and press `Tab`.

A Application Switcher opens, showing an icon for each open app.

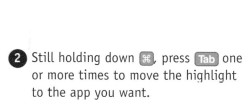

2 Still holding down ⌘, press `Tab` one or more times to move the highlight to the app you want.

Note: Press and hold ⌘+`Shift` and press `Tab` to move backward through the apps.

3 When you reach the app you want, release ⌘.

Application Switcher closes, and the selected app comes to the front.

4 If necessary, click **Window** and select the window you want.

Note: You can press ⌘+` to switch among the windows in the current app.

TIPS

Are there other ways of switching among apps?

You can use the keyboard and the trackpad — or mouse, if you have connected one — together. Press and hold ⌘, press `Tab` once to open Application Switcher, and then click the app you want to bring to the front.

Can I do anything else with Application Switcher other than switching to an app?

You can also hide an app or quit an application from Application Switcher. Press and hold ⌘, press `Tab` to open Application Switcher, and then select the app you want to affect. Still holding ⌘, press `H` to hide the app or press `Q` to quit the app.

Switch Apps Using Mission Control

OS X's Mission Control feature helps you manage your desktop and switch among apps and windows. When you activate Mission Control, it shrinks the open windows so that you can see them all and click the one you want. You can use Mission Control to display all open windows in all apps or just the windows in a particular app.

Mission Control also shows different desktop spaces, enabling you to switch among desktop spaces or move an app window from one desktop space to another.

Switch Apps Using Mission Control

See All Your Open Apps and Windows

1 Swipe up on the trackpad with three fingers.

Note: You can also press F3 to activate Mission Control.

Note: On some Mac keyboards, you press F3 to launch Mission Control. You can also press Control + ⬆.

Note: You can also launch Mission Control by using a hot corner. See Chapter 2 for instructions on setting and using hot corners.

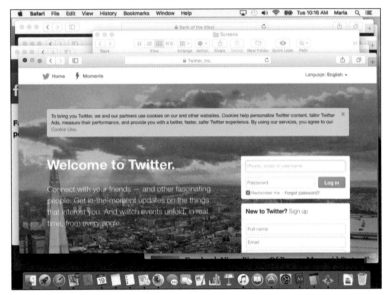

Mission Control opens and displays all open apps and windows.

A The Spaces bar at the top of the window shows the open desktops and any apps that are full screen.

B The current desktop or app is highlighted.

2 Move the pointer over the Spaces bar.

Thumbnails of the desktops and full-screen apps appear.

C To preview a window in an app, position the pointer over the window so that a blue outline appears around it. Then press **Spacebar** to preview the window. Press **Spacebar** again to close the preview.

3 Click the window you want to use.

The window appears, and you can work with it.

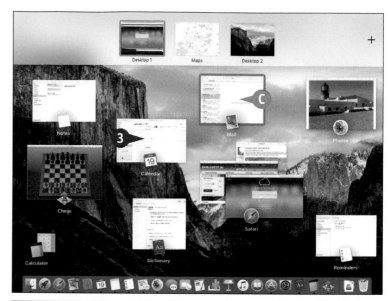

See All the Windows in the Active App

1 Click the Dock icon of the app you want to see.

2 Press **Control**+**F3**.

Note: You can also press **Control**+**↓** to display the windows of the active app.

OS X displays thumbnails of that app's windows.

3 Click the window you want to see.

OS X restores all the windows from all the apps, placing the window you clicked at the front.

TIP

What other actions can I take with Mission Control?

After pressing **Control**+**F3** to show all windows of the current app, you can press **Tab** to show all windows of the next app. Press **Shift**+**Tab** to show all windows of the previous app. You can press **⌘**+**F3** to move all open windows to the sides of the screen to reveal the desktop. Press **⌘**+**F3** when you want to see the windows again.

Set Up Dictation and Text to Speech

OS X's Dictation feature enables you to dictate text, which can be a fast and accurate way of entering text into documents. The Text to Speech feature enables you to have the system voice read on-screen items to you.

Before using Dictation and Text to Speech, you use Dictation & Speech preferences to enable the features. You can choose options such as whether to use the Enhanced Dictation feature, select your dictation language and the system voice, and define keyboard shortcuts for starting dictation and speaking.

Set Up Dictation and Text to Speech

1 Press **Control**+click **System Preferences** (🟦) on the Dock.

The contextual menu opens.

2 Click **Dictation & Speech.**

The System Preferences window opens and displays the Dictation & Speech pane.

3 Click **Dictation.**

The Dictation pane appears.

4 Click **Input** (⌄) and select the correct input.

5 Click **On** (◯ changes to ◉).

The Would You Like to Use Enhanced Dictation? dialog opens.

6 Click **Use Enhanced Dictation**.

The dialog closes.

OS X starts to download the files for Enhanced Dictation.

7 Click **Language** (◆) and select your language.

8 Click **Shortcut** (◆) and select the shortcut for starting dictation.

9 Click **Text to Speech**.

The Text to Speech pane opens.

10 Click **System Voice** (⬦) and select the voice you prefer.

Note: You can install other voices by clicking **Customize** on the System Voice pop-up menu.

11 Click **Play** to hear the voice.

12 Drag the **Speaking Rate** slider to adjust the speed if necessary.

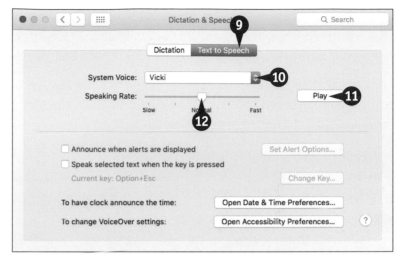

13 Click **Announce when alerts are displayed** (☐ changes to ☑) to hear alerts.

A You can click **Set Alert Options** to choose the voice, phrase, and delay for alerts.

14 Click **Speak selected text when the key is pressed** (☐ changes to ☑) to make your MacBook speak selected text.

B You can click **Change Key** to set the keystroke.

15 Click **Close** (●).

System Preferences closes.

TIP

Should I use Enhanced Dictation?

Using Enhanced Dictation is usually a good idea. Enhanced Dictation uses your MacBook to perform the speech recognition instead of sending your speech to Apple servers, and so has three main advantages over standard Dictation. First, you can dictate when your MacBook is offline as well as when it is online. Second, you can dictate continuously instead of having to pause between sentences or phrases. Third, you need not worry about the potential privacy implications of sharing your speech with Apple.

Using Dictation and Text to Speech

With the Dictation and Text to Speech features enabled and configured on your MacBook, you can use them freely as you work or play. When you are using an app that accepts text input, you can press your keyboard shortcut to turn on Dictation, and then dictate text into a document.

To make Text to Speech read to you, you select the text you want to hear and then press the appropriate keyboard shortcut. If you have enabled the announcing of alerts, your MacBook automatically speaks their text as well.

Using Dictation and Text to Speech

Use Dictation

1 Open the app into which you want to dictate text. For example, click **Notes** (⬜) on the Dock to open Notes.

2 Open the document into which you will dictate text. For example, in Notes, click the appropriate note.

3 Position the insertion point.

4 Press the keyboard shortcut you set for starting Dictation.

Note: The default keyboard shortcut is pressing Fn twice.

A The Dictation window opens.

5 Speak into your microphone.

Note: To enter a word with an initial capital letter, say "cap" followed by the word — for example, say "cap director" to enter "Director." To enter punctuation, say the appropriate word, such as "period," "comma," or "semicolon." To create a new paragraph, say "new paragraph."

B Dictation inserts the text in the document.

6 Click **Done**.

The Dictation window closes.

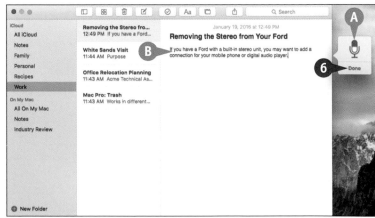

Make Text to Speech Read Text

1 In an app that contains text, select the text you want to hear.

2 Press the keyboard shortcut you set for Text to Speech.

Note: The default keyboard shortcut is **Option** + **Esc**.

Text to Speech reads the selected text to you.

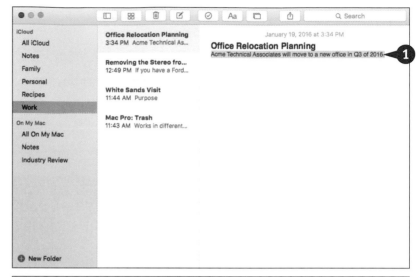

Hear Alerts from Text to Speech

C After an alert appears, Text to Speech waits as long as specified in Dictation & Speech preferences.

If you have not dismissed the alert, Text to Speech announces the app and then reads the text of the alert.

1 Click **Close** or **Snooze**, as appropriate, to dismiss the alert.

TIP

How accurate is Dictation?

Dictation can be highly accurate, but your results depend on how clearly you speak and how faithfully your microphone transmits the sound. For best results, use a headset microphone and position it to the side of your mouth, outside your breath stream.

When reviewing dictated text, read it for sense to identify incorrect words and phrases. Because all the text is spelled correctly, it can be easy to overlook mistakes caused by Dictation inserting the wrong words or phrases instead of what you said.

Remove Apps

O S X enables you to remove apps you have added, but not apps included with the operating system. If you no longer need apps you have installed, you can remove them to reclaim the disk space they occupy and to prevent them from causing your MacBook to run more slowly.

You can remove most apps by simply moving them to the Trash. But if an app has an uninstall utility, you should run that utility to remove the app and its ancillary files.

Remove Apps

Remove an App by Moving It to the Trash

1 Click **Launchpad** (🚀) on the Dock.

The Launchpad screen appears.

A If necessary, click a dot to move to another screen in Launchpad. You can also swipe left or right with two fingers on the trackpad.

2 Click the app and drag it to the Trash.

Finder places the app in the Trash.

Note: You can also drag an app to the Trash from the Applications folder. Alternatively, click the app in the Applications folder, click **Action** (⚙ ⌄), and then select **Move to Trash**.

Remove an App by Using an Uninstall Utility

1 Click **Finder** (🙂) on the Dock.

A Finder window opens.

2 Navigate to the folder that contains the uninstall utility.

Note: With the Finder active, you can press ⌘+Shift+A to open a window showing the Applications folder.

Note: See the tip for instructions on where to find the utility.

3 Press Option+double-click the uninstall utility.

The uninstall utility opens, and the Finder window closes.

4 Follow the steps of the uninstall utility. For example, click **Uninstall**.

5 When the uninstall utility finishes running, quit it. For example, press ⌘+Q.

TIP

Where do I find the uninstall utility for an app?
If the app has a folder within the Applications folder, look inside that folder for an uninstall utility. If there is no folder, open the disk image file, CD, or DVD from which you installed the app and look for an uninstall utility there. Some apps use an installer for both installing the app and uninstalling it, so if you do not find an uninstall utility, try running the installer and see if it contains an uninstall option. You may also need to download an uninstall utility from the app developer's website.

Identify Problem Apps

Sometimes you may find that your MacBook starts to respond slowly to your commands, even though no app has stopped working. When this occurs, you can use the Activity Monitor utility to see what app is consuming more of the processors' cycles than it should. To resolve the problem, you can quit that app and then restart it.

If you cannot quit the app normally, you can force quit it. You can force quit it either from Activity Monitor or by using the Force Quit Applications dialog.

Identify Problem Apps

① Click **Launchpad** (🚀) on the Dock.

The Launchpad screen appears.

② Type *ac*.

Launchpad displays only those items whose names include words starting with *ac*.

③ Click **Activity Monitor** (📊).

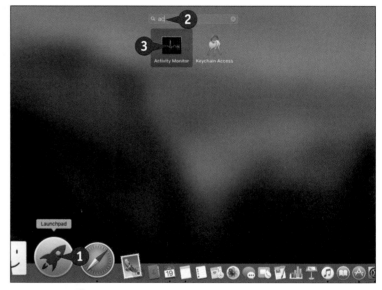

The Activity Monitor window opens, listing all your running apps and processes.

Ⓐ The title bar shows *(My Processes)* to indicate you are viewing only your processes.

④ Click **View**.

The View menu opens.

⑤ Click **All Processes**.

Note: You should view all processes because another user's processes may be slowing your MacBook.

Ⓑ The title bar shows *(All Processes)*.

Ⓒ Other users' processes and system processes appear as well.

⑥ Click **CPU**.

The details of your MacBook's central processing units, or CPUs, appear.

Ⓓ The CPU Load graph shows how hard the CPU is working.

⑦ Click **% CPU** once or twice, as needed, so that Descending Sort (⌄) appears on the column heading.

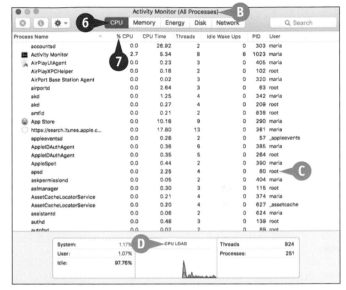

Activity Monitor sorts the processes by CPU activity in descending order.

⑧ Identify the app that is using the most processor cycles.

⑨ Click that app's Dock icon.

The app appears.

⑩ Save your work in the app, and then quit it.

⑪ Click the Activity Monitor window.

⑫ Click the **Activity Monitor** menu and click **Quit Activity Monitor** to close Activity Monitor.

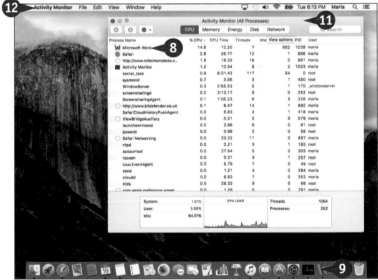

TIP

How do I see whether my MacBook is running short of memory?
Click **Memory** on the Activity Monitor tab bar and then look at the Memory Pressure readout. Click the **Memory** column heading to sort the processes by the amount of memory they are using.

Force a Crashed App to Quit

When an app is working normally, you can quit it by clicking the Quit command on the app's menu or by pressing `Control`+`Q`. But if an app stops responding to the trackpad and keyboard, you cannot quit it this way. Instead, you use the Force Quit command that OS X provides for this situation.

When an app stops responding, it may freeze, so that the window does not change, or it may display the spinning cursor for a long time, indicating that the app is busy.

Force a Crashed App to Quit

Force Quit an App from the Dock

1 Pressing and holding `Option`, click the app's icon on the Dock. Keep holding down the trackpad button until the Dock menu appears.

2 Click **Force Quit**.

OS X forces the app to quit.

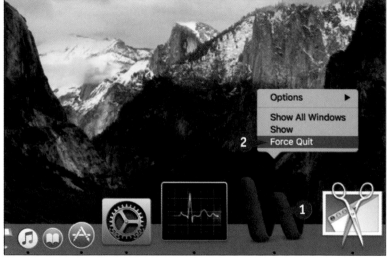

Force Quit an App from the Force Quit Applications Dialog

1 Click **Apple** (🍎).

The Apple menu opens.

2 Click **Force Quit**.

Note: You can open the Force Quit Applications dialog from the keyboard by pressing `Option`+`⌘`+`Esc`.

The Force Quit Applications dialog opens.

3 Click the app you want to force quit.

4 Click **Force Quit**.

A dialog opens to confirm that you want to force quit the app.

5 Click **Force Quit**.

OS X forces the app to quit.

6 Click **Close** (●).

The Force Quit Applications dialog closes.

TIP

How do I recover the unsaved changes in a document after force quitting the app?

When you force quit an app, you normally lose all unsaved changes in the documents you were using in the app. However, some apps automatically store unsaved changes in special files called *recovery files*, which the apps open when you relaunch them after force quitting. For some apps, you may also be able to return to an earlier version of the document.

Revert to an Earlier Version of a Document

OS X includes a feature called *versions* that enables apps to save different versions of the same document in the same file. You can display the different versions of the document at the same time and go back to an earlier version if necessary.

Only apps written to work specifically with OS X Lion, 10.7, and subsequent versions of OS X can use the versions feature. Such apps include TextEdit — the text editor and word processor included with OS X — and the apps in Apple's iWork suite.

Revert to an Earlier Version of a Document

1 In the appropriate app, open the document. For example, open a word processing document in TextEdit.

2 Click the app's name on the menu bar.

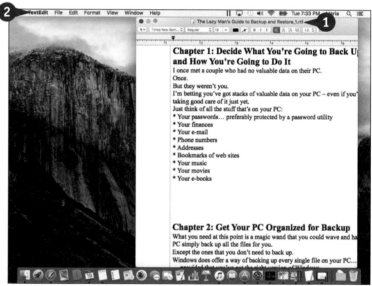

The app's menu opens.

3 Click **Revert To**.

Note: You can also highlight **Revert To** without clicking.

The Revert To submenu opens.

A You can click a version on the menu to go straight to that version.

4 Click **Browse All Versions**.

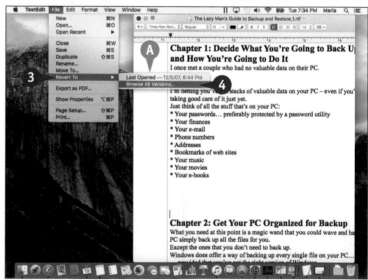

B OS X displays earlier versions of the document on the right, with newer versions at the front, and older versions at the back.

C The current version appears on the left.

5 Position the pointer over the time bars, and then click the version you want.

The version comes to the front.

6 Click **Restore**.

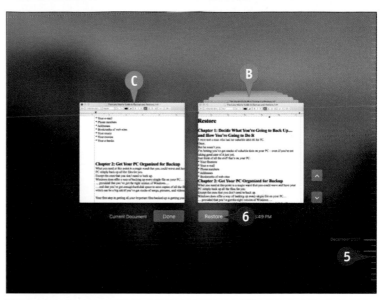

OS X restores the version of the document.

The version opens in the app so that you can work with it.

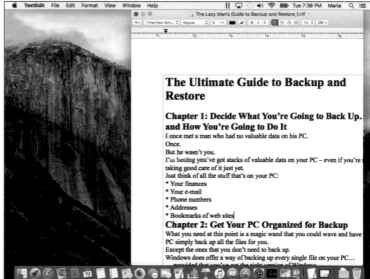

How can I tell whether an app supports versions?

With the app open, click **File** and see if the Revert To command appears on the menu. If the command appears, the app supports versions; if not, it does not.

How can I examine a document more closely before reverting to it?

When OS X displays the document versions, click the document you want to examine. The document's window enlarges so that you can see the document better. Click the background when you want to return the document window to its previous size.

Using Dashboard

The Dashboard feature offers an easy way to access *widgets*, small applications that provide very specific functionality. To use a widget, you activate Dashboard, which fills the desktop and presents the widgets installed on it. Use the widgets you want; when you are done, close Dashboard again. OS X includes a number of useful widgets by default, such as Weather, Calculator, Address Book, and Flight Tracker. There is even a widget to help you manage your widgets.

Using Dashboard

1 Click **Launchpad** (🚀) on the Dock.

The Launchpad screen appears.

2 Click **Dashboard** (⚫).

Note: You can also open Dashboard by opening Mission Control and then clicking the **Dashboard** space.

Dashboard opens, occupying the full screen.

Ⓐ You can click an interactive widget, such as the Calculator widget, and use it by clicking its buttons.

Ⓑ You can view an informational widget, such as the Clock widget.

3 To configure a widget, move the pointer over it.

The Info button (ⓘ) appears if the widget is configurable.

4 Click **Info** (ⓘ).

116

The widget turns over, showing its configuration options.

⑤ Change the widget's configuration options as needed. For example, on the Weather widget, you can choose the location, switch between Fahrenheit and Celsius, and choose whether to include lows in the 6-day forecast.

⑥ Click **Done**.

The widget turns over, and you see the effects of your changes.

⑦ When you finish using widgets, click **Back** (⊙).

Dashboard disappears.

The screen that you were using before invoking Dashboard reappears.

How can I make Dashboard more useful?

If you do not find Dashboard useful in its default state, do not worry — you are not alone. To make Dashboard more useful, add to it widgets that perform useful functions by using the technique explained in the next section, "Configure Dashboard." Consider adding third-party widgets such as the Mac-monitoring iStat Pro widget, the battery-life widget called Mighty Monitor, and the countdown timer widget called Countdown. If you enjoy games, look at widgets such as the Asteroids widget and the Missile Command widget.

Configure Dashboard

You can configure Dashboard to contain the widgets you find most useful. Dashboard includes a variety of built-in widgets that you can access instantly. You can download other widgets from online sources.

You can also change the layout in which the widgets appear in Dashboard. For example, you may want to position related widgets in groups so that you can find them easily.

Configure Dashboard

1 Click **Launchpad** (🚀) on the Dock.

The Launchpad screen appears.

2 Click **Dashboard** (●).

Note: You can also open Dashboard by opening Mission Control and then clicking the **Dashboard** space.

Dashboard opens, occupying the full screen.

3 Click and drag the widgets to where you want them to appear.

4 Click **Add** (⊕).

The screen of available widgets appears.

Ⓐ You can click **More Widgets** to display more widgets online.

5 Click the widget you want to add to Dashboard.

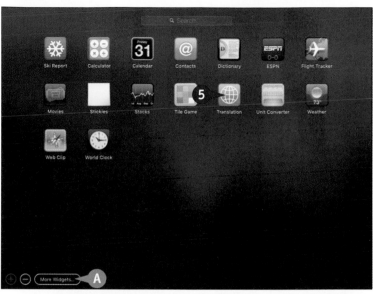

Ⓑ The widget appears on Dashboard, and you can start using it.

6 When you finish using widgets, click **Back** (▶).

Dashboard disappears.

The screen that you were using before invoking Dashboard reappears.

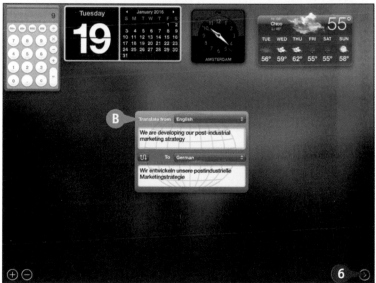

TIP

How can I remove a widget from Dashboard?

To remove a widget from Dashboard, open Dashboard and click **Remove** (⊖). A Delete icon (⊗) appears on each widget. Click **Delete** (⊗) on the widget you want to remove. The widget disappears from Dashboard and moves to the list of available widgets, from which you can add it again later if necessary. When you finish removing widgets, click **Remove** (⊖) again to return Dashboard to its normal mode.

CHAPTER 5

Managing Your Files and Folders

The Finder enables you to manage your files, folders, and drives. You can take many actions in the Finder, including copying, moving, and deleting files and folders.

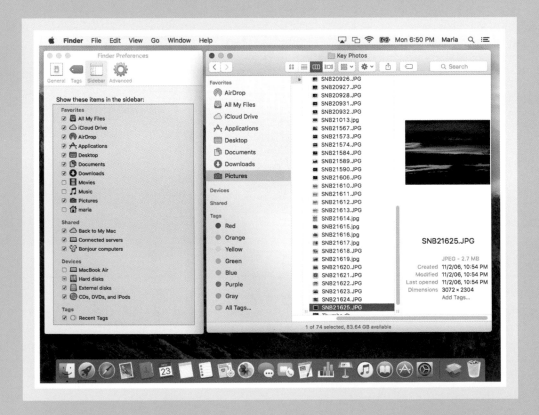

Understanding Where to Store Files

OS X automatically creates a structure of folders in each user account for storing files. Your home base is your Home folder, which contains folders such as Desktop, Documents, Downloads, and Music. You can navigate easily among your folders by using the sidebar or the Go menu. To help you find your files, the Finder also includes a view called All My Files, which shows your files arranged by their type or another attribute you choose.

Understanding Where to Store Files

1 Click **Finder** (🙂) on the Dock.

A Finder window opens to your default folder or view.

2 Click **All My Files**.

The Finder window displays the All My Files view, which shows all your files.

3 Click **Documents**.

The contents of the Documents folder appear.

Note: The Documents folder is your storage place for word processing documents, spreadsheets, and similar files.

4 Click **Go**.

The Go menu opens.

5 Click **Home**.

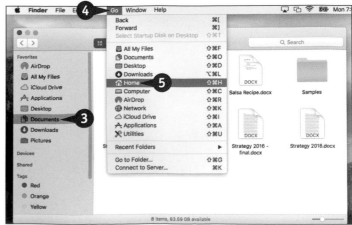

The contents of your Home folder appear.

Ⓐ The Desktop folder contains items on your desktop.

Ⓑ The Downloads folder contains files you download via apps such as Safari or Mail.

Ⓒ The Movies folder contains movies, such as iMovie projects.

Ⓓ The Pictures folder contains images.

Ⓔ The Public folder is for sharing files with others.

⑥ Double-click **Music**.

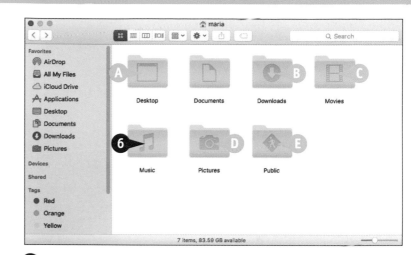

The contents of your Music folder appear.

Ⓕ The iTunes folder contains your music library.

Ⓖ The GarageBand folder appears if you have used GarageBand, the music-composition app.

Ⓗ The Audio Music Apps folder contains support files for GarageBand and other music apps.

Ⓘ You can click **Back** (〈) to move back along the path of folders you have followed.

⑦ Click **Close** (●).

The Finder window closes.

How do I choose what folder the Finder opens by default?
Click the desktop to activate the Finder. Click **Finder** to open the Finder menu, and then click **Preferences**. Click **General** to display the General pane. Click the **New Finder windows show** pop-up menu (◉), and then select the folder you want new Finder windows to display. Click **Close** (●) to close the Finder Preferences window.

Using the Finder's Views

The Finder provides four views to help you find and identify your files and folders. You can switch from view to view by using the View buttons, the View menu or the contextual menu, or keyboard shortcuts.

Icon view shows each file or folder as a graphical icon. List view shows folders as a collapsible hierarchy. Column view enables you to navigate quickly through folders and see where each item is located. Cover Flow view is great for identifying files visually by looking at their contents.

Using the Finder's Views

Icon View

① Click **Finder** (🙂) on the Dock.

A Finder window opens showing your default folder or view.

② Click the folder you want to display.

The folder appears — in this case, the Pictures folder.

③ Click **Icons** (🔡) on the toolbar.

The files and folders appear in Icon view.

List View

① Click **List** (☰) on the toolbar.

The files and folders appear in List view.

② Click **Expand** (▶ changes to ▼) next to a folder.

The folder's contents appear.

Note: If the disclosure triangles do not appear next to folders, click **View**, highlight **Arrange By**, and select **None**.

③ When you need to hide the folder's contents again, click **Collapse** (▼ changes to ▶).

Note: Click a column header in List view to sort by that column.

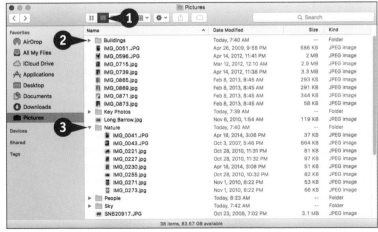

Column View

1 In the Finder window, click **Columns** (▥) on the toolbar.

The files and folders appear in Column view.

2 Click a folder in the first column after the sidebar.

The folder's contents appear in the next column.

3 Click another folder if necessary.

The folder's contents appear.

4 Click a file.

A A preview of the file appears.

Cover Flow View

1 In the Finder window, click **Cover Flow** (▥) on the toolbar.

The files and folders appear in Cover Flow view.

2 Click a file in the list view.

A preview or icon appears in the Cover Flow area.

B Click to display the previous document.

C Click to display the next document.

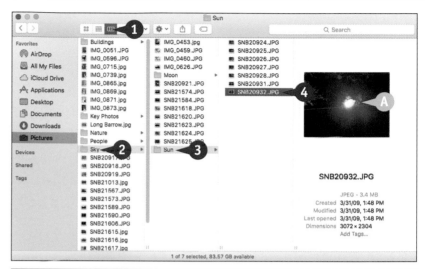

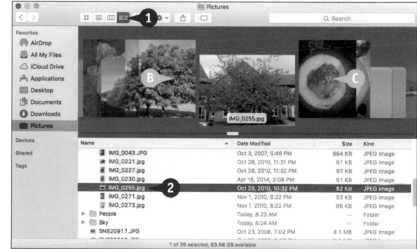

TIP

Can I change the size of icons used in Icon view?

Yes. If both the status bar and toolbar are displayed, you can change icon size by dragging the slider on the right side of the status bar. If the toolbar is hidden, the status bar appears below the window's title bar. To display the status bar, click **View** and **Show Status Bar**. To display the toolbar, click **View** and **Show Toolbar**.

To set a default size for Icon view, switch to Icon view and then click **View** and **Show View Options**. In the View Options window, click and drag the **Icon size** slider. Click **Use as Defaults**. Click **Close** (●) to close the View Options window.

Work with Finder Tabs

The Finder enables you to open multiple tabs within the same window. This capability is useful when you need to work in multiple folders at the same time. You can navigate quickly among the tabs by using the tab bar.

Finder tabs are especially useful if you switch a Finder window to full-screen mode. You can drag files or folders from one Finder tab to another to copy or move the items.

Work with Finder Tabs

1 Click **Finder** () on the Dock.

A Finder window opens.

2 Click the folder you want to view in the window.

3 Press ⌘+**T** or click **File** and **New Tab**.

Note: The Finder hides the tab bar by default when only one tab is open. You can display the tab bar by clicking **View** and clicking **Show Tab Bar** or pressing **Shift**+⌘+**T**.

Ⓐ The tab bar appears.

Ⓑ A new tab opens.

4 Click the folder you want to view.

Note: You can use a different view in each tab.

5 Click **New Tab** (+).

Note: To close a tab, position the pointer over it and then click **Close** (×). You can also press ⌘+**W** or click **File** and select **Close Tab**.

A new tab opens.

6 Drag the tab along the tab bar to where you want it.

Note: You can drag a tab to another Finder window if you want. You can also drag a tab out of a Finder window to turn it into its own window.

7 Click **View** and **Full Screen**. Alternatively, press `Control` + `⌘` + `F`.

The Finder window appears full screen, giving you more space for working with files, folders, and tabs.

Note: To exit full-screen view, move the pointer to the top of the screen so that the menu bar appears, and then click **View** and **Exit Full Screen**. Alternatively, press `Esc` or press `Control` + `⌘` + `F` again.

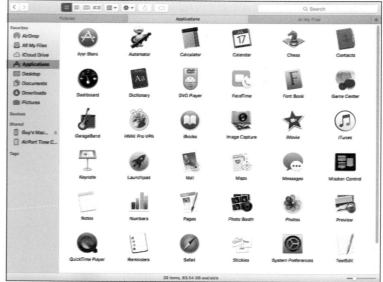

How do I copy or move files using Finder tabs?

Select the files in the source tab, and then drag them to the destination tab on the tab bar. To put the files into the folder open in the destination tab, drop the files on the destination tab in the tab bar. To navigate to a subfolder, position the pointer over the destination tab until its content appears, and then drag the items to the subfolder.

View a File with Quick Look

OS X's Quick Look feature enables you to preview files in Finder windows without actually opening the files in their apps. You can use Quick Look to determine what a file contains or to identify the file for which you are looking. You can preview a file full screen with Quick Look or preview multiple files at the same time. Quick Look works for many widely used types of files, but not for all types.

View a File with Quick Look

1 Click **Finder** (🙂) on the Dock.

A Finder window opens to your default folder or view.

2 Click the file you want to look through.

3 Click **Action** (⚙ ⌄).

The Action pop-up menu opens.

Note: You can also press [Spacebar] to open a Quick Look window for the selected item.

4 Click **Quick Look**.

A Quick Look window opens, showing a preview of the file or the file's icon.

Note: When you use Quick Look on an audio file or a video file, OS X starts playing the file.

5 If you need to scroll to see more of the file, drag the scroll box on the scroll bar or swipe up on the trackpad.

A You can click **Open with** to open the file in its default app.

6 To view the file in full-screen view, click **Full Screen** (◉).

The Quick Look window expands to fill the screen.

Note: To see more of the file in full-screen view, scroll down, swipe up with two fingers, or press **Page down**.

7 Click **Exit Full Screen** (⬈) when you finish using full-screen view.

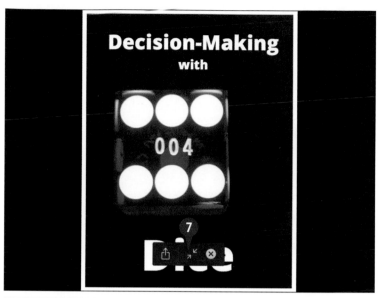

8 Click **Close** (✖) to close the Quick Look window.

Note: Instead of closing the Quick Look window, you can press ➡, ⬅, ⬆, or ⬇ to display another file or folder.

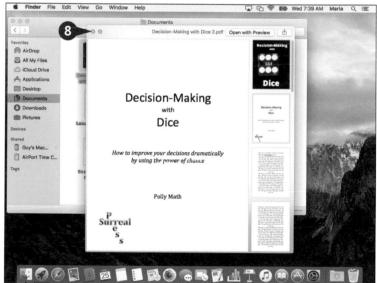

TIP

How do I use Quick Look on more than one file at a time?

Use Quick Look's full-screen view, which enables you to browse the files easily. Select the files you want to view with Quick Look, launch Quick Look, and click **Full Screen** (◎) to enter full-screen view. Click **Play** (▶) to play each preview for a few seconds, or click **Next** (➡) and **Previous** (⬅) to move from preview to preview. Click **Index Sheet** (⊞) to see the index sheet showing all previews, and then click the item you want to see.

Search for a File or Folder

OS X includes a powerful search feature called Spotlight that enables you to find the files and folders you need. Spotlight automatically indexes the files on your MacBook and connected drives so that it can deliver accurate results within seconds when you search.

You can use Spotlight either directly from the desktop or from within a Finder window. Depending on what you need to find, you can use either straightforward search keywords or complex search criteria.

Search for a File or Folder

Search Quickly from the Desktop

1. Click **Spotlight** (Q).

   The Spotlight pop-up window opens.

2. Type one or more keywords.

   Spotlight displays a list of matches.

3. In the left pane, click the result you want to preview.

   Ⓐ The right pane shows a preview.

4. Double-click the file you want to open.

   The file opens in the application associated with it.

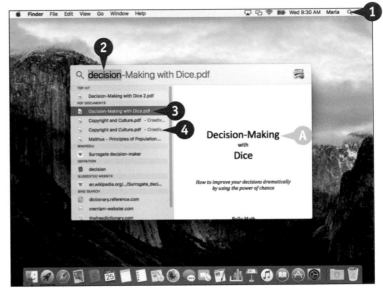

Search from a Finder Window

1. Click **Finder** (🙂) on the Dock.

   A Finder window opens.

2. Click the folder or location you want to search.

3. Click in the search field.

4. Type the keywords for your search.

   Ⓑ The Finder window's title bar changes to Searching.

   Ⓒ A list of search results appears.

   Ⓓ You can click a suggested search criterion on the pop-up menu to restrict the search.

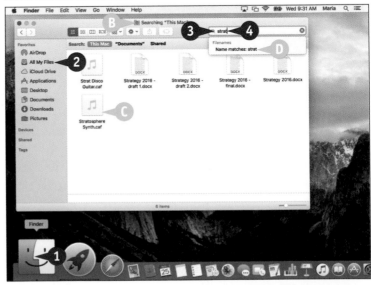

5 To change where Spotlight is searching, click a button on the Search bar.

E You can quickly view a file by pressing `Control` +clicking it and then clicking **Quick Look** or by clicking it and pressing `Spacebar`.

F You can open a file by double-clicking it.

6 To refine the search, click **Add** (⊕).

A line of controls appears.

7 Click the first pop-up menu (◉) and click **Kind**, **Last opened date**, **Last modified date**, **Created date**, **Name**, or **Contents**.

8 Click the second pop-up menu (◉) and select search criteria — for example, *Kind is Document*.

Note: To add more search criteria, click **Add** (⊕).

The search results appear.

G You can click **Save** to save the search for future use.

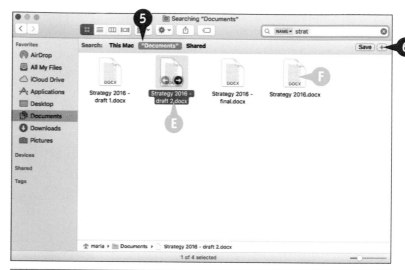

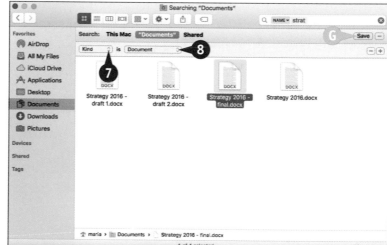

What does Spotlight index?
Spotlight indexes both the metadata and the contents of files. Metadata includes information such as the filename, file extension, and file label; the date created, date received, and date last viewed; and the subject, title, and comment assigned to the file. Contents include any text, enabling you to search by keyword in documents that contain text.

Can I change where Spotlight searches for files?
You can customize the list of folders that Spotlight searches. See the next section for instructions on customizing Spotlight.

Control Which Folders Spotlight Searches

OS X's Spotlight feature indexes your MacBook's files so that you can easily search them from either the Spotlight icon on the menu bar or from a Finder window. To improve the search results that Spotlight returns, you can customize the folders that Spotlight searches. You can exclude folders you do not want to search and choose whether to use Spotlight Suggestions in Spotlight itself and in the Look Up feature, which enables you to look up words in documents or web pages.

Control Which Folders Spotlight Searches

1 Press **Control** + click **System Preferences** (⚙) on the Dock.

The contextual menu opens.

2 Click **Spotlight**.

Note: Alternatively, click **Apple** (), click **System Preferences**, and then click **Spotlight** (🔍).

The System Preferences window opens with the Spotlight pane at the front.

3 Click **Search Results**.

The Search Results pane appears.

4 Click the check box for any item you want to exclude from search results (☑ changes to ☐).

5 Click **Allow Spotlight Suggestions in Spotlight and Look up** (☐ changes to ☑) if you want Spotlight suggestions to appear in Spotlight and in Look Up.

A You can click **Keyboard Shortcuts** to display the Spotlight category in the Shortcuts pane in Keyboard preferences. Here, you can disable or change the keyboard shortcuts for Spotlight.

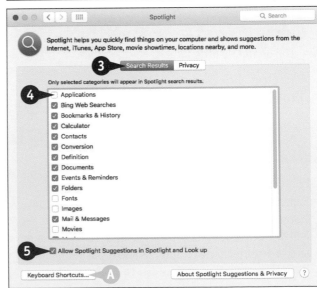

6 Click **Privacy**.

The Privacy pane appears.

7 Click **Add** (✚).

Note: Adding a folder to the exclusion list prevents even a search in a Finder window showing that folder's contents from finding matches. This can be confusing to users, because the files are right there and clearly match the search criteria.

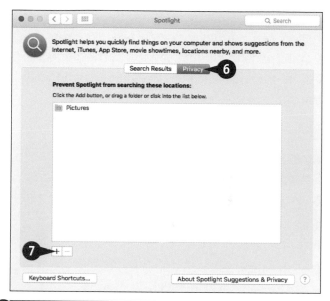

A dialog opens.

8 Click the folder you want to add.

Note: You can select two or more folders by clicking the first and then ⌘+clicking each of the others.

9 Click **Choose**.

The dialog closes, and the folder appears in the list.

10 Click **Close** (●).

System Preferences closes.

Is there another way to add locations to the Privacy list?

Instead of using the dialog to build the list of locations you do not want Spotlight to search, you can work from a Finder window. Click **Finder** (🙂) on the Dock to open a Finder window, and position it so that you can see both it and the Spotlight preferences pane. Click and drag from the Finder window to the Spotlight preferences pane the folders or disks you want to protect to add them to the list. You can select multiple items to save time.

Create a New Folder

O S X builds a hierarchy of folders in your user account but also enables you to create as many new folders and subfolders as you need. You can create folders and subfolders in your user account or in other parts of the file system, such as on an external drive connected to your MacBook. If the folders are for your personal use, keep them in your user account — as long as your MacBook's drive has enough space — or on a removable drive.

Create a New Folder

1 Click **Finder** () on the Dock.

A Finder window opens to your default folder.

2 Click the folder in which you want to create the new folder.

3 Click **Action** (✿ ∨) on the toolbar.

The Action pop-up menu opens.

4 Click **New Folder**.

Note: You can also create a new folder by pressing ⌘+Shift+N, or by clicking **File** on the Finder menu bar and clicking **New Folder**.

Ⓐ A new folder appears in the Finder window.

The new folder shows an edit box around the default name, Untitled Folder.

5 Type the name you want to give the folder.

6 Press **Return**.

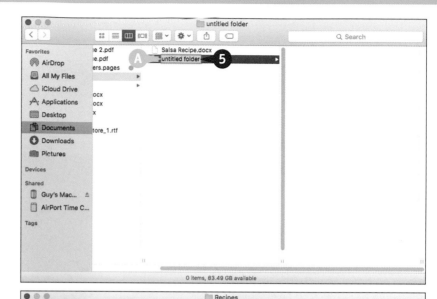

The folder takes on the new name.

7 Click or double-click the folder, depending on the view you are using.

The folder opens. You can now add files to the folder or create subfolders inside it.

Why can I not create a new folder inside some other folders?

Most likely, you do not have permission to create a folder in that folder. Each user can create new items in the folders in his user account, and administrators can create folders in some other folders. But OS X protects other folders, such as the System folder and the Users folder, from anybody creating new folders.

Copy a File

The Finder enables you to copy a file from one folder to another. Copying is useful when you need to share a file with other people or when you need to keep a copy of the file safe against harm.

You can copy either by clicking and dragging or by using the Copy and Paste commands. You can copy a single file or folder at a time or copy multiple items.

Copy a File

Copy a File by Clicking and Dragging

1 Click **Finder** (🗿) on the Dock.

A Finder window opens.

2 Click the folder that contains the file you want to copy.

3 Click **File**.

The File menu opens.

4 Click **New Finder Window**.

A new Finder window opens.

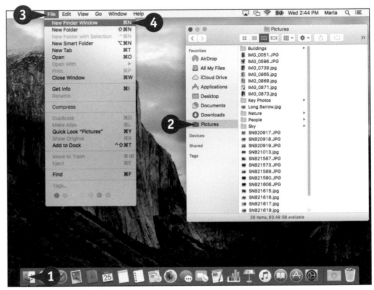

5 In the second Finder window, navigate to the destination folder.

6 Arrange the Finder windows so that you can see both.

7 Select the file or files.

8 Press and hold (Option) while you click the file and drag it to the destination folder.

Note: Pressing and holding (Option) while dragging causes OS X to copy the file on a local drive instead of moving the file.

Note: The pointer displays a plus sign (🔂) to indicate copying.

The copy or copies appear in the destination folder.

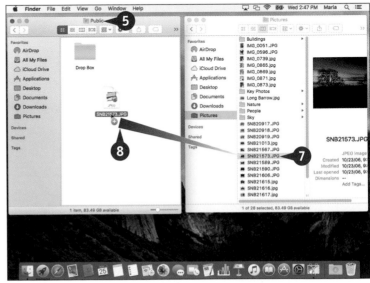

Copy a File by Using Copy and Paste

1 Click **Finder** ( ) on the Dock.

A Finder window opens.

2 Click the folder that contains the file you want to copy.

3 Click the file.

Note: You can also copy the selected item by pressing ⌘+C and paste the copied or cut item by pressing ⌘+V.

4 Click **Action** (⚙ ∨).

The Action pop-up menu opens.

5 Click **Copy**.

Finder copies the file's details to the clipboard.

6 Click the folder in which you want to create the copy.

7 Click **Action** (⚙ ∨).

The Action pop-up menu opens.

8 Click **Paste Item**.

A copy of the file appears in the destination folder.

Note: You can use the Paste command in either the same Finder window or tab or another Finder window or tab — whichever you find more convenient.

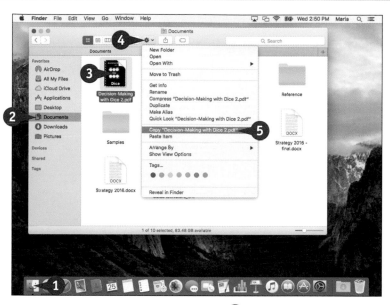

How do I copy a folder?

Use the same techniques as for files: Either press Option +click and drag the folder or folders to the destination folder, or use the Copy command to copy the folder and the Paste command to paste it into the destination folder.

Can I make a copy of a file in the same folder as the original?

To make a copy of a file in the same folder as the original, click the file, click **Action** (⚙ ∨), and then click **Duplicate**. Finder automatically adds *copy* to the end of the copy's filename to distinguish it from the original.

Move a File

The Finder makes it easy to move a file from one folder to another. You can move a file quickly by clicking it in its current folder and then dragging it to the destination folder.

When the destination folder is on the same drive as the source folder, the Finder moves the file to that folder. But when the destination folder is on a different drive, the Finder copies the file by default. To override this and move the file, you press ⌘ as you drag.

Move a File

Move a File Between Folders on the Same Drive

1 Click **Finder** (🙂) on the Dock.

A Finder window opens.

2 Click the folder that contains the file you want to move.

3 Click **File**.

The File menu opens.

4 Click **New Finder Window**.

A new Finder window opens.

5 In the second Finder window, open the destination folder.

6 Click and drag the Finder windows so that you can see both.

7 Click the file and drag it to the destination folder.

The file appears in the destination folder and disappears from the source folder.

Move a File from One Drive to Another

1 Click **Finder** (🙂) on the Dock.

A Finder window opens.

2 Click the folder that contains the file you want to move.

3 Press **Control** + click **Finder** (🙂) on the Dock.

The contextual menu opens.

4 Click **New Finder Window**.

A new Finder window opens.

5 In the second Finder window, click the drive to which you want to copy the file.

6 Click the destination folder.

7 Arrange the Finder windows so that you can see both.

8 Press and hold ⌘ while you click the file and drag it to the destination folder.

The file appears in the destination folder and disappears from the source folder.

TIP

Can I move files by using menu commands rather than clicking and dragging?

If you find it awkward to click and drag files from one folder to another, you can use menu commands instead. Select the file or files you want to move, and then click **Edit** and **Copy** to copy them. Open the destination folder and click **Edit** to open the Edit menu. Press and hold **Option** and click **Move Item Here** or **Move Items Here**.

Rename a File or Folder

The Finder enables you to rename any file or folder you have created. To keep your MacBook's file system well organized, it is often helpful to rename files and folders.

OS X prevents you from renaming system folders, such as the System folder itself, the Applications folder, or the Users folder. OS X also prevents renaming the standard folders in each user account, such as the Documents folder and the Pictures folder, because apps expect these folders to be available.

Rename a File or Folder

1 Click the desktop.

The Finder becomes active.

2 Click **File**.

The File menu opens.

3 Click **New Finder Window**.

A new Finder window opens.

4 Click the folder that contains the file or folder you want to rename.

5 Click the file or folder.

6 Press **Return**.

Note: You can also display the edit box by clicking the file's name to select it, pausing, and then clicking again. You must pause between the clicks; otherwise, the Finder registers a double-click and opens the file.

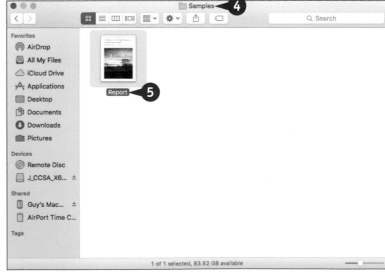

An edit box appears around the filename.

7 Edit the file's current name, or simply type the new name over the current name.

8 Press Return.

A The file takes on the new name.

You can now open the file by double-clicking it or pressing ⌘+O, or rename another file or folder.

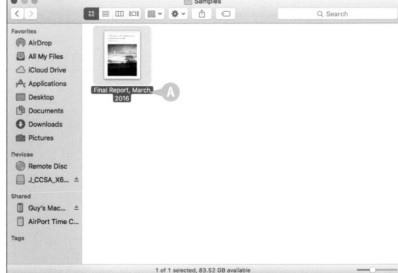

Can I rename several files at the same time?

There is no convenient way to rename several files at the same time from the Finder manually. Each file in a folder must have a unique name, so you cannot apply the same name to two or more files simultaneously. Some applications and scripts have features for renaming multiple files at once, usually by giving them sequential names using numbers appended to a base name — for example, Carlsbad Trip 01, Carlsbad Trip 02, and so on.

View the Information About a File or Folder

O S X keeps a large amount of information about each file and folder. When you view the file or folder in most Finder views, you can see the item's name and some basic information about it, such as its kind, size, and date last modified.

To see further information about the file or folder, you can open the Info window. This window contains multiple sections that you can expand by clicking **Expand** (▶) or collapse by clicking **Collapse** (▼).

View the Information About a File or Folder

1 Click **Finder** ( ) on the Dock.

A Finder window opens.

2 Click the folder that contains the file whose info you want to view.

3 Click the file.

4 Click **Action** (⚙ ✓).

The Action pop-up menu opens.

5 Click **Get Info**.

Note: You can also open the Info window for the selected item by pressing ⌘+ I .

The Info window opens.

6 View the preview.

7 Review the tags. Press Return to add tags.

Note: See the next section, "Organize Your Files with Tags," for more on tags.

8 Review the general information:

Kind shows the file's type. *Size* shows the file's size on disk. *Where* shows the folder that contains the file. *Created* shows when the file was created. *Modified* shows when the file was last changed.

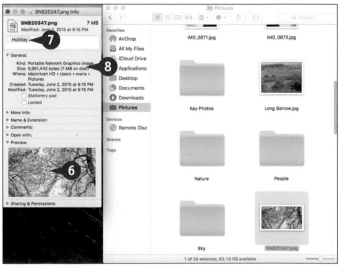

9 Review the details in the More Info section.

Note: The More Info details are especially useful for photos.

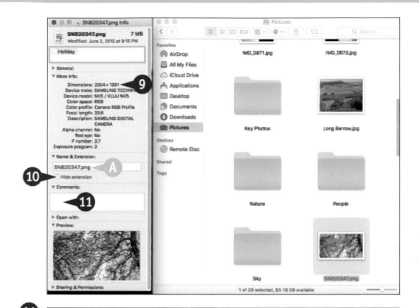

Ⓐ You can change the filename or extension. Normally, it is best not to change the extension.

10 Click **Hide extension** (☐ changes to ☑) if you want to hide the extension.

11 Type any comments to help identify the file.

12 Click **Open with** (◉) and select the app with which to open this file.

13 Click **Change All** if you want to use the app for all files of this type.

14 Click **Close** (●).

The Info window closes.

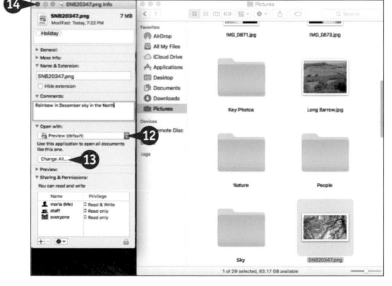

How do I use the Sharing & Permissions settings?

To adjust the permissions for the file or folder, click the Privilege row for the user or group you want to affect. You can then select the appropriate level of permissions: **Read & Write**, **Read only**, or **No Access**. Click **Add** (✚) to add a user or group to the list. Click **Remove** (—) to remove the selected user or group from the list.

Organize Your Files with Tags

You can organize your files and folders by giving them descriptive names and storing them in appropriate places. But OS X and its apps give you another means of organizing your files and folders: tags.

OS X includes a set of default tags that you can customize to better describe your projects. You can then apply one or more tags to a file to enable you to locate it more easily either on your MacBook or in iCloud.

Organize Your Files with Tags

Customize Your Tags

1 Click the desktop.

The Finder becomes active.

2 Click **Finder**.

The Finder menu opens.

3 Click **Preferences**.

The Finder Preferences window opens.

4 Click **Tags**.

The Tags pane appears.

5 Click a tag you want to rename, and then type the new name.

6 Click the check box (⊟ changes to ✅) to make the tag appear in the list in the Finder.

7 Drag the tags into the order in which you want them to appear.

8 Drag tags to the Favorite Tags list at the bottom to control which tags appear in Finder menus.

Ⓐ You can click **Add** (➕) to add a new tag to the list.

9 Click **Close** (●).

The Finder Preferences window closes.

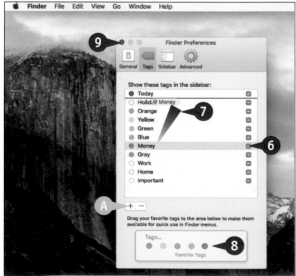

Apply Tags to Files and Folders

1. If the Tags section of the sidebar is not displayed, position the pointer over Tags and click **Show**.

2. Click the file or folder and drag it to the appropriate tag.

   Finder applies the tag.

Note: You can also apply tags from the File menu or from the contextual menu.

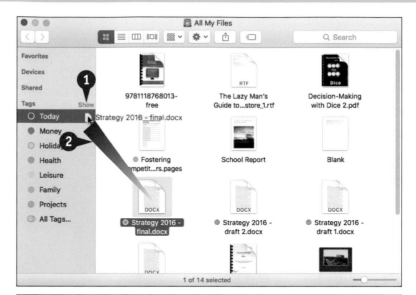

View Files and Folders by Tags

1. If the Tags section of the sidebar is not displayed, position the pointer over Tags and click **Show** when it appears.

2. Click the appropriate tag.

   Ⓑ The Finder window shows the tagged files and folders.

TIP

How do I apply tags to a new document I create?
In the app, click **File** and **Save** or press ⌘ + S to display the Save As dialog. Type the filename, then click **Tags** and click each tag you want to apply. You can then choose the folder in which to save the document and click **Save** to save it.

Compress Files

OS X includes a compression tool that enables you to shrink files. Compression is especially useful for files you need to transfer across the Internet, place on a limited-capacity medium such as a USB drive, or archive for storage.

Using the Finder, you can compress a single file or multiple files. Compressing creates a compressed file in the widely used Zip format, often called a *Zip file,* that contains a copy of the files. The original files remain unchanged.

Compress Files

Compress Files to a Zip File

1 Click **Finder** (🙂) on the Dock.

   A Finder window opens.

2 Click the folder that contains the file or files you want to compress.

3 Select the file or files.

4 Click **Action** (✿ ⌄).

   The Action pop-up menu opens.

5 Click **Compress**.

Ⓐ The compressed file appears in the folder.

Note: If you selected one file, OS X gives the file the same name with the .zip extension. If you selected multiple files, OS X names the Zip file Archive.zip.

6 Click the file and press Return.

   An edit box appears.

7 Type the new name and press Return.

   The file takes on the new name.

Extract Files from a Zip File

1. Click **Finder** (🙂) on the Dock.

   A Finder window opens.

2. Click the folder that contains the Zip file.

Note: If you receive the Zip file attached to an e-mail message, save the file as explained in Chapter 7.

3. Double-click the Zip file.

Archive Utility unzips the Zip file, creates a folder with the same name as the Zip file, and places the contents of the Zip file in it.

4. Click the new folder to see the files extracted from the Zip file.

TIP

When I compress a music file, the Zip file is bigger than the original file. What have I done wrong?
You have done nothing wrong. Compression removes extra space from the file, and can squeeze some graphics and text files down by as much as 90 percent. But if you try to compress an already compressed file, such as an MP3 audio file or an MPEG video file, Archive Utility cannot compress it further — and the Zip file packaging adds a small amount to the file size.

Using the Trash

OS X provides a special folder called the Trash in which you can place files and folders you intend to delete. Like a real-world trash can, the Trash retains files until you actually empty it. So if you find you have thrown away a file that you need after all, you can recover the file from the Trash. The Trash icon appears at the right end of the Dock by default, giving you quick access to the Trash.

Using the Trash

Place a File in the Trash

1 Click **Finder** (🙂) on the Dock.

A Finder window opens to your default folder or view.

2 Click the folder that contains the file you want to throw in the Trash.

3 Click the file you want to delete.

4 Click **Action** (✱ ⌄).

The Action pop-up menu opens.

5 Click **Move to Trash**.

Ⓐ The file disappears from the folder and moves to the Trash.

Note: You can also place a file in the Trash by clicking and dragging it to the Trash icon on the Dock, or from the keyboard by clicking the file and then pressing ⌘ + Delete.

Recover a File from the Trash

1 Click **Trash** (🗑) on the Dock.

The Trash window opens.

2 Click the file you want to recover.

3 Click **Action** (⚙ ⌄).

The Action pop-up menu opens.

4 Click **Put Back**.

The Finder restores the file to its previous folder.

Note: If you want to put the file in a different folder, drag it to that folder. For example, drag the file to the desktop.

5 Click **Close** (●) or press ⌘+W.

The Trash window closes.

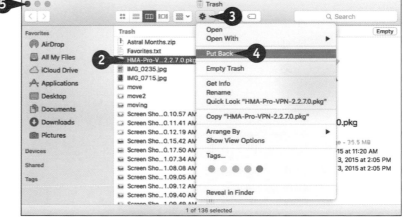

TIP

What else can I do with the Trash?

You can use the Trash to eject a removable disk, CD, or DVD in an optical drive you have connected to your MacBook. When you click a removable disk, CD, or DVD and drag it toward the Trash, the Trash icon changes to an Eject icon (⏏). Drop the item on the Eject icon to eject it. When you click and drag a recordable CD or DVD to which you have added files toward the Trash, OS X displays a Burn icon (☢). Drop the disc on the Burn icon to start burning it.

Customize the Finder Toolbar

The toolbar that appears at the top of the Finder window contains buttons that you can use to access commands quickly and easily. For example, the various View buttons appear there along with the Action menu button. Although the Finder toolbar includes a number of buttons by default, you can configure the toolbar so that it contains the buttons you use most frequently.

Configure the Finder Window Toolbar

1 Click **Finder** () on the Dock.

A Finder window opens to your default folder or view.

2 Click **View**.

The View menu opens.

3 Click **Customize Toolbar**.

The Customize Toolbar dialog opens.

4 To add a button to the toolbar, drag it from the Customize Toolbar dialog and drop it on the toolbar where you want it to appear.

Note: You can click a button on the toolbar and drag it to a new position.

A If you need to restore the toolbar to its original state, click the **... or drag the default set into the toolbar** box and drag it to the toolbar.

The button appears on the toolbar.

5 To remove a button from the toolbar, drag its icon from the toolbar into the Customize Toolbar dialog.

6 Click **Show** ($\updownarrow$) and then click the appearance you want: **Icon and Text**, **Icon Only**, or **Text Only**.

7 Click **Done**.

The Customize Toolbar dialog closes, and the toolbar appears in its customized form.

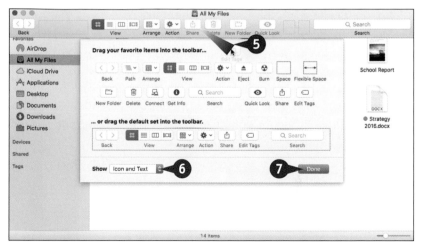

What does the Path button do?

The Path button enables you to easily see and navigate the path to the folder the Finder window is displaying. The path appears as a vertical menu of locations starting from the active folder — for example, New : Documents : Maria : Users: Macintosh HD : MacBook. You can also display the path by pressing ⌘+clicking the location name in the title bar.

How do I use the Space item and the Flexible Space item?

Drag a Space item to where you need a fixed amount of space on the toolbar. Drag a Flexible Space item to where you need a space whose width will adjust automatically depending on the number of other controls on the toolbar.

Customize the Sidebar

The sidebar on the left side of Finder windows gives you quick access to files, folders, and apps. The sidebar contains several locations and folders by default, but you can customize the sidebar to contain only the items you find most useful.

The sidebar contains four sections. Favorites are items you access frequently and cloud storage locations such as iCloud Drive or Dropbox. Devices include memory sticks and other external devices. Shared includes drives or computers your MacBook accesses over a network. Tags shows your list of tags for identifying and accessing items.

Customize the Sidebar

1 Click **Finder** (🙂) on the Dock.

A Finder window opens to your default folder or view.

Note: If the sidebar does not appear, click **View** and then click **Show Sidebar**. Alternatively, press ⌘+**Option**+**S**.

2 Optionally, move the pointer over the border of the sidebar, then click and drag to change the width.

3 Click the folder that contains the item you want to add to the sidebar.

4 Click the item you want to add.

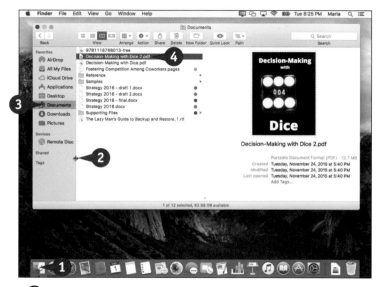

5 Click **File**.

The File menu opens.

6 Click **Add to Sidebar**.

The item appears at the bottom of the sidebar.

7 Optionally, click the item and drag it to a different position on the sidebar.

The item appears in its new position.

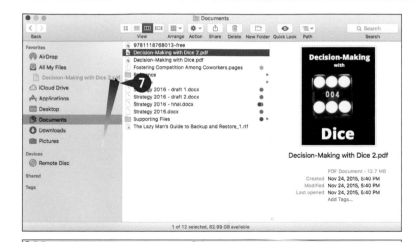

8 To remove an item from the sidebar, press Control +click the item.

The contextual menu opens.

9 Click **Remove from Sidebar**.

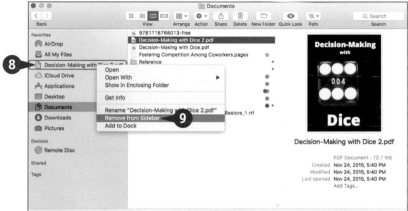

TIP

Which items can I add to the sidebar?
You can add most any item you can access through the Finder. To find out whether you can add a particular item, click it in a Finder window, click **File** to open the File menu, and see if the Add to Sidebar command appears. If so, click **Add to Sidebar** to add the item to the sidebar.

Configure Finder Preferences

The Finder is the application that controls the OS X desktop, how files and folders are managed, and many other aspects of the way your MacBook operates. Like most applications, the Finder has a set of preferences you can configure to change the way it looks and works. You change Finder preferences using its Preferences command. The Preferences window has several tabs that you use to configure specific aspects of how the Finder looks and behaves.

Configure Finder Preferences

1 Click the desktop.

The Finder becomes active.

2 Click **Finder**.

The Finder menu opens.

3 Click **Preferences**.

The Finder Preferences window opens.

4 Click **General** (⬛).

The General tab appears.

5 In the Show These Items on the Desktop list, select (☑) each item you want to appear on the desktop.

6 Click **New Finder windows show** (⬍) and select the default location for new Finder windows, such as **Documents**.

7 Select **Open folders in tabs instead of new windows** (☑) if you want each folder to open in a new tab in the current window rather than in a new window.

8 Click **Tags** (⬤).

The Tags tab appears.

9 Select (☑) each tag you want the sidebar to show.

Ⓐ You can click **Add** (+) to add a tag.

Ⓑ You can click **Remove** (—) to remove the selected tag.

10 Drag your favorite tags into the Tags box at the bottom of the Tags pane for quick use.

11 Click **Sidebar** (▦).

The Sidebar tab appears.

Note: The Sidebar tab in Finder preferences displays the default list of items for the sidebar. To add or remove individual locations or files, use the technique explained in the previous section.

12 Select (☑) each item you want the sidebar to show.

13 Deselect (☐) each item you want to remove from the sidebar.

14 Click **Advanced** (⚙).

The Advanced tab appears.

15 Select (☑) **Show all filename extensions** to make the Finder always display all filename extensions.

16 Select (☑) **Show warning before changing an extension** to receive a warning when you change a filename extension. This is normally helpful.

17 Select (☑) **Show warning before emptying the Trash** to confirm emptying the Trash.

18 Click **When performing a search** (⬍) and then click **Search This Mac**, **Search the Current Folder**, or **Use the Previous Search Scope**, as needed.

19 Click **Close** (⬤).

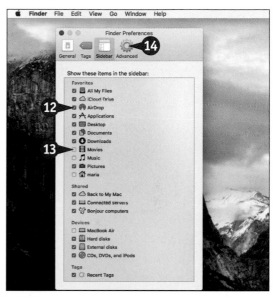

TIP

Which folder should I use as my start folder for new Finder windows?
Choose whichever folder you find most convenient — for example, the folder you keep your most important documents in. Click **New Finder windows show** (⬍) and select **Other**. In the dialog that opens, click the folder you want to use, and then click **Close**.

CHAPTER 6

Surfing the Web

If your MacBook is connected to the Internet, you can browse or *surf* the sites on the World Wide Web. For surfing, OS X provides a web browser app called Safari. Using Safari, you can quickly move from one web page to another, search for interesting sites, and download files to your MacBook.

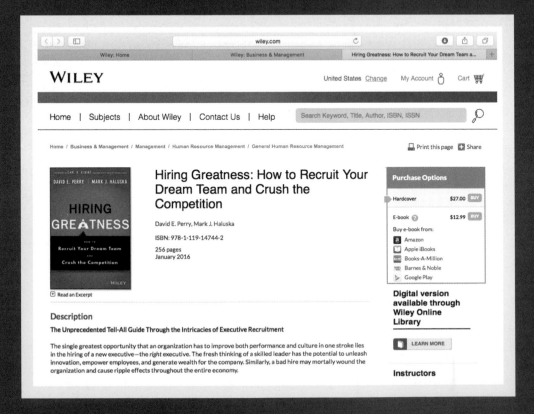

Open a Web Page

The Safari app included with OS X enables you to browse the Web in various ways. The most straightforward way to reach a web page is to type or paste its unique address, which is called a *uniform resource locator* or *URL,* into the address box in Safari.

This technique works well for short addresses but is slow and awkward for complex addresses. Instead, you can click a link or click a bookmark for a page you have marked.

Open a Web Page

1 Click **Safari** (◉) on the Dock.

Safari opens.

2 Click anywhere in the address box or press ⌘+L.

Safari selects the current address.

3 Type the URL of the web page you want to visit.

Note: You do not need to type the http:// part of the address. Safari adds this automatically for you when you press Return.

4 Press Return.

Safari displays the web page.

Follow a Link to a Web Page

You can click a link on a web page in Safari to navigate to another page or another marked location on the same page. Most web pages contain multiple links to other pages, which may be either on the same website or on another website. Some links are underlined, whereas others are attached to graphics or to different-colored text. When you position the pointer over a link, the pointer changes from the standard arrow (↖) to a hand with a pointing finger (👆).

Follow a Link to a Web Page

1 In Safari, position the pointer over a link (↖ changes to 👆).

Note: If you want to see the address of a link over which you move the pointer, display the status bar by clicking **View** and then clicking **Show Status Bar**. The address appears in the status bar.

2 Click the link.

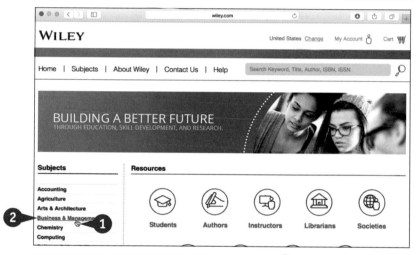

Safari shows the linked web page.

A You can click the address box to see the full address of the web page to which you have navigated.

Note: The address box in Safari normally shows the base name of the website you are visiting, such as wiley.com, rather than the full address of the web page.

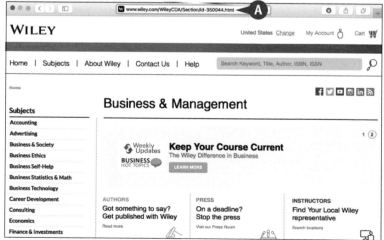

Open Several Web Pages at Once

Safari enables you to open multiple web pages at the same time, which is useful for browsing quickly and easily. You can open multiple pages either on separate tabs in the same window or in separate windows. You can drag a tab from one window to another.

Use separate tabs when you need to see only one of the pages at a time. Use separate windows when you need to compare two pages side by side.

Open Several Web Pages at Once

Open Several Pages on Tabs in the Same Safari Window

1 Go to the first page you want to view.

Note: You can also click **Add** (**+**) or press **⌘**+**T** to open a new tab showing your home page. Type a URL in the address box, and then press **Return** to go to the page.

2 Press **Control**+click a link.

The contextual menu opens.

3 Click **Open Link in New Tab**.

Ⓐ Safari opens the linked web page in a new tab.

Note: You can repeat steps **2** and **3** to open further pages on separate tabs.

4 To change the page Safari is displaying, click the tab for the page you want to see.

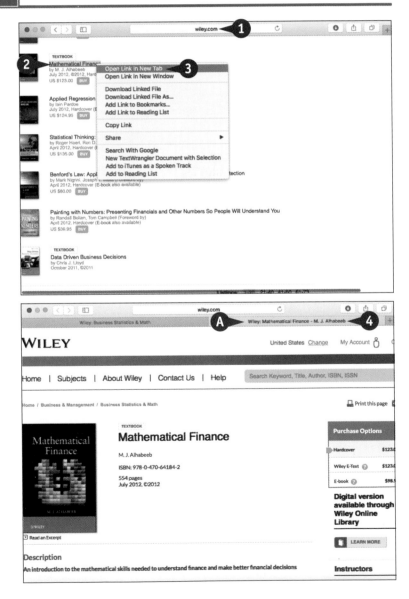

Open Several Pages in Separate Safari Windows

1 Go to the first page you want to view.

2 Press **Control**+click a link.

The contextual menu opens.

3 Click **Open Link in New Window**.

Note: You can also open a new window by pressing ⌘+N.

B Safari opens the linked web page in a new window.

4 To move back to the previous window, click it. If you cannot see the previous window, click **Window** and then click the window on the Window menu.

Note: You can also move back to the previous window by closing the new window you just opened.

Note: Press ⌘+` to cycle forward through windows and ⌘+Shift+` to cycle backward.

Note: You can click **Window** and **Merge All Windows** to merge all windows onto tabs in a single window.

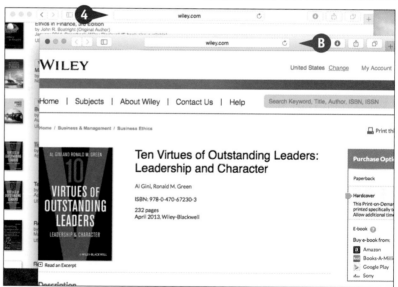

TIP

Can I change the way that Safari tabs and windows behave?

Yes. Click **Safari** and select **Preferences** to open the Preferences window, and then click **Tabs**. Click **Open pages in tabs instead of windows** (⬦) and then click **Never**, **Automatically**, or **Always**, as needed. Click **⌘+click to open a link in a new tab** (☐ changes to ☑) to use ⌘ for opening a new tab. Click **When a new tab or window opens, make it active** (☐ changes to ☑) if you want to switch to the new tab or window on opening it. Click **Use ⌘+1 through ⌘+9 to switch tabs** (☐ changes to ☑) to switch tabs quickly by pressing shortcuts. Click **Close** (⬤) to close the Preferences window.

Navigate Among Web Pages

Safari makes it easy to navigate among the web pages you browse. Safari tracks the pages that you visit, so that the pages form a path. You can go back along this path to return to a page you viewed earlier; after going back, you can go forward again as needed.

Safari keeps a separate path of pages in each open tab or window, so you can move separately in each tab or window.

Navigate Among Web Pages

Go Back One Page

1 In Safari, click **Previous Page** (❮).

Safari displays the previous page you visited in the current tab or window.

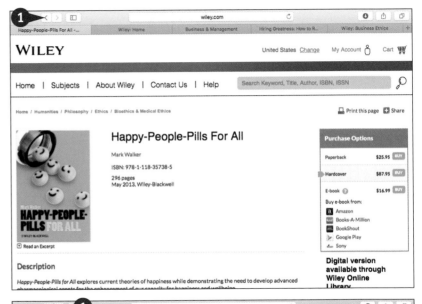

Go Forward One Page

1 Click **Next Page** (❯).

Note: The Next Page button is available only when you have gone back. Until then, there is no page for you to go forward to.

Safari displays the next page for the current tab or window.

Go Back Multiple Pages

1. Click **Previous Page** (❮) and keep holding down the trackpad button.

   A pop-up menu opens showing the pages you have visited in the current tab or window.

2. Click the page you want to visit.

   Safari displays the page.

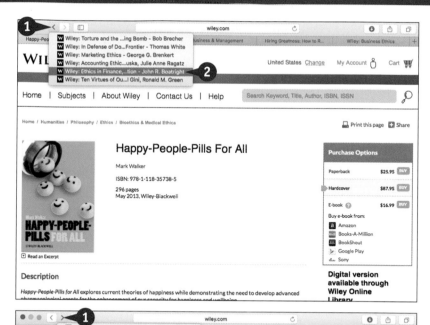

Go Forward Multiple Pages

1. Click **Next Page** (❯) and keep holding down the trackpad button.

   A pop-up menu opens showing the pages further along the path for the current tab or window.

2. Click the page you want to visit.

   Safari displays the page.

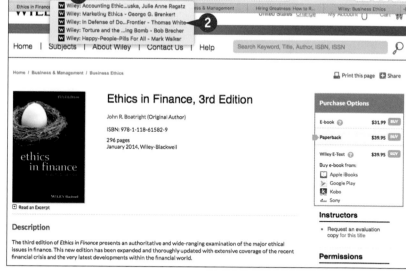

TIP

How can I navigate with the keyboard?
You can use these following keyboard shortcuts:

- Press ⌘+[to display the previous page.
- Press ⌘+] to display the next page.
- Press ⌘+Shift+H to display your home page.
- Press ⌘+Shift+[to display the previous tab.
- Press ⌘+Shift+] to display the next tab.

- Press ⌘+W to close the current tab and display the previous tab. If the window has no tabs, this command closes the window.
- Press ⌘+Shift+W to close the current window and display the previous window, if there is one.
- Press ⌘+1 to display the first tab, ⌘+2 to display the second tab, and so on up to ⌘+9.

Return to a Recently Visited Page

To help you return to web pages you have visited before, Safari keeps the History list of all the pages you have visited recently.

Normally, each person who uses your MacBook has a separate user account, so each person has his own History. But if you share a user account with other people, you can clear the History list to prevent them from seeing what web pages you have visited. You can also shorten the length of time for which History tracks your visits.

Return to a Recently Visited Page

Return to a Page on the History List

1 In Safari, click **History**.

The History menu opens.

A If a menu item for the web page you want appears on the top section of the History menu, before the day submenus, simply click the item.

2 Highlight or click the day on which you visited the web page.

The submenu opens, showing the sites you visited on that day.

3 Click the web page to which you want to return.

Safari displays the web page.

Clear Your Browsing History

1 Click **History**.

The History menu opens.

Note: You may have to scroll down the History menu to reach the Clear History command.

2 Click **Clear History.**

The Clearing History Will Remove Related Cookies and Other Website Data dialog opens.

3 Click **Clear** (⬍) and then click **the last hour**, **today**, **today and yesterday**, or **all history** to specify what you want to clear.

4 Click **Clear History**.

Safari clears the History list for the period you chose.

Note: If you want to browse without History storing the list of web pages you visit, click **File** and then click **New Private Window**. Any sites you browse in the Private Browsing window will not be stored.

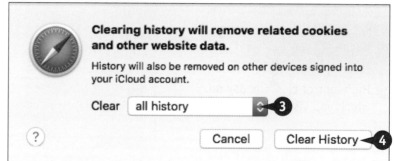

TIP

What does the Show History command do?

Click **History** and select **Show History** to open a History window for browsing and searching the sites you have visited. Type a term in the search box in the lower-right corner to search. Click the disclosure triangle (▶ changes to ▼) to expand the list of entries in a day. Double-click a history item to open its page in the same window, or press Control +click a history item and click **Open in New Tab** or **Open in New Window** to open the page in a new tab or a new window.

Play Music and Videos on the Web

Many websites contain music files or video files that you can play directly in the Safari browser. Safari can play many widely used types of audio files and video files, and most sites provide easy-to-use buttons — such as a Play/Pause button and a volume slider — to enable you to control playback. This section shows the SoundCloud music website and the YouTube video website as examples.

Play Music and Videos on the Web

Play Music

1. In Safari, navigate to a music website and browse to find a song you want to play.

Note: This example uses the SoundCloud site, www.soundcloud.com. There are many other music sites.

2. Click **Play** (such as ▶).

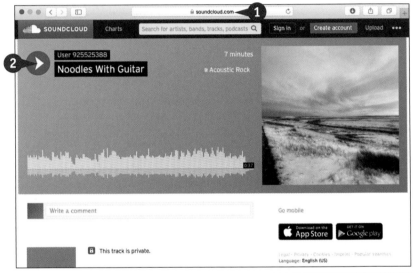

The song starts playing.

A. The progress indicator shows playback progress.

3. Click **Pause** (such as ⏸) if you want to pause the music.

B. Many sites enable you to indicate whether you like the music.

C. Some sites enable you to comment on the music.

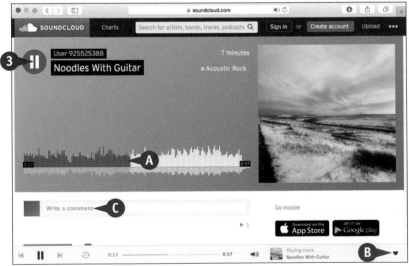

Play Videos

1 In Safari, navigate to a video website and browse to find a video you want to play.

Note: This example uses the YouTube website, www.youtube.com. There are various other video websites; see the tip for information on some.

2 Click the video to open it.

The video starts playing automatically.

D You can click **Settings** (⚙) to change the playback speed or the quality.

3 Click **Full Screen** (⬛).

The video appears full screen.

4 Move the pointer over the video.

The playback controls appear, and you can use them to control playback.

E You can click **Share** (➦) to share the video with others.

F You can click **Exit Full Screen** (⬛) to return from full screen to a window.

G You can click **AirPlay** (▣) to play the video to a TV connected to an Apple TV.

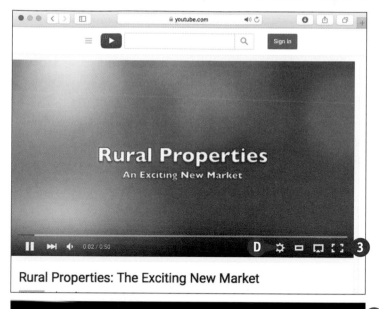

TIP

What are the main video sites on the Web?

As of this writing, the most popular video websites include YouTube (www.youtube.com), NetFlix (www.netflix.com), Vimeo (www.vimeo.com), and DailyMotion (www.dailymotion.com).

Depending on the types of videos you want to watch, you may do better by searching online using suitable search terms than by simply going to the most popular sites.

Change Your Home Page

When you open a new window, Safari automatically displays your *home page*, the page it is configured to show at first. You can set your home page to any web page you want or to an empty page. You can also control what page Safari shows when you open a new tab or a new window. Your choices are to display the Favorites screen, your home page, an empty page, or the same page from which you opened the new tab or window.

Change Your Home Page

1 In Safari, navigate to the web page that you want to make your home page.

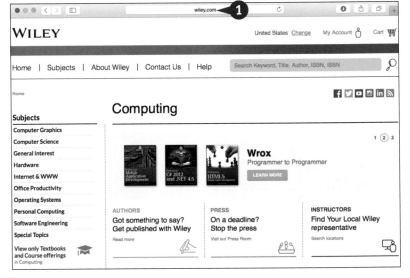

2 Click **Safari**.

The Safari menu opens.

3 Click **Preferences**.

Note: You can also press ⌘+, to open the Preferences window.

The Preferences window opens.

4 Click **General**.

The General pane opens.

5 Click **Set to Current Page**.

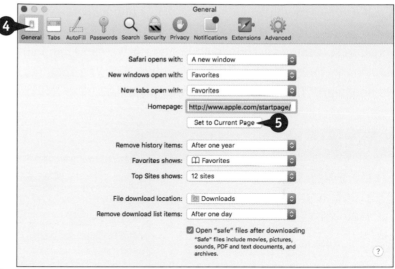

Safari changes the Home Page text field to show the page you chose.

6 Click **New windows open with** (🔼) and click **Favorites**, **Homepage**, **Empty Page**, or **Same Page**, as appropriate.

7 Click **New tabs open with** (🔼) and select **Top Sites**, **Homepage**, **Empty Page**, or **Same Page**, as appropriate.

8 Click **Close** (●).

The Preferences window closes.

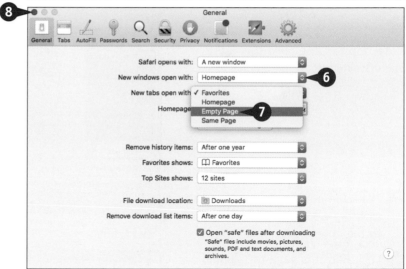

TIPS

How can I display my home page in the current window?

Click **History** on the menu bar and then click **Home**. Alternatively, press ⌘ + Shift + H.

What setting should I choose for Remove History Items in General preferences?

Choose the setting that best matches the length of time you want to keep history items so you can browse or search them. Your choices are **After one day**, **After one week**, **After two weeks**, **After one month**, **After one year**, or **Manually**. If you select Manually, click **History** and then click **Clear History** whenever you want to clear your History items.

Create Bookmarks for Web Pages

Safari enables you to create markers called *bookmarks* for the addresses of web pages you want to be able to revisit easily. When you find such a web page, you can create a bookmark for its address, assign the bookmark a descriptive name, and store it on the Favorites bar, on the Bookmarks menu, or in a Bookmark folder. You can then return to the web page's address by clicking its bookmark. The content of the web page may have changed by the time you return.

Create Bookmarks for Web Pages

Create a New Bookmark

1. In Safari, navigate to a web page you want to bookmark.

2. Click **Bookmarks**.

   The Bookmarks menu opens.

3. Click **Add Bookmark**.

   Note: You can also press ⌘+D to open the Add Bookmark dialog.

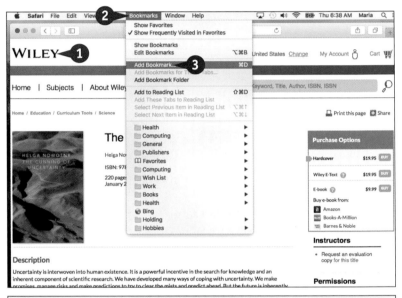

The Add Bookmark dialog opens, with the web page's title added to the upper box.

4. Click **Add this page to** (￮) and select the location or folder in which to store the bookmark.

5. Type a descriptive name for the bookmark.

6. Click **Add**.

   The Add Bookmark dialog closes.

   Safari creates the bookmark.

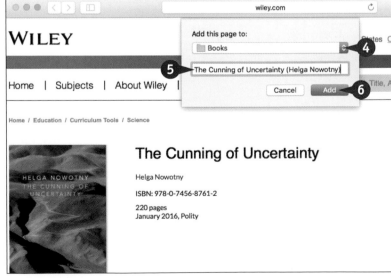

Organize Your Bookmarks

1 Click **Show sidebar** (⊞).

Safari displays the sidebar.

2 Click **Bookmarks** (📖).

Safari displays the Bookmarks pane.

3 Click **Edit**.

A You can click **New Folder** to create a new folder, type the name for the folder, and then press **Return**.

4 Double-click a collapsed folder to display its contents, or double-click an expanded folder to collapse it to the folder.

5 Click and drag a bookmark to the folder in which you want to place it.

Note: You can click and drag the bookmark folders into a different order. You can also place one folder inside another folder.

6 Click **Previous Page** (❮).

Safari returns you to the page you were viewing before.

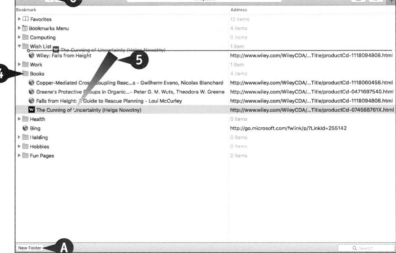

TIP

How do I go to a bookmark I have created?

If you placed the bookmark on the Favorites bar, click the bookmark on the Favorites bar; if the Favorites bar is not displayed, click **View** and **Show Favorites Bar** to display it. If you put the bookmark on the Bookmarks menu, click **Bookmarks**, and then click the bookmark on the Bookmarks menu or one of its submenus. If you cannot easily locate the bookmark, click **Show sidebar** (⊞) to display the sidebar, and then click **Bookmarks** (📖) to display the bookmarks. Locate the bookmark, and then double-click it.

Using Reader View and Reading List

Safari's Reader View enables you to minimize distractions by displaying only the text of a web page in an easily readable format. Reader View works on many, but not all, web pages.

Safari also enables you to save a web page in its current state so that you can read it later. You can quickly add the current web page to Reading List, which you can then access via the Reading List pane in the sidebar.

Using Reader View and Reading List

Switch a Web Page to Reader View

1 In Safari, navigate to a web page you want to read.

2 Click **Show Reader View** (≡).

Note: If the Show Reader View button does not appear, it is because Safari has determined that the page does not have content suitably formatted for Reader View.

Note: You can also switch to Reader View by clicking **View** and **Show Reader** and switch back by clicking **View** and **Hide Reader**. Alternatively, press ⌘+**Shift**+**R** to toggle Reader View on or off.

    Safari switches the web page to Reader View.

Ⓐ The web page's contents appear in easy-to-read fonts.

Ⓑ Links appear in bold blue font and work as usual.

3 When you finish using Reader View, click **Hide Reader View** (▤).

    Safari switches the web page back from Reader View.

Add a Web Page to Reading List

1 Navigate to a web page.

2 Move the pointer over the Show Reader View button (≡).

3 Click **Add Page to Reading List** (⊕).

Safari displays a brief animation showing the page moving from the address box to the Show Sidebar button (▢).

Note: You can also click **Bookmarks** and select **Add to Reading List** or press ⌘ + **Shift** + **D**.

Note: You can click **Bookmarks** and select **Add These Tabs to Reading List** to add all the tabs in the current window to Reading List.

Open Reading List and Display a Page

1 Click **Show sidebar** (▢).

Safari displays the sidebar.

2 Click **Reading List** (∞).

The Reading List pane opens.

3 Click the item you want to read.

The item appears.

ⓒ When you are ready to remove an item from Reading List, position the pointer over its entry and click **Delete** (✕).

TIP

Why does Reading List show me a different version of a web page than a bookmark shows?

Reading List stores the web page as it exists when you give the Add the Reading List command, so when you return to the page, you see it exactly as it was when you stored it. By contrast, clicking a bookmark displays the current version of the web page, which may have changed from the version you saw when you created the bookmark. For example, if you click a bookmark to go to a news site's home page, you will see the latest stories.

Share Web Pages or Links with Others

Safari enables you to share web pages or their addresses quickly by using the Share button on the toolbar. You can send the page or its URL to someone else via AirDrop, e-mail, or instant messaging; post the page to Twitter, Facebook, or LinkedIn; or add the page to Notes or Reminders.

When sharing via Mail, you can send the page as it is, send a Reader version of the page, send a PDF file showing the page, or send a link to the page.

Share Web Pages or Links with Others

Share a Page via AirDrop

1. Navigate to the web page you want to share.

2. Click **Share** (⬆).

   The Share pop-up menu opens.

3. Click **AirDrop**.

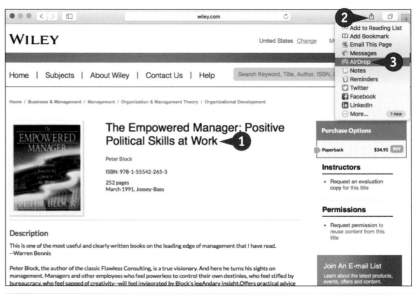

   The AirDrop dialog opens.

4. Click the person to whom or the device to which you want to send the page.

   AirDrop sends an invitation to receive the page.

   Ⓐ The Waiting readout appears.

   If the person accepts, AirDrop sends the page.

   The Sent readout appears.

5. Click **Done**.

   The AirDrop dialog closes.

Share a Link via E-Mail

1 Navigate to the web page you want to share.

2 Click **Share** (⬆).

The Share pop-up menu opens.

3 Click **Email This Page.**

Mail creates a new message.

Ⓑ The page's title appears in the Subject box.

4 Add the recipient's address.

5 If Image Size appears, click **Image Size** (⬍) and then click the image size, such as **Actual Size** or **Small**.

6 Click **Send Web Content As** (⬍) and select what to send: **Web Page**, **Reader**, **PDF**, or **Link Only**.

Note: Sending a link enables the recipient to view the latest version of the page.

7 Type any message needed.

8 Click **Send** (✐).

Mail sends the message.

TIP

How do I post a page on Twitter or Facebook?

Click **Share** (⬆) to open the Share pop-up menu. To share the link on Twitter, click **Twitter**. Type the text of the tweet, click **Add Location** if you want to add your location, and then click **Send**. To share the link on Facebook, click **Facebook**. Select the sharing group, such as **Family** or **Friends**. Type the text of the post, click **Add Location** if you want to add your location, and then click **Post**.

Follow Links Others Share with You

O S X and its apps enable you to follow links that other people share with you. When you receive a link in an e-mail message in Mail, you can preview the link to see if you want to follow it. You can then open the link in Safari or add it to Reading List.

If you open a Finder window or tab to the AirDrop folder, you can receive links via AirDrop. You can save these links and optionally open them in Safari.

Follow Links Others Share with You

Follow a Link Shared via AirDrop

1 Click **Finder** (![icon]) on the Dock.

A Finder window opens.

2 Click **AirDrop**.

The AirDrop screen appears.

Note: You can minimize the AirDrop window or open another tab in front of it without deactivating AirDrop.

3 When you receive a link via AirDrop, click **Accept**.

Safari displays the linked page.

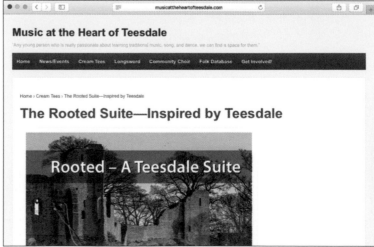

Follow a Link Shared via E-Mail

1 In Mail, click the message that contains the link.

2 Position the pointer over the link.

3 Click the pop-up button (⤵).

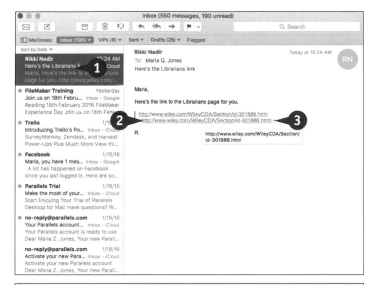

The preview of the page appears.

4 Click **Open with Safari**.

Ⓐ You can click **Add to Reading List** to add the web page to Reading List instead of opening it.

Safari displays the page.

TIP

What other actions can I take with a link in Mail?
In Mail, you can press `Control`+click a link in a message to open the contextual menu, which contains actions you can take with the link. Click **Open Link** to open the link without previewing the page. Click **Open Link Behind Mail** to open the link in Safari but keep Mail displayed so that you can finish reading your mail. Click **Copy Link** to copy the link so that you can paste it into a document.

Download a File

M any websites provide files to download, and Safari makes it easy to download files from websites to your MacBook's file system. For example, you can download apps to install on your MacBook, pictures to view on it, or songs to play.

OS X includes apps that can open many file types, including music, graphic, movie, document, and PDF files. To open other file types, you may need to install extra apps or add plug-in software components to extend the features of the apps you already have.

Download a File

1 In Safari, go to the web page that contains the link for the file you want to download.

2 Click the link.

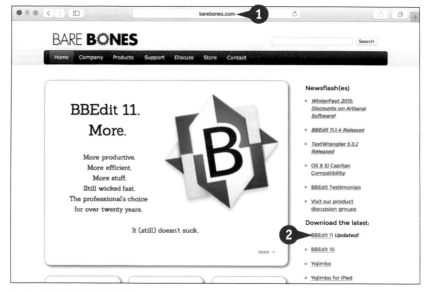

Safari starts the download.

Note: The indicator on the Downloads button (⬇) shows the progress of the download.

3 Click **Downloads** (⬇) to open the Downloads window.

4 When the download is complete, press `Control`+click the file in the Downloads window.

The contextual menu opens.

5 Click **Open**.

Note: Depending on the file type and the preferences you have set, Safari may open the file automatically for you.

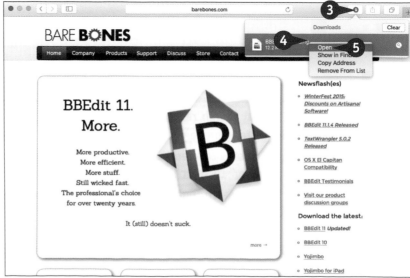

The file opens.

Depending on the file type, you can then work with the file, enjoy its contents, or install it.

Note: If the file is an app, you can install it as discussed in Chapter 4. If the file is a data file, such as a document or a picture, OS X opens the file in the app for that file type.

⑥ If the file disappears from the Downloads window and Safari does not open the file for you, click **Downloads** on the Dock.

The Downloads stack opens.

⑦ Click the file you downloaded.

The file opens.

TIP

What should I do when clicking a download link opens the file instead of downloading it?
If clicking a download link on a web page opens the file instead of downloading it, press `Control`+click the link to display the contextual menu. Click **Download Linked File** if you want to save the file in your Downloads folder. If you prefer to save the file in a different folder or under a different name of your choice, click **Download Linked File As**, and then specify the folder and filename in the dialog that opens.

Configure Safari for Security and Privacy

The Web is packed with fascinating sites and useful information, but it is also full of malefactors and criminals who want to attack your MacBook and steal your valuable data.

To keep your MacBook safe, you can prevent Safari from automatically opening supposedly safe files you download. Safari also enables you to choose which websites can use WebGL, a technology for displaying three-dimensional graphics in the browser. You can also choose which Internet plug-ins to use and which websites can use them.

Configure Safari for Security and Privacy

1 With the Safari app running, click **Safari**.

The Safari menu opens.

2 Click **Preferences**.

The Preferences window opens.

3 Click **General**.

The General pane opens.

4 Click **Open "safe" files after downloading** (☑ changes to ☐).

5 Click **Security**.

The Security pane opens.

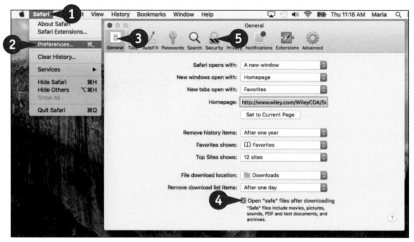

6 Click **Warn when visiting a fraudulent website** (☐ changes to ☑).

7 Click **Enable JavaScript** (☑ changes to ☐) if you want to disable JavaScript. See the tip for advice.

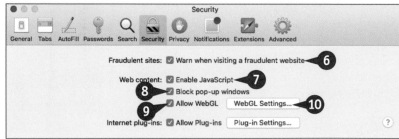

8 Click **Block pop-up windows** (☐ changes to ☑) if you want to block pop-up windows.

Note: Some websites need pop-up windows to function properly.

9 Click **Allow WebGL** (☐ changes to ☑) if you want to let websites use the WebGL language to display 3D graphics in Safari.

10 Click **WebGL Settings**.

The Allow Websites to Use WebGL with the Settings Below dialog opens.

11 For each site in the Currently Open Websites list, click ⬍ and then click **Ask**, **Block**, **Allow**, or **Allow Always**, as needed.

12 For each site in the Configured Websites list, click ⬍ and then click **Ask**, **Block**, **Allow**, or **Allow Always**, as needed.

13 Click **When Visiting Other Websites** (⬍), and then click **Ask**, **Block**, **Allow**, or **Allow Always**, as needed.

Note: For safety, choose **Ask** for the When Visiting Other Websites option.

14 Click **Done**.

The Allow Websites to Use WebGL with the Settings Below dialog closes.

The Security pane appears.

15 Select (☑) or clear (☐) **Allow Plug-ins**, as needed.

16 If you allow plug-ins, click **Plug-in Settings**.

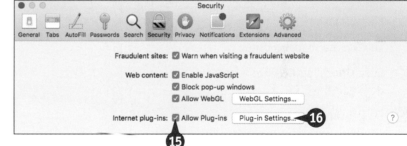

TIP

What is JavaScript, and should I disable it?
JavaScript is a scripting language used by many websites to provide interactive features. While it is possible for malefactors to perform some unwelcome actions with JavaScript, the language is widely used for positive purposes and usually can do little harm. What is more of a threat to your MacBook's security is Java, a full-featured programming language that can run on many computer platforms and is often used by Web-delivered services. JavaScript is completely different from Java but is sometimes tainted by association with Java.

continued ►

To protect your MacBook from Web-based attacks, you can refuse unwanted cookies files, which websites can use to track your actions and movements; block pop-up windows, which malicious websites can use to distribute malevolent software; and control whether websites need your permission to use location services on your MacBook. You can also remove cookies and data that either specific websites or all websites have stored on your MacBook.

Configure Safari for Security and Privacy (continued)

The Plug-In Settings dialog opens.

17 In the left pane, click the plug-in you want to configure.

A You can click the plug-in's check box to disable the plug-in (☑ changes to ☐).

18 In the right pane, click each ⬍ and then click **Ask**, **Block**, **Allow**, or **Allow Always**, as needed.

19 Click **When Visiting Other Websites** (⬍), and then click **Ask**, **Block**, **Allow**, or **Allow Always**, as needed.

20 Click **Done**.

The Plug-In Settings dialog closes.

The Security pane appears.

21 Click **Privacy**.

The Privacy pane opens.

22 In the Cookies and Website Data area, click **Allow from websites I visit** (◯ changes to ◉). See the tip in this section.

23 In the Website Use of Location Services area, click **Prompt for each website once each day** (◯ changes to ◉), **Prompt for each website one time only** (◯ changes to ◉), or **Deny without prompting** (◯ changes to ◉), as needed.

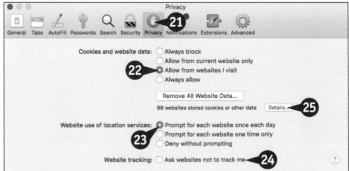

24 Click **Ask websites not to track me** (☐ changes to ☑) if you want to request not to be tracked. Websites may not honor this request.

25 If you want to view the details of cookies and data that websites have stored, click **Details**.

The Details dialog opens.

B You can click **Search** (🔍) and search by name.

C You can click a site and then click **Remove**.

D You can click **Remove All** to remove all sites.

26 Click **Done**.

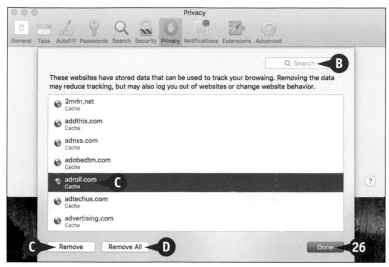

The Privacy pane appears.

27 If you want to remove all website data from your MacBook, click **Remove All Website Data**.

A confirmation dialog opens.

28 Click **Remove Now**.

The confirmation dialog closes.

29 Click **Close** (●).

The Safari Preferences window closes.

TIP

What are cookies, and should I block them?

A *cookie* is a small text file that a website uses to store information about what you do on the site — for example, what products you have browsed or added to your shopping cart. Cookies from sites you visit are usually helpful to you. However, cookies from third-party sites, such as those that advertise on sites you visit, may threaten your privacy. For this reason, choose **Allow from websites I visit** rather than **Always block** in the Cookies and Website Data area of the Privacy pane.

CHAPTER 7

Sending and Receiving E-Mail

OS X includes Mail, a powerful e-mail app. After setting up your e-mail accounts, you can send and receive e-mail messages and files.

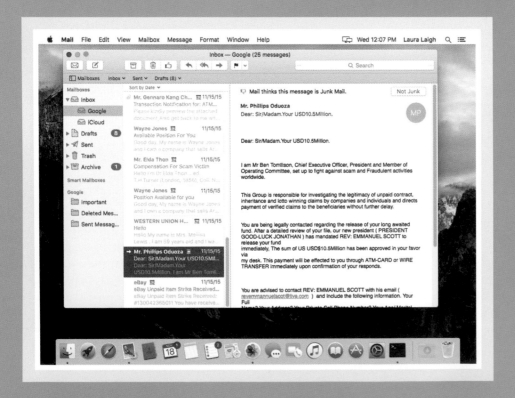

Set Up Your E-Mail Accounts

The Mail app enables you to send and receive e-mail messages easily using your existing e-mail accounts. If you add an iCloud account to your user account during initial setup or in System Preferences, OS X can automatically set up e-mail in Mail. If you have other e-mail accounts, you can add them manually.

To set up some types of e-mail accounts, Mail requires only your e-mail address and password. For other types, you also need to enter the addresses and types of your provider's mail servers.

Set Up Your E-Mail Accounts

1 Click **Mail** () on the Dock.

The Choose a Mail Account Provider dialog opens.

Note: If Mail opens and displays your inbox, your e-mail account is already set up and working.

2 Click the account type (◯ changes to ◉). Your choices are **iCloud**, **Exchange**, **Google**, **Yahoo!**, **AOL**, or **Other Mail Account**.

Note: For an Office 365 account, click **Exchange** (◯ changes to ◉) and use the server name **outlook.office365.com**.

3 Click **Continue**.

A dialog opens that allows you to sign in to the account. This example shows the Sign In dialog that appears for a Google account.

Ⓐ In some dialogs, you can click **More Options** to display other options, such as setting up a new e-mail account on the service.

Note: If you select Other Mail Account, you must choose between IMAP and POP for your incoming mail server type and enter the mail server's address.

4 Type your e-mail address.

5 Click **Next**.

The service prompts you for your password.

6 Type your password.

7 Click **Next**.

188

The Select the Apps You Want to Use with This Account dialog opens.

8 Click the check box (☐ changes to ☑) for each app you want to use with this account.

9 Click **Done**.

Mail displays your inbox, and you can begin reading and sending e-mail.

B You can click a message in the message list to display its contents.

C Mail automatically identifies possible events and contacts in e-mail messages you receive. The Event readout shows any events. You can click **add** to review the information and add the event to your calendar, or click **Close** (⊗) to remove the prompt.

Note: When you receive a calendar invitation, the message includes the name of the event and the Calendar icon. You can click **Accept**, **Maybe**, or **Decline** to give your response.

D You can click **Mailboxes** (▦) to display your mailboxes, and then click the mailbox you want to view.

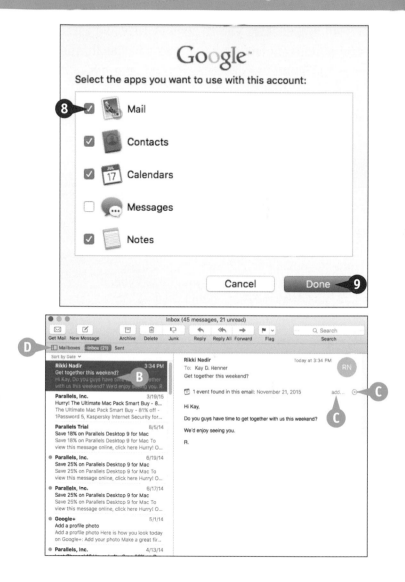

TIPS

How do I add more e-mail accounts?

You can add more e-mail accounts by clicking **Mail** on the menu bar, clicking **Add Account**, and then following the prompts. Alternatively, press Control + click **System Preferences** (⚙) on the Dock, click **Internet Accounts**, click **Add** (+), and follow the prompts.

Which account type should I choose for my incoming mail server?

Check your ISP's website or call customer service to find out what type of mail server to use. Most ISPs use either POP (Post Office Protocol) or IMAP (Internet Mail Access Protocol), but others use Exchange or Exchange IMAP.

Send an E-Mail Message

The Mail app enables you to send an e-mail message to anybody whose e-mail address you know. After starting a new message, you can specify the recipient's address either by typing it directly into the To field or by selecting it from your list of contacts in the Contacts app.

You can send an e-mail message to a single person or to multiple people. You can send copies to Cc, or carbon-copy, recipients or send hidden copies to Bcc, or blind carbon-copy, recipients.

Send an E-Mail Message

1 In Mail, click **New Message** (✍).

Note: You can also press ⌘+N or click **File** on the menu bar and then click **New** to start a new message.

A new message window opens.

2 Click **Add Contact** (⊕).

The Contacts panel opens.

3 Click the contact.

4 Click the e-mail address.

Note: In the Contacts panel, a name in lighter gray has no e-mail address in the contact record.

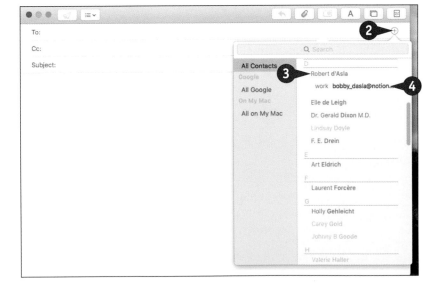

The contact name appears as a button in the To field.

Note: You can add other addresses to the To field as needed.

5 To add a Cc recipient, click the Cc field.

6 Start typing a name or e-mail address.

Mail displays matches from Contacts.

7 Click the appropriate match or finish typing.

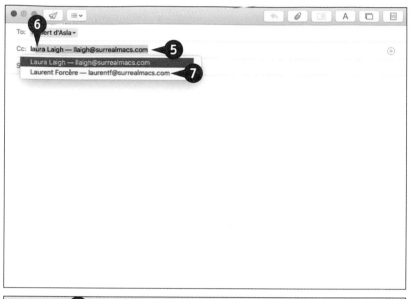

The name or address appears in the Cc box.

8 Type the subject for the message.

9 Type the body text of the message.

10 Click **Send** (✐).

Mail sends the message and stores a copy in your Sent folder.

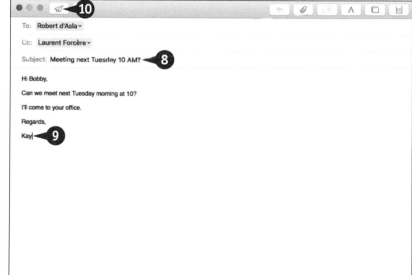

TIP

How can I send Bcc (blind carbon-copy) messages?

Mail hides the Bcc field in the New Message window by default. To display the Bcc field, click **Customize** (≡∨) on the toolbar of a message window and then click **Bcc Address Field** on the pop-up menu. The Bcc field appears below the Cc field, and you can add recipients either by clicking **Add Contact** (⊕) or by typing their names or e-mail addresses.

Each Bcc recipient sees only his own address, not the addresses of other Bcc recipients. The To recipients and Cc recipients see none of the Bcc recipients' names and addresses.

Send an E-Mail Message Using Stationery

Mail includes dozens of stationery templates that enable you to create messages easily that have a graphical look and consistent, attractive formatting. Mail divides the stationery templates into five categories — Birthday, Announcements, Photos, Stationery, and Sentiments — but you can use any template for any purpose.

To use stationery, you first create a new message. Next, you open the Stationery pane and apply the appropriate stationery template. You can then place your text in the template's text placeholders and your photos in any photo placeholders.

Send an E-Mail Message Using Stationery

1. In Mail, click **New Message** (✏️).

Note: You can also press ⌘+N or click **File** on the menu bar and then click **New** to start a new message.

Note: Using stationery, especially including photos, can greatly increase message size, which may cause problems for some recipients. Some e-mail apps cannot display stationery correctly.

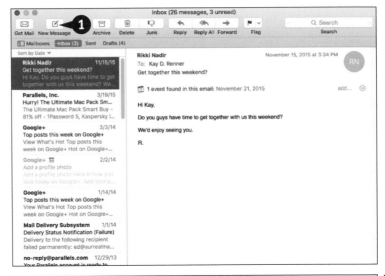

A new message window opens.

2. Add the recipient or recipients to the To box.

Note: You can add a recipient either by clicking **Add Contact** (⊕) and then clicking the contact in the Contacts panel or by typing the recipient's name or e-mail address.

3. Type the subject.

4. Click **Stationery** (▦).

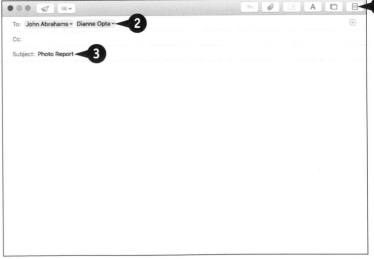

The Stationery pane opens.

5 Click a category of stationery.

The stationery designs in that category appear.

6 Click a stationery design.

The design appears in the lower part of the message window.

7 Click **Stationery** (▦).

The Stationery pane closes.

8 Replace the sample text with your own text.

9 Click **Photo Browser** (▢) if the stationery includes photo placeholders.

The Photo Browser opens.

10 Click and drag a photo from the Photo Browser to each placeholder.

11 Click **Photo Browser** (▢) to close the Photo Browser.

12 Click **Send** (✐).

Mail sends the message.

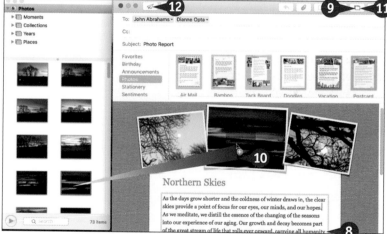

TIP

How can I apply font formatting to a message?

You can apply font formatting by using either the Format bar or the Fonts window. The Format bar, which you display or hide by clicking **Show Format Bar** (A) on the toolbar, enables you to change the font family, font size, and font color, and apply boldface, italics, or underline. The Fonts window, which you display or hide by pressing ⌘+T, enables you to apply a wider range of font formatting and to change the document color.

Receive and Read Your Messages

M ail enables you to receive your incoming messages easily and read them in whatever order you prefer. A message sent to you goes to your mail provider's e-mail server. To receive the message, you cause Mail to connect to the e-mail server and download the message to your MacBook.

When working with e-mail, it often helps to display the mailbox list on the left side of the Mail window. You can use this list to navigate among mailboxes and to see which activities Mail is currently performing.

Receive and Read Your Messages

Display the Mailbox List and Receive Messages

① In Mail, click **Mailboxes** (▦).

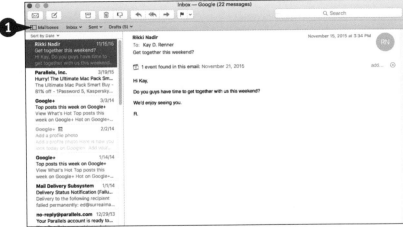

Ⓐ The mailbox list appears.

② Click the mailbox you want to view.

③ Click **Get Mail** (✉).

Mail connects to the e-mail server and downloads any messages.

Ⓑ Depending on how you have configured notifications, a notification banner or alert may appear as a message arrives.

Ⓒ The Mail Activity readout shows what Mail is doing.

Ⓓ The new messages appear in your inbox.

Ⓔ A blue dot indicates an unread message.

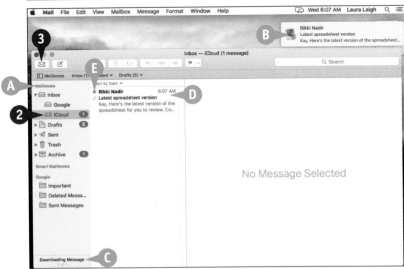

Read Your Messages

1 Click a message in the message list.

F The message appears in the reading pane.

2 Double-click a message in the message list.

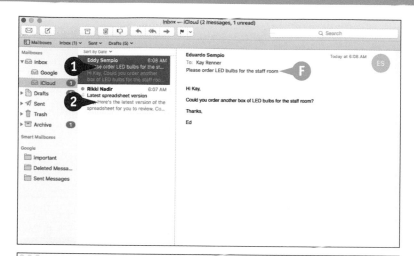

The message's text and contents appear in a separate window.

3 Read the message.

4 Click **Close** (●).

The message window closes.

G You can click **Mailboxes** (▦) when you want to hide the mailbox list again.

Is there an easy way to tell whether I have new messages?

If you have unread messages, the Mail icon on the Dock shows a red circle containing the number of unread messages.

How can I change Mail's frequency of checking for new messages?
Click **Mail** and **Preferences** to open the Preferences window, and then click **General**. Click the **Check for new messages** pop-up menu (⬦), and then select the method or interval: **Automatically**, **Every minute**, **Every 5 minutes**, **Every 15 minutes**, **Every 30 minutes**, **Every hour**, or **Manually**. Click **Close** (●) to close the Preferences window.

Reply to a Message

Mail enables you to reply to any e-mail message you receive. When you reply, you can include either the whole of the original message or just the part of it that you select.

If you are one of multiple recipients of the message, you can choose between replying only to the sender and replying to both the sender and all the other recipients other than Bcc recipients. You can also adjust the list of recipients manually if necessary, removing existing recipients and adding other recipients.

Reply to a Message

1 In the inbox, click the message to which you want to reply.

Note: You can also double-click the message to open it in a message window, and then start the reply from there.

2 Click **Reply** (⤺).

Note: If the message has multiple recipients, you can click **Reply All** (⤺⤺) to reply to the sender and to all the other recipients except Bcc recipients.

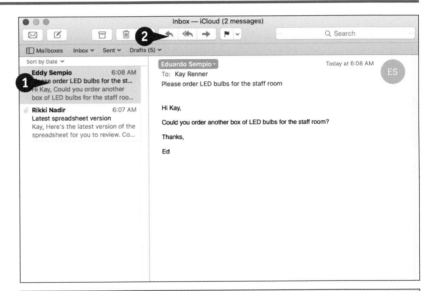

Mail creates the reply and opens it in a window.

Ⓐ The recipient's name appears as a button.

Ⓑ You can position the pointer over the contact's name, click the pop-up button (⬇) that appears, and then click a different address if necessary.

③ Type the text of your reply.

It is usually best to type your text at the beginning of the reply rather than after the message you are replying to.

Note: You can also add other recipients to the message as needed. If you have chosen to reply to all recipients, you can remove any recipients as necessary.

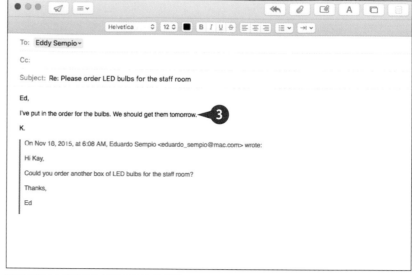

④ Click **Send** (✈).

Mail sends the reply and saves a copy in your Sent folder.

Note: Click **Message** and then click **Send Again** to send the same message again — for example, because a mail server rejects it. You can change recipients or the message contents as needed.

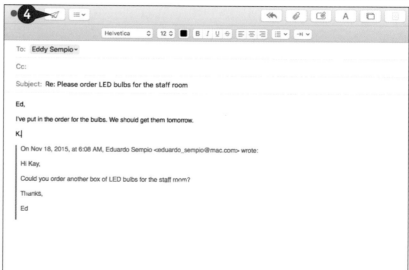

TIP

Can I reply to only part of a message rather than send the whole of it?
Yes. Select the part you want to include, and then click **Reply** (↩) or **Reply All** (↩), as appropriate. Mail creates a reply containing only the part you selected. If Mail still includes all of the message, click **Mail**, click **Preferences**, click **Composing**, and then click **Include selected text, if any; otherwise include all text** (◯ changes to ◉) instead of **Include all of the original message text**.

Forward a Message

Mail enables you to forward to other people a message that you receive. You can either forward the entire message or forward only a selected part of it.

When you forward a message, you can add your own comments to the message. For example, you might want to explain to the recipient which person or organization sent you the original message, why you are forwarding it, and what action — if any — you expect him to take.

Forward a Message

1 If necessary, click **Mailboxes** (🗔) and then click the mailbox that contains the message you want to forward.

Ⓐ The Replied arrow (↰) indicates you have replied to a message.

Ⓑ The Forwarded arrow (➡) indicates you have forwarded a message.

2 Click the message.

The message's content appears in the reading pane.

Note: You can also forward a message that you have opened in a message window.

3 Click **Forward** (➡).

Note: You can click **Message** and then click **Redirect** to redirect a message to someone else without the Fwd: indicator appearing.

A window opens showing the forwarded message.

The subject line shows Fwd: and the message's original subject, so the recipient can see it was forwarded.

4 Enter the recipient's name or address. You can either type the address or click **Add Contact** (⊕) and then select the address from the Contacts panel.

5 Edit the subject line of the message if necessary.

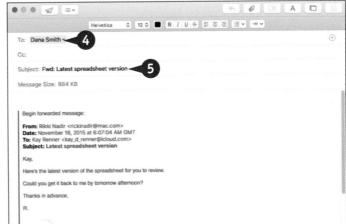

6 Optionally, edit the forwarded message to shorten it or make it clearer to the recipient.

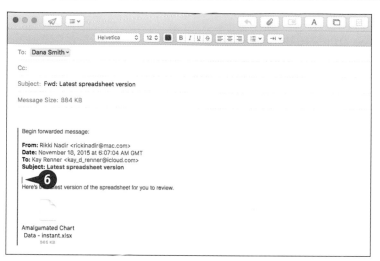

7 Type any message you want to include to the recipient.

8 Click **Send** (✈).

Mail sends the forwarded message to the recipient.

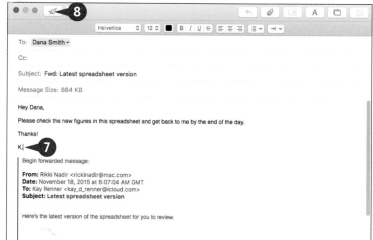

What does the Forward as Attachment command on the Message menu do?

The Forward as Attachment command enables you to send a copy of a message as an attachment to a message instead of in the message itself. This command is useful when you want to send a forwarded message that includes formatting in a plain text message.

Can I forward only part of a message rather than all of it?

To forward only part of a message, select the part you want to forward, and then click **Forward** (➡). Mail includes only the part you selected.

Send a File via E-Mail

As well as enabling you to communicate via e-mail messages, Mail gives you an easy way to transfer files to other people. You can attach one or more files to an e-mail message so that the files travel as part of the message. The recipient can then save the file on her computer and open it.

Mail's Send Large Attachments with Mail Drop feature enables you to transfer large files without running up against the size constraints that some mail servers impose.

Send a File via E-Mail

1 In Mail, click **Compose New Message** (⊡).

Note: If you have multiple accounts, Mail creates the new message as being sent by the account that is currently active. To use a different account, click that account in the Mailboxes pane.

A new message window opens.

2 Add the recipient's name or address. You can either type the address or click **Add Contact** (⊕) and then select the address from the Contacts panel.

3 Type the subject for the message.

4 Type any message body that is needed.

5 Click **Attach** (⌀).

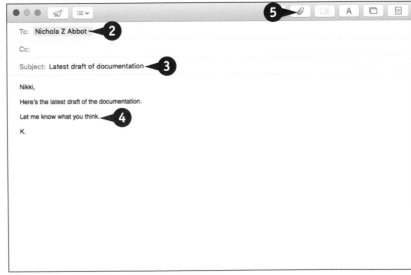

A dialog opens.

6 Click the file you want to attach to the message.

7 Click **Choose File**.

The dialog closes.

A Mail attaches the file to the message.

Note: Depending on the file type, the attachment may appear as an icon in the message or as a picture.

B The Message Size readout appears below the Subject line.

8 Click **Send** (⍋).

Mail sends the message with the file attached.

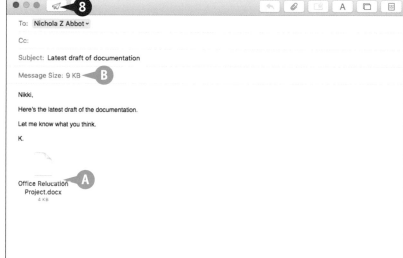

What does Send Large Attachments with Mail Drop do?

Send Large Attachments with Mail Drop uploads large attachments to Apple's Internet storage instead of including them in the message. If the message's recipient is using an iCloud account, she receives the attachments in the e-mail message via automatic download; if the recipient is using another type of account, she receives a link to download the file manually.

To enable Send Large Attachments with Mail Drop, click **Mail** on the menu bar and then click **Preferences**. Click **Accounts** to display the Accounts pane, click the account in the left pane, and then click **Advanced**. Click **Send large attachments with Mail Drop** (☐ changes to ☑), and then click **Close** (⬤).

Receive a File via E-Mail

Afile you receive via e-mail appears as an attachment to a message in your inbox. You can use the Quick Look feature to examine the file and decide whether to keep it or delete it. Quick Look can display the contents of many types of files well enough for you to determine what they contain.

To keep an attached file, you can save it to your MacBook's drive. You can then remove the attached file from the e-mail message to help keep down the size of your mail folder.

Receive a File via E-Mail

1 In your inbox, click the message.

The message appears in the reading pane.

2 Press **Control**+click the attachment.

The contextual menu opens.

3 Click **Quick Look Attachment**.

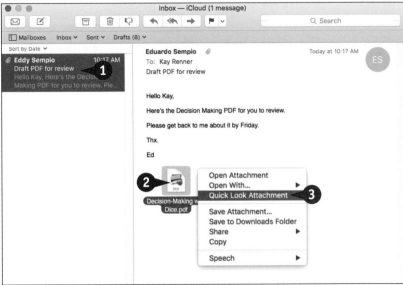

A Quick Look window opens showing the attachment's contents.

A You can click **Full Screen** (⊙) if you want to view the document full-screen.

B You can click **Open With** to open the file in a suitable app — for example, click **Open with Preview** to open a PDF file in the Preview app.

4 When you finish previewing the file, click **Close** (⊗).

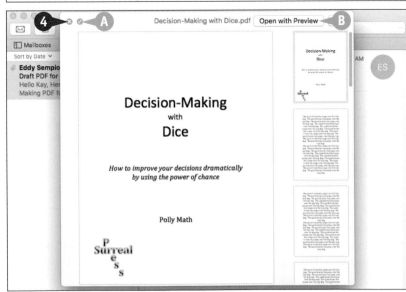

The Quick Look window closes.

⑤ Press **Control**+click the attachment.

The contextual menu opens.

⑥ Click **Save Attachment**.

The Save As dialog opens.

Note: If the Save As dialog opens at its small size, click **Expand Dialog** (ⱽ) to expand it.

⑦ Navigate to the folder in which you want to save the file.

⑧ Optionally, click the **Tags** box and click each tag you want to assign to the file.

⑨ Click **Save**.

Mail saves the file.

Note: If you want to remove the attachment from the message, click **Message** and then click **Remove Attachments**.

TIPS

Should I check incoming files for viruses and malevolent software?
Yes, you should always check incoming files with antivirus software. Most antivirus and security apps scan incoming files automatically, but they also enable you to scan individual files manually. Even though OS X generally has fewer problems with viruses and malevolent software than Windows PCs, it is possible for a file to cause damage, steal data, or threaten your privacy.

Is there a quick way to see what messages have attachments?
In the inbox, click the **Sort by** pop-up menu, and then click **Attachments**. Mail sorts the inbox so that the messages with attachments appear first.

View E-Mail Messages by Conversations

Mail enables you to view an exchange of e-mail messages as a conversation instead of viewing each message as a separate item. Conversations, also called *threads*, let you browse and sort messages on the same subject more easily by separating them from other messages in your mailboxes.

If you decide to organize your messages by conversations, you can expand or collapse all conversations to see the messages you want.

View E-Mail Messages by Conversations

1 In Mail, click the mailbox that contains the messages you want to view.

A The messages in the folder appear.

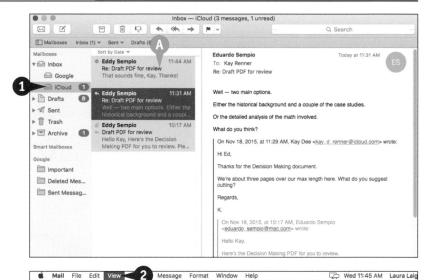

2 Click **View**.

The View menu opens.

3 Click **Organize by Conversation**.

Mail organizes the messages into conversations, so that each exchange appears as a single item rather than as separate messages.

Ⓑ The number to the right of a conversation indicates how many messages it contains.

④ Click the conversation.

Note: You can expand all conversations in the folder by clicking **View** and clicking **Expand All Conversations**. Click **View** and click **Collapse All Conversations** to collapse them again.

Ⓒ All the messages in the conversation appear in summary.

⑤ Click the number to the right of the conversation.

Ⓓ Mail expands the conversation so that you can see each of the messages it contains.

Ⓔ You can click a message to display it in the reading pane.

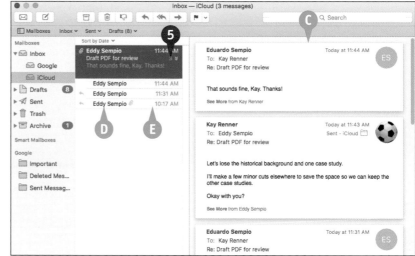

TIP

Are there other advantages to viewing an exchange as a conversation?
When you view an exchange as a conversation, you can manipulate all the messages in a single move instead of having to manipulate each message individually. For example, click the conversation and drag it to a folder to file all its messages in that folder, or click the message and press ⌘ + Delete to delete the entire conversation.

Reduce the Amount of Spam You Receive

Spam is unwanted e-mail messages, also called *junk mail*. Spam ranges from messages offering specialized products, such as pharmaceuticals, to attempts to steal your financial details, passwords, or personal information.

Mail includes features that enable you to reduce the amount of spam that reaches your inbox. You can configure Mail to identify junk mail automatically, and you can learn to spot identifying features of spam messages. Unfortunately, it is not yet possible to avoid spam completely.

Reduce the Amount of Spam You Receive

Set Mail to Identify Junk Mail Automatically

1 With the Mail app active, click **Mail**.

The Mail menu opens.

2 Click **Preferences**.

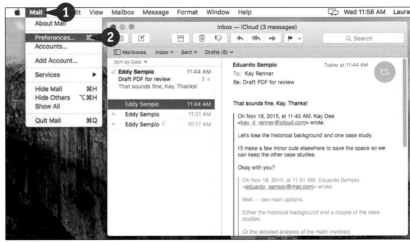

The Preferences window opens.

3 Click **Junk Mail** (🗑).

4 Click **Enable junk mail filtering** (☐ changes to ☑).

5 Click **Mark as junk mail, but leave it in my Inbox** (◯ changes to ◉) to review junk mail in your inbox.

6 Click each of the three check boxes (☐ changes to ☑).

7 Click **Trust junk mail headers in messages** (☐ changes to ☑).

8 Click **Close** (●).

The Preferences window closes.

Review Your Junk Mail

1. Click **Inbox** or the inbox of a particular account, such as **Google**.

2. Click a message.

3. See whether Mail has identified the message as junk mail.

4. See if the message is addressed to you.

5. Check whether the message greets you by name or with a generic greeting.

6. Read the message's content for veracity.

7. If a message appears to be spam, and Mail has not identified it as junk, click **Junk** (🗩).

8. Click **Delete** (🗑) to delete the message.

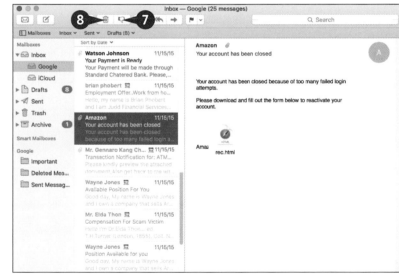

CHAPTER 8

Chatting and Calling

OS X includes Messages for instant messaging and FaceTime for video chat with users of Macs and iOS devices. You can also configure Handoff with your iPhone so that you can phone and send SMS messages using your MacBook.

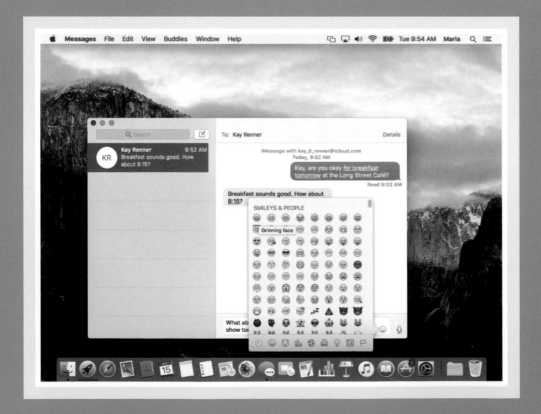

Set Up Messages

The Messages app enables you to chat with your contacts via instant messaging. Using Messages, you can connect via Apple's iMessage service to contacts on Macs and iOS devices or to contacts on other online messaging services, such as Google Talk, Yahoo! Messenger, and AOL.

If you have set up iCloud on your MacBook, Messages should already be configured for your iCloud account, and you can add any other messaging accounts as needed. If you have not set up iCloud, you must add an account to Messages before you can use the app.

Set Up Messages

Set Up Messages with Your Apple ID

1 Click **Messages** (💬) on the Dock.

The iMessage window opens.

Note: If the Messages window opens instead of the iMessage window, go to the next subsection.

2 Type your Apple ID.

Ⓐ You can click **Create new Apple ID** to create an Apple ID if you do not have one.

3 Type your password.

4 Click **Sign In**.

The Messages window opens.

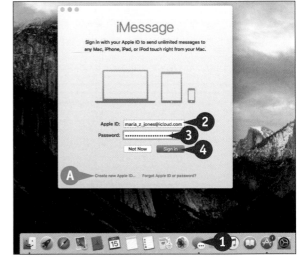

Add Another Messaging Account

1 Click **Messages** (💬) on the Dock.

The Messages window opens.

2 Click **Messages**.

The Messages menu opens.

3 Click **Add Account**.

The Choose a Messages Account Provider dialog opens.

4 Click a Messages account provider (◯ changes to ◉). Your choices are **Google**, **Yahoo!**, **AOL**, and **Other messages account**.

5 Click **Continue**.

Note: If you selected Other Messages Account, click **Account Type** (🔁) and then click **AIM** or **Jabber**, as appropriate.

A dialog for entering the account information appears. This example uses Google, for which the Sign In dialog appears.

6 Type the e-mail address for the messaging account.

7 Click **Next**.

The Password dialog opens.

8 Type your password.

9 Click **Next**.

Note: If the 2-Step Verification dialog opens, type the code sent to your mobile device.

A dialog opens enabling you to select the services to use with the messaging account.

10 Click an option, such as **Mail**, **Contacts**, **Calendars**, **Messages**, or **Notes** (☐ changes to ☑).

11 Click **Done**.

Messages sets up the account, and you can start using it.

TIPS

What is iMessage?

iMessage is Apple's instant-messaging service. To use iMessage, you need only an Apple ID, such as your iCloud account ID. With iMessage, you can send instant messages to any iPhone user or anyone who uses an Apple ID on a Mac, iPhone, iPad, or iPod touch.

How can I use Messages with people on my local network?

You can use Bonjour, an Apple communications technology, to communicate with other Mac users and iOS device users on your local network. To set up Bonjour, click **Messages**, and then click **Preferences**. In the Preferences window, click **Accounts**, click **Bonjour**, and then click **Enable Bonjour instant messaging** (☐ changes to ☑).

Chat with a Buddy

Messages enables you to chat with your contacts, or *buddies*, via instant messaging. The easiest way to start using Messages is by sending text messages. Depending on the messaging services and the computers or devices your buddies are using, you may be able to chat via audio or video as well.

To start chatting, you send your buddy an invitation. If your buddy accepts the invitation, the reply appears in the Messages window. You can conduct multiple chats simultaneously, switching from chat to chat as needed.

Chat with a Buddy

1 Click **Messages** (🗨) on the Dock.

The Messages window opens.

2 Click **Compose New Message** (✎).

A New Message entry appears in the left pane.

3 Click **Add Contact** (⊕).

The Contacts panel opens.

4 Click the buddy with whom you want to chat.

The buddy's addresses appear.

5 Click the appropriate address.

Ⓐ The buddy's name appears as a button in the To area.

Note: If the buddy's button appears red, it means that the buddy is not registered with iMessage. You may need to use a different address to contact the buddy.

6 Type the text you want to send, and then press **Return**.

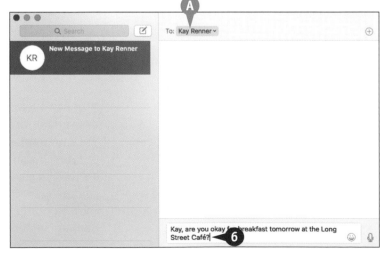

B Your message appears in a bubble on the right side of the right pane.

Note: You can make messages display buddy pictures by clicking **View** on the menu bar and then clicking **Show All Buddy Pictures in Conversations**.

C A reply from your buddy appears on the left side of the right pane.

7 Type a reply to your buddy's reply.

8 Click **Special Characters** (☺).

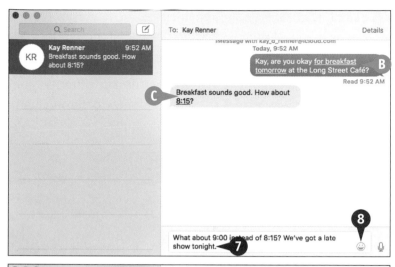

The Special Characters panel opens.

9 Click the category of special characters you want: **Recents and Favorites** (🕐), **Smileys & People** (☺), **Animals & Nature** (🐾), **Food & Drink** (🍴), **Activity** (⚽), **Objects** (💡), **Symbols** (🔣), or **Flags** (🏳).

10 Click the special character you want to use.

The special character appears in the message.

11 Press Return.

Messages sends the message.

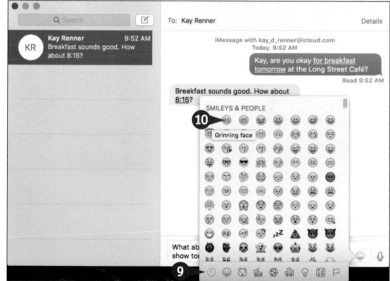

TIP

How can I turn off notifications for a conversation?

In the left pane, press Control +click the conversation you want to affect, and then click **Do Not Disturb** on the contextual menu.

From the contextual menu, you can also give other commands, such as clicking **Open Conversation in Separate Window** to move this conversation to a separate window or **Delete Conversation** to delete this conversation.

Send and Receive Files with Messages

A s well as chat, Messages enables you to send files easily to your buddies and receive files they send to you. During a chat, you can send a file either by using the Send File command or by dragging a file from a Finder window into Messages.

When a buddy sends you a file, you can decide whether to receive it. Messages automatically stores the files you receive in the Downloads folder in your user account, but you can change the destination to another folder if you so choose.

Send and Receive Files with Messages

Send a File

1. Start a text chat with the buddy to whom you want to send a file, or accept a chat invitation from that buddy.

2. Click **Buddies**.

   The Buddies menu opens.

3. Click **Send File**.

The Send File dialog opens.

4. Click the file you want to send.

5. Click **Send**.

A A button for the file appears in the text box.

6 Type any message needed.

7 Press **Return**.

Messages sends the message, including a button for transferring the file.

If your buddy accepts the file, Messages transfers it.

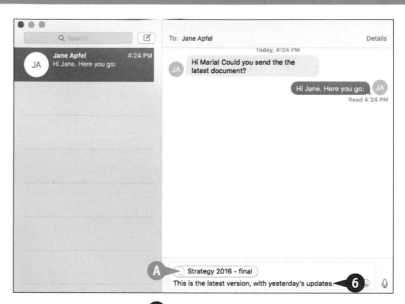

Receive a File

B When your buddy sends you a file, it appears as a button in the Chat window.

1 Click **Window**.

The Window menu opens.

2 Click **File Transfers**.

C The File Transfers window opens.

3 Press **Control**+click the file.

The contextual menu opens.

4 Click **Show in Finder**.

A Finder window opens to the folder containing the file, and you can work with the file as usual.

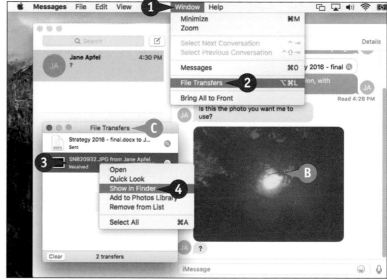

TIP

Can I change the folder in which Messages puts files I download?

Yes, you can change the folder from its default location, the Downloads folder in your user account. To change the folder, click **Messages**, and then click **Preferences**. The Preferences window opens. Click **General** in the upper-left corner. The General preferences pane opens. Click **Save Received Files To** (⬍), and then click **Other**. A dialog opens. Click the folder you want to put your downloaded files in, and then click **Select**. Click **Close** (⬤) to close the Preferences window.

Sign In to FaceTime and Set Preferences

Apple's FaceTime technology enables you to make audio and video calls easily across the Internet. FaceTime works with all recent Macs and with current and recent iOS devices — the iPhone, iPod touch, and iPad.

Your MacBook includes a built-in video camera and microphone, so it is ready to use FaceTime right out of the box. Before you can make calls, you may need to sign in to FaceTime. You may also want to choose preferences for FaceTime.

Sign In to FaceTime and Set Preferences

Open and Set Up FaceTime

1 Click **FaceTime** ( ) on the Dock.

Note: If the FaceTime icon does not appear on the Dock, click **Launchpad** ( ) on the Dock, and then click **FaceTime** ( ) on the Launchpad screen.

The FaceTime window opens.

2 Type your Apple ID.

Note: If you need to create a new Apple ID, click **Create New Apple ID**.

3 Type your password.

4 Click **Sign In**.

FaceTime signs you in.

5 Click **FaceTime** on the menu bar.

The FaceTime menu opens.

6 Click **Preferences**.

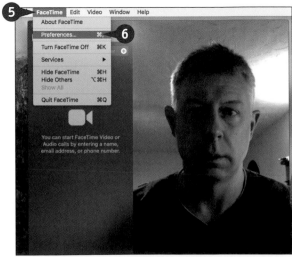

The Preferences window for FaceTime opens, showing the Settings tab.

Ⓐ You can click **Add Email** and type another e-mail address to enable people to contact you via that address.

⑦ Click **Ringtone** (⬍) and choose the ringtone you want to use.

⑧ Click **Blocked**.

The Blocked tab appears.

Ⓑ To remove an address from the blocked list, click the address and then click **Remove** (—).

Ⓒ To block an address, click **Add** (+), and then click the contact you want to block. The contact's addresses appear in the list.

⑨ Click **Close** (⬤).

The Preferences window closes.

TIP

How do I stop using FaceTime temporarily on one of my Macs?

If you use multiple Macs, you may want to stop using FaceTime temporarily on one of the Macs so that you can use it solely on the other Mac.

You can do this by disabling your account for FaceTime on the Mac you want to stop using. Click **FaceTime** (▣) on the Dock to launch FaceTime, then click **FaceTime** on the menu bar and click **Preferences** to open the Preferences window. On the Settings tab, click **Enable this account** (☑ changes to ☐), and then click **Close** (⬤).

Make and Receive FaceTime Calls

When you have set up FaceTime with your Apple ID, you can make and receive FaceTime calls from your MacBook. You can call any iPhone user or any user of a Mac or other iOS device who has enabled FaceTime.

To make a call, you open FaceTime, click the contact, and then select the e-mail address or phone number to use for contacting him. To receive a call, you simply answer when FaceTime alerts you to the incoming call.

Make and Receive FaceTime Calls

Make a FaceTime Call

1 Click **FaceTime** (🔲) on the Dock.

Note: If no FaceTime icon appears on the Dock, click **Launchpad** (🚀), and then click **FaceTime** (🔲).

2 Click the **Search** box.

3 Start typing the contact's name.

The list of matches appears.

4 Click **Video** (🎥) for the contact.

FaceTime places the call.

5 When your contact answers, begin chatting.

6 When you are ready to finish the call, move the mouse to display the pop-up controls, and then click **End** (📞).

Receive a FaceTime Call

When you receive a FaceTime call, a FaceTime window appears.

1 Click **Accept**.

Note: In the Contacts app, you can assign a specific ringtone and a specific text tone to a contact. These tones can help you identify which contact is calling or messaging you.

The call begins.

A You can move the mouse to display the pop-up controls and then click **Full Screen** () to enlarge the FaceTime window to full screen.

2 Chat with your caller.

B You can click **Mute** (■) to mute the audio.

3 When you are ready to finish the call, click **End** (■) on the pop-up controls.

TIP

Must I keep FaceTime running all the time to receive incoming calls?

No. After you set up FaceTime with your Apple ID, FaceTime runs in the background even when the app itself is not open. When FaceTime detects an incoming call, it plays a ringtone and displays a window in front of your other open windows. You can then decide whether to accept the call or reject it.

Configure and Use Handoff with Your iPhone

If you have an iPhone, iPad, or iPod touch, you can enjoy the impressive integration that Apple has built into the iOS operating system and into OS X. Apple calls this integration Continuity. Continuity involves several features including Handoff, which enables you to pick up your work or play seamlessly on one device exactly where you have left it on another device. For example, you can start writing an e-mail message on your Mac and then complete it on your iOS device. This section shows you Continuity and Handoff using an iPhone, which offers more extensive features than an iPad or an iPod touch.

Understand Which iPhone Models and Mac Models Can Use Continuity

To use Continuity, your iPhone must be running iOS 8, iOS 9, or a later version. Your Mac must be running OS X 10.10, which is called Yosemite; OS X 10.11, which is called El Capitan; or a later version. Your Mac must have Bluetooth 4.0 hardware. In practice, this includes a Mac mini or MacBook Air from 2011 or later, a MacBook Pro or iMac from 2012 or later, a Mac Pro from 2013 or later, or a MacBook from 2015 or later.

Enable Handoff on Your iPhone

To enable your iPhone to communicate with your Mac, you need to enable the Handoff feature. Press **Home** to display the Home screen, tap **Settings** (⚙) to open the Settings app, tap **General** (⚙) to display the General screen, and then tap **Handoff & Suggested Apps**. On the Handoff & Suggested Apps screen, set the **Handoff** switch to On (◯), and then set the **Installed Apps** switch in the Suggested Apps list to On (◯) or Off ( ).

Enable Handoff on Your Mac

You also need to enable Handoff on your Mac. To do so, click **Apple** (🍎) on the menu bar and then click **System Preferences** to open the System Preferences window. Click **General** (⚙) to display the General pane. Click **Allow Handoff between this Mac and your iCloud devices** (☐ changes to ☑). You can then click **System Preferences** on the menu bar and click **Quit System Preferences** to quit System Preferences.

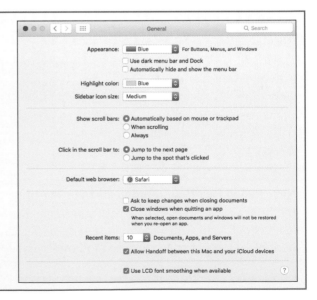

Make and Take Phone Calls on Your Mac

When you are using your Mac within Bluetooth range of your iPhone, Continuity enables you to make and take phone calls on your Mac instead of your iPhone. For example, when someone calls you on your iPhone, your Mac displays a call window automatically, and you can pick up the call on your Mac.

Send and Receive Text Messages from Your Mac

Your Mac can already send and receive messages via Apple's iMessage service, but when your iPhone's connection is available, your Mac can send and receive messages directly via Short Message Service (SMS) and Multimedia Messaging Service (MMS). This capability enables you to manage your messaging smoothly and tightly from your Mac.

CHAPTER 9

Organizing Your Life

To help you keep your daily life organized, your MacBook includes the Calendar, Contacts, Reminders, and Maps apps.

Navigate the Calendar App

The Calendar app enables you to input your appointments and events and track them easily. After launching the app, you can navigate to the dates with which you need to work. You can sync your calendar data with your iOS devices, such as an iPhone or iPad.

Calendar has a streamlined user interface that makes it easy to move among days, weeks, months, and years. You can click the **Today** button to display the current day, or use the Go to Date dialog to jump directly to a specific date.

Navigate the Calendar App

Open Calendar and Navigate by Days

1 Click **Calendar** (🗓) on the Dock.

Calendar opens.

2 Click **Day**.

Calendar displays the current day, including a schedule of the day's events.

3 Click **Next** (❯) to move to the next day or **Previous** (❮) to move to the previous day.

Calendar displays the day you chose.

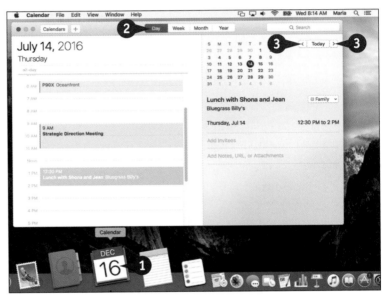

View and Navigate by Weeks

1 Click **Week**.

Calendar displays the week for the date you were previously viewing.

2 Click **Next** (❯) to move to the next week or **Previous** (❮) to move to the previous week.

Calendar displays the week you chose.

View and Navigate by Months

1 Click **Month**.

Calendar displays the current month.

2 Click **Next** (>) to move to the next month or **Previous** (<) to move to the previous month.

Calendar displays the month you chose.

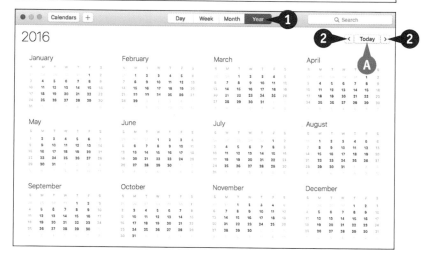

View and Navigate by Years

1 Click **Year**.

Calendar displays the year for the date you were last viewing.

2 Click **Next** (>) to move to the next year or **Previous** (<) to move to the previous year.

Calendar displays the year you chose.

Note: In Week view, Month view, or Year view, double-click a day to display it in Day view.

Ⓐ You can click **Today** to display today's date.

TIP

Which keyboard shortcuts can I use to navigate in Calendar?

Press ⌘+**1** to display the calendar by day, ⌘+**2** by week, ⌘+**3** by month, or ⌘+**4** by year. Press ⌘+**→** to move to the next day, week, month, or year, or ⌘+**←** to move to the previous one. Press ⌘+**Shift**+**T** to open the Go to Date dialog, which enables you to jump to a specific date. Press ⌘+**T** to jump to today's date.

Create a New Calendar

Calendar enables you to create as many calendars as you need to separate your events into logical categories. Calendar comes with two iCloud calendars already created for you: the Home calendar and the Work calendar. Any calendars in other online accounts you have set up on your MacBook appear automatically as well. You can create new calendars as needed alongside these calendars.

After creating a new calendar, you can create events in it. You can also change existing events from another calendar to the new calendar.

Create a New Calendar

1 Click **Calendar** (🗓) on the Dock.

Calendar opens.

2 Click **File** on the menu bar.

The File menu opens.

3 Click or highlight **New Calendar**.

The New Calendar submenu opens.

4 Click the calendar service, such as **iCloud**, in which to create the new calendar.

Note: If the Calendars pane is open, you can create a new calendar by pressing Control + clicking in open space in the Calendars pane and then clicking **New Calendar** on the contextual menu.

Calendar displays the Calendars pane if it was hidden.

Calendar creates a new calendar and displays an edit box around its default name, Untitled.

5 Type the name for the calendar and press Return.

Calendar applies the name to the calendar.

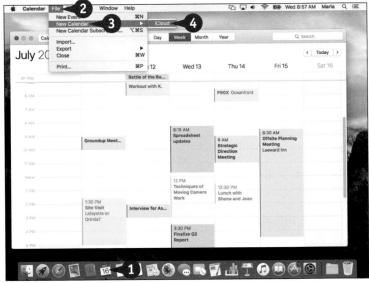

6 Press **Control**+click the calendar's name.

The contextual menu opens.

7 Click **Get Info**.

A dialog opens showing information for the calendar.

8 Click **Color** (⬩) and then select the color you want the calendar to use.

9 Type a description for the calendar.

A Click **Ignore alerts** (☐ changes to ☑) if you want to suppress alerts for the calendar.

10 Click **OK**.

The dialog closes.

You can now add events to the calendar.

TIP

What do the check boxes in the Calendars pane do?
The check boxes control what calendars Calendar displays. Click a check box (☑ changes to ☐) to remove a calendar's events from display.

Create an Event

Calendar makes it easy to organize your time commitments by creating an event for each appointment, meeting, trip, or special occasion. Calendar displays each event as an item on its grid, so you can see what is supposed to happen when.

You can create an event either for a specific length of time, such as 1 or 2 hours, or for an entire day. And you can create either an event that occurs only once or an event that repeats one or more times, as needed.

Create an Event

1 Click **Calendar** (📅) on the Dock.

Calendar opens.

2 Navigate by days, weeks, months, or years to reach the day on which you want to create the event.

3 Click **Day**.

Calendar switches to Day view.

4 Click the event's start time and drag to its end time.

Calendar creates an event where you clicked and applies a default name, New Event.

When you release the trackpad button, the event's details appear in the right pane.

5 Type the name for the event and then press Return.

6 Click **Add Location** and enter the location.

7 Click **Calendar** (🔽) and then click the calendar to which you want to assign the event.

8 Click **Add Alert, Repeat, or Travel Time**.

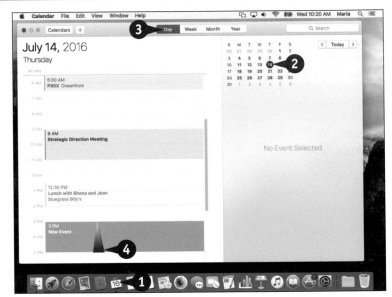

Controls for setting the alert, repeat, and travel time appear.

A You can click **all-day** (☐ changes to ☑) to make the event an all-day event.

B In an iCloud calendar, you can click **travel time** and specify the travel time required.

9 If you want a reminder, click **alert** and specify the details of the alert, such as **10 minutes before**.

10 Click **Add Invitees** and specify anybody to invite to the event.

11 To add further information, click **Add Notes, URL, or Attachments**.

12 Click **Add Note** and type any notes needed.

13 Click **Add URL** and type or paste the URL for the event.

14 Click **Add Attachment**, click the file in the Open dialog, and then click **Open**.

15 When you finish entering details, click outside the details pane.

The details pane closes.

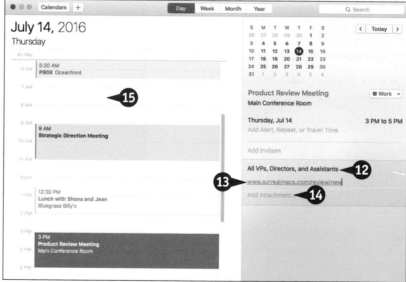

TIP

How do I create a repeating event?

In the details pane, click **repeat** and click **Every Day**, **Every Week**, **Every Month**, or **Every Year**. Use the controls that appear for setting the details of the repetition — for example, click **end repeat**, click **After**, and specify **8 times**. For other options, click **Custom** to open the Custom dialog. You can then click **Frequency** (⬍) and select **Daily**, **Weekly**, **Monthly**, or **Yearly**, and then specify the repetition patterns, such as **Every 2 Weeks**.

Share a Calendar with Other People

Calendar enables you to share any calendar stored on iCloud with other people so that they know when you are busy. You can share an iCloud calendar either as a private calendar, available only to the people whose names or e-mail addresses you specify, or as a public calendar, available to everyone.

If you store your calendars on your MacBook rather than in iCloud, you can publish any calendar to a calendar server on the Internet to share it with others.

Share a Calendar with Other People

Open the Dialog for Sharing a Calendar

1. Click **Calendar** (🗓) on the Dock.

   Calendar opens.

2. Click **Calendars**.

   The Calendars pane opens.

3. Press `Control` + click the calendar you want to share.

   The contextual menu opens.

4. Click **Share Calendar**.

   The Share dialog opens.

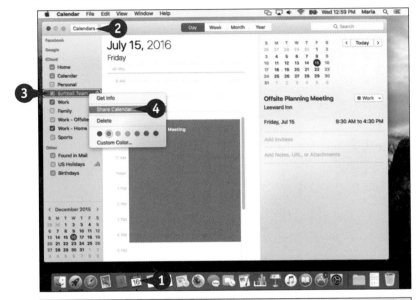

Share a Calendar with Specific People

1. In the Share dialog, start typing a name or e-mail address.

2. Click the e-mail address for the contact.

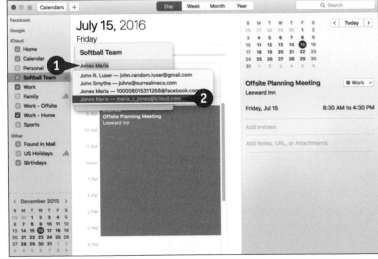

The contact's name appears as a button in the Shared With list.

3 Click the pop-up button (⌄) on the contact's button.

The pop-up menu opens.

4 Click **View & Edit** to enable the contact to edit the calendar. Click **View Only** to enable the contact to only view the calendar.

A You can add other contacts as needed by clicking **Share With** (⊕).

5 Click **Done**.

Calendar shares the calendar with the people you specified.

Make a Calendar Public

1 In the Share dialog, click **Public Calendar** (☐ changes to ☑).

The URL field appears, showing the web address for the shared calendar.

B You can click **Share** (⬆) to share the URL.

2 Click **Done**.

The Share dialog closes, and the Calendar app makes the calendar public.

How do I publish a calendar stored on my MacBook?

Click **Calendars** to display the Calendars pane, then click the calendar. Click **Edit** on the menu bar, and then click **Publish** to open the Publish Calendar dialog. In the **Publish calendar as** box, type the name under which to share the calendar. Click **Base URL** and type or paste the URL for the calendar server, click **Login** and type your login name, and then click **Password** and type your password. Choose options, such as clicking **Publish changes automatically** (☐ changes to ☑), at the bottom of the Publish Calendar dialog, and then click **Publish** to publish the calendar.

Subscribe to a Shared Calendar

Calendar enables you to subscribe to calendars that others have shared on iCloud or published on the Internet. By subscribing to a calendar, you add it to Calendar so that you can view the events in the calendar along with those in your calendars.

You can subscribe to a calendar either by typing or pasting its URL into Calendar or by clicking a link in a message that you have received.

Subscribe to a Shared Calendar

① Click **Calendar** (▦) on the Dock.

Calendar opens.

② Click **File**.

The File menu opens.

③ Click **New Calendar Subscription**.

Note: Many organizations, sports teams, and artists make their calendars available on their websites. You can either copy the calendar's URL or download the calendar.

The Enter the URL of the Calendar You Want to Subscribe To dialog opens.

④ Type or paste in the calendar's URL.

Note: If you receive a link to a published calendar, click the link in Mail. Calendar opens and displays the Enter the URL of the Calendar You Want to Subscribe To dialog with the URL inserted. Click **Subscribe**.

⑤ Click **Subscribe**.

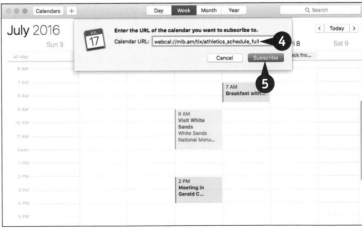

A dialog opens showing the details of the calendar.

6 If necessary, edit the default name to display for the calendar.

7 Click **Color** (⟨⟩) and select the color to use for the calendar.

8 Click **Location** (⟨⟩) and choose where to store the calendar. Your choices are **iCloud** or **On My Mac**.

9 Click **Alerts** (☐ changes to ☑) if you want to remove alerts.

10 Click **Attachments** (☐ changes to ☑) if you want to remove attachments.

11 Click **Auto-refresh** (⟨⟩) and select your preferred option for automatically refreshing the calendar, such as **Every day** or **Every week**.

12 Click **Ignore alerts** (☐ changes to ☑) if you want to ignore alerts set in the calendar.

13 Click **OK**.

Calendar adds the calendar, and its events appear.

TIPS

How do I update a published calendar?
You can update all your published calendars at the same time by clicking **View** on the menu bar and then clicking **Refresh Calendars**. You can also give the Refresh Calendars command by pressing ⌘+R.

How do I unsubscribe from a published calendar?
Click **Calendars** to display the Calendars pane, press Control +click the calendar, and then click **Unsubscribe** on the contextual menu.

Add Someone to Your Contacts

O S X's Contacts app enables you to track and manage your contacts. Contacts stores the data for each contact on a separate virtual address card that contains storage slots for many different items of information, from the person's name and phone numbers to the e-mail addresses and photo.

To add a contact, you create a new contact card and enter the person's data on it. You can also add contact information quickly from vCard address card files that you receive.

Add Someone to Your Contacts

1 Click **Contacts** (■) on the Dock.

The Contacts app opens.

2 Click **Add** (**+**).

The Add pop-up menu opens.

3 Click **New Contact**.

Note: You can also create a new contact card by clicking **File** on the menu bar and then clicking **New Card** on the File menu.

Contacts creates a new card and selects the First placeholder.

4 Type the contact's first name.

Note: Press Tab to move the selection from the current field to the next.

5 Type the contact's last name.

6 If the contact works for a company, type the company name.

A You can click **Company** (☐ changes to ☑) when creating a card for a company or organization rather than for an individual. Contacts then uses the company name for sorting.

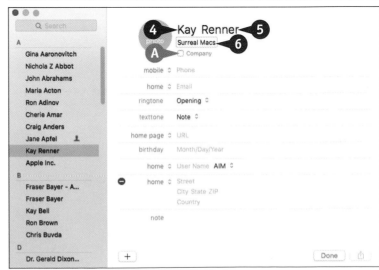

7 Click the pop-up menu ($\updownarrow$) next to the first Phone field and select the type of phone number, such as **work** or **mobile**.

8 Type the phone number.

9 Add other phone numbers as needed.

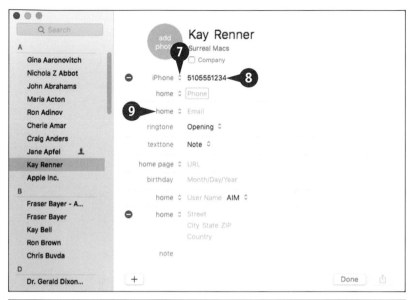

10 Click the pop-up menu ($\updownarrow$) next to the first Email field and then click the type of e-mail address, such as **work** or **home**.

11 Type the e-mail address.

12 Add the physical address and other information.

13 Click **Done**.

Contacts closes the card for editing.

The card appears in the contacts list.

Note: Only the fields that contain data appear in the card.

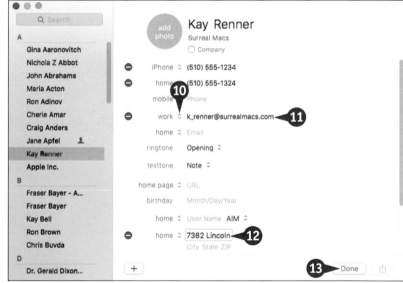

TIPS

How do I add a vCard to Contacts?

If you receive a vCard file, which has the .vcf file extension and contains a virtual address card, in Mail, press Control +click the card, highlight **Open With** on the contextual menu, and then select **Contacts**. A dialog opens prompting you to confirm that you want to import the card into Contacts. Click **Import**.

How do I delete a contact from Contacts?

To delete a contact, click the card, click **Edit**, and then select **Delete Card** or press Delete . A confirmation dialog opens. Click **Delete**.

Change a Contact's Information

Contacts makes it easy to change the information for a contact. So when you learn that a contact's details have changed, or you need to add extra information, you can open the contact record and make the changes needed.

Contacts enables you to add a wide variety of different fields to a contact record to store the information about a contact. You can also add a photo to a contact record.

Change a Contact's Information

1 Click **Contacts** (▊) on the Dock.

The Contacts app opens.

2 In the left pane, click the contact whose information you want to change.

3 Click **Edit**.

Contacts opens the contact's card for editing.

4 To change an existing field, click it and then type the updated information.

Ⓐ You can add a field by clicking **Add** (➕) and then clicking the field on the contextual menu or the More Fields submenu.

5 To remove an existing field, click **Remove** (➖) next to it.

6 To add a photo for the contact, click **add photo**.

Note: If the contact card already has a photo, click the photo to edit or replace it.

A dialog opens.

7 Click **Faces**.

The faces you have identified in the Photos app appear.

Note: Click **Defaults** to assign one of OS X's user account pictures. Click **iCloud Photos** to use a picture you have stored in iCloud. Click **Camera** to take a photo with your MacBook's camera.

8 Click the face you want to use.

9 Click **Edit**.

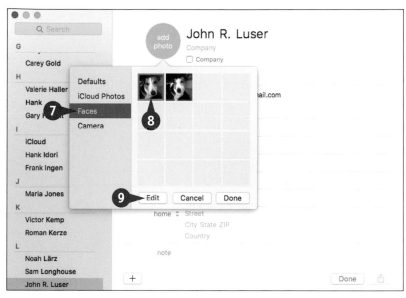

The photo opens for editing.

10 Click and drag the slider to zoom in or out.

11 Click and drag the photo to change the part that appears.

B You can click **Effect** ( ) to apply an effect to the photo.

12 Click **Done**.

Contacts adds the photo to the contact record.

13 Click **Done**.

Contacts closes the contact record for editing.

TIPS

How can I add information that does not fit in any of Contacts' fields?

You can use the Notes field for any information, but you can also create custom fields. Click the pop-up menu ( ) next to an empty field, and then click **Custom** to open the Add Custom Label dialog. Type the name for the field and click **OK**. You can then type the data for the field.

Are there other ways of adding photos to contact records?

Yes. You can click and drag a photo from the Photos app, a Finder window, an e-mail message, or a web page to the photo placeholder.

Organize Contacts into Groups

Contacts enables you to organize your contacts into separate groups, making it easier to find the contacts you need. Groups are useful if you have several different categories of contacts, such as family, friends, and colleagues. You can assign any contact to as many groups as needed.

After creating groups, you can view a single group at a time or search within a group. You can also send an e-mail message to all the members of a group.

Organize Contacts into Groups

Create a Group of Contacts

1 Click **Contacts** (■) on the Dock.

The Contacts app opens.

2 Click **View**.

The View menu opens.

3 Click **Show Groups**.

Note: You can also press ⌘+⊞ to display or hide the Groups pane.

The Groups pane opens on the left side of the Contacts window.

4 Position the pointer over the account in which you want to create the group, such as **iCloud**.

The Add button (⊕) appears.

5 Click **Add** (⊕).

Contacts adds a group and displays an edit box around the default name, *untitled group*.

6 Type the name and press **Return**.

The name appears.

Note: Your contact groups appear on any iOS device you sync with the same iCloud account. iOS devices enable you to create and edit contacts, but not to manipulate groups.

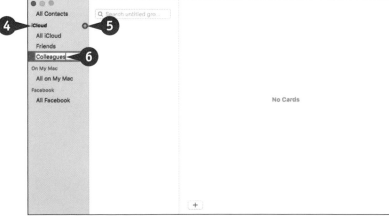

Add Contacts to a Group

1 Click **All Contacts**.

Contacts displays all your contacts.

2 Click and drag one or more contacts to the new group.

Note: To add multiple contacts to the group, click the first, and then press ⌘+click each of the others. Click and drag the selected contacts to the group.

View a Group or Search Within It

1 Click the group.

Contacts displays the contacts in the group.

2 To search within the group, click in the search box and type a search term.

Contacts displays matching contacts.

3 Click the contact you want to view.

A The contact's details appear.

TIPS

How do I remove a contact from a group?
Click the group and then click the contact. Click **Edit** and select **Remove from Group**. Contacts removes the contact from the group but does not delete the contact record.

How do I delete a group?
Click the group, click **Edit**, and then select **Delete Group**. Contacts displays a confirmation message. Click **Delete**. Deleting a group does not affect the contacts it contains; the contacts remain available through the All Contacts group or any other groups to which they belong.

Create Notes

Your MacBook is a great device for taking notes wherever you go. The Notes app enables you to create notes stored in an online account, such as your iCloud account, and sync them across your devices. Alternatively, you can store notes on your MacBook itself, which is useful if you do not have reliable Internet connectivity or if you distrust online storage.

You can create straightforward notes in plain text, but you can also add formatting, check boxes, photos, and sketches.

Create Notes

Open the Notes App and View an Existing Note

1 Click **Notes** (🗒) on the Dock.

Note: If Notes (🗒) does not appear on the Dock, click **Launchpad** (🚀) and then click **Notes** (🗒) on the Launchpad screen.

The Notes window opens.

2 Click an existing note.

Ⓐ The contents of the note appears in the right pane.

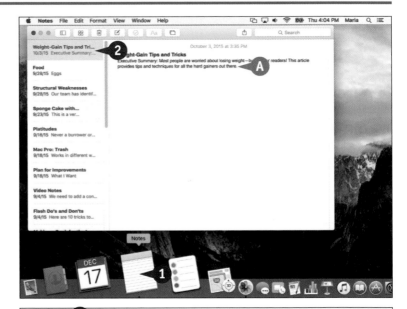

Work with Folders and Display the "On My Mac" Account

1 Click **Show Folders** (▣).

Note: You can also toggle the display of the Folders pane by clicking **View** on the menu bar and then clicking **Show Folders**.

Ⓑ The folders pane appears.

2 Click **New Folder** (⊕).

Notes creates a new folder and displays an edit box around the default name, Untitled.

3 Type the name for the folder.

4 Click elsewhere or press **Return** to apply the name.

5 Click **Notes**.

The Notes menu opens.

6 Click **"On My Mac" Account**, placing a check mark on the menu item.

C The On My Mac account appears in the folders pane.

D You can click **New Folder** (⊕) to create other new folders if necessary.

Note: You can drag a folder from one account to another in the folders pane.

Create a New Note

1 In the folders pane, click the folder in which you want to create the new note.

Note: If you do not have the folders pane displayed, you cannot control which folder Notes creates the new note in. You can move the note to another folder later if necessary.

2 Click **Create a Note** (⬚).

Notes creates a new blank note.

3 Type the title of the note and press Return.

Note: To set the style Notes uses for the first paragraph of a note, click **Format** on the menu bar; click **New Notes Start With**; and then click **Title**, **Heading**, or **Body**, as needed.

4 Start typing the text of the note.

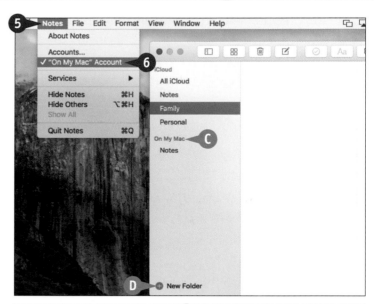

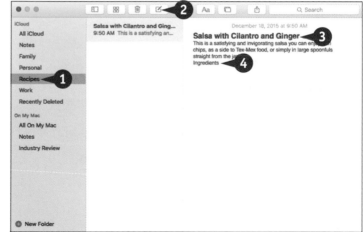

TIPS

Can I use styles and formatting in all my notes?
Styles are available only in notes you store in iCloud or in the On My Mac account. Basic formatting — boldface, italic, and underline — works for notes on Google, Exchange, and IMAP accounts as well as for notes in iCloud.

How do I save my notes?
The Notes app automatically saves your notes when you make changes. You do not need to save the notes manually.

continued ▶

The Notes app includes six built-in styles that enable you to format your notes with a title, headings, body text, bulleted lists, dashed lists, and numbered lists. By using these styles to format notes instead of using direct formatting, such as bold and italic, you can create structured notes that you can easily use in a word processing app.

You can also insert round check boxes to create checklists, lists from which you can check off completed items.

Create Notes (continued)

5 When you need to change style for a paragraph, click **Styles** (Aa).

The Styles pop-up panel opens.

6 Click the style you want to apply: **Title**, **Heading**, **Body**, **Bulleted List**, **Dashed List**, or **Numbered List**.

Note: Notes automatically switches to the Body style for the paragraph after a Title paragraph or a Heading paragraph. Notes continues the Body, Bulleted List, Dashed List, and Numbered List styles until you change styles manually.

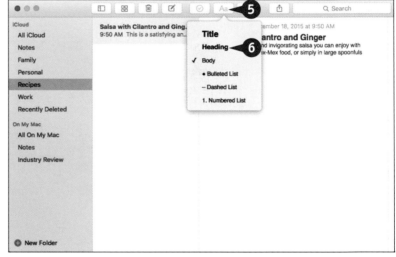

The Styles pop-up panel closes.

Notes applies the style to the paragraph.

7 To create a checklist, click and drag to select the paragraphs for the list.

8 Click **Make a checklist** (⊘).

A round check box (◯) appears before each paragraph.

E You can click a check box to select it (◯ changes to ⊘).

9 To add a photo or video, click where you want to position it.

10 Click **Add a photo or video** (▱).

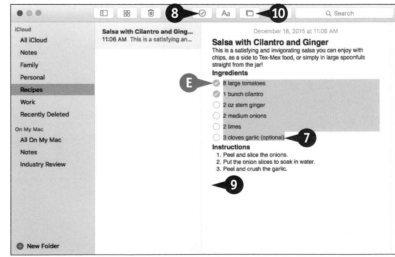

The Photos browser opens.

11 Click the photo and drag it to the note.

The photo appears in the note.

12 Click **Close** (●).

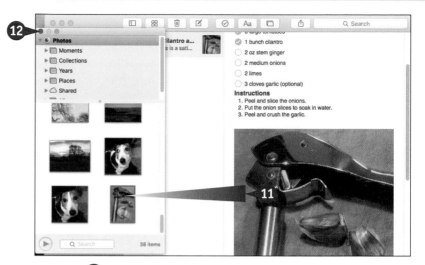

The Photos browser closes.

13 When you want to apply other formatting, click and drag to select the text you want to affect.

14 Click **Format**.

The Format menu opens.

15 Click or highlight **Font**, **Text**, or **Indentation**. This example uses **Font**.

The submenu opens.

16 Click the formatting you want to apply. For example, click **Italic**.

Notes applies that formatting to the text.

17 When you finish working with Notes, click **Close** (●).

The Notes app closes.

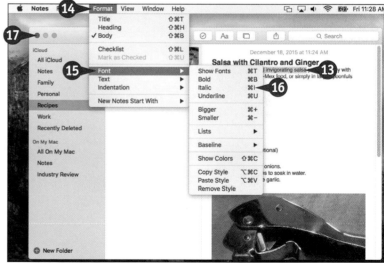

How do I move a note from one folder or account to another?

Click **Show Folders** (▢) to display the folders pane. Click the current folder, then click the note and drag it to the destination folder.

How do I delete a note?

Either click the note in the Notes list and then click **Delete** (🗑) on the toolbar, or press Control + click the note and then click **Delete** on the contextual menu.

Notes moves the note to the Recently Deleted folder, from which you can recover it if necessary. After 30 days, Notes permanently deletes the note.

Track Your Commitments with Reminders

OS X's Reminders app gives you an easy way to track what you have to do and your progress on your tasks. Reminders enables you to link a reminder to a specific time, a specific location, or both. Linking a reminder to a location is useful when you sync your reminders from your MacBook with an iPhone, iPad, or iPod touch that you carry from location to location.

Track Your Commitments with Reminders

Open Reminders and Manage Your Reminders Lists

1 Click **Reminders** (📖) on the Dock.

Note: If the Reminders icon (📖) does not appear on the Dock, click **Launchpad** (🚀), and then click **Reminders** (📖).

The Reminders app opens.

Ⓐ The sidebar on the left shows your various lists of reminders.

Note: If the sidebar does not appear, click **View** on the menu bar and then click **Show Sidebar** to display it.

Ⓑ The main pane shows the reminders in the selected list.

2 Click **Add List** (➕).

Ⓒ A new reminders list appears, provisionally titled New List.

3 Type the name for the list, and then press Return.

Note: You can click and drag your lists of reminders into a different order if you want.

Note: To delete a list of reminders, Control +click the list, click **Delete**, and then click **Delete** in the confirmation dialog.

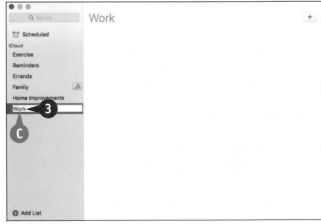

Create a Reminder

1. In the sidebar, click the list in which to create the new reminder.

2. Click **Add** (+).

   A new reminder appears in the list.

3. Type the text of the reminder.

   The Info button (ⓘ) appears to the right of the reminder.

4. Click **Info** (ⓘ).

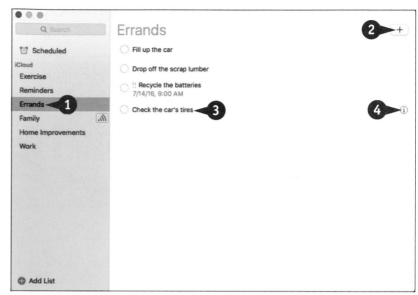

The Info panel appears.

5. Click **On a Day** (☐ changes to ☑).

   The date and time controls appear.

6. Click the date and specify the date for the reminder.

7. Click the time and specify the time for the reminder.

8. If you want the reminder to repeat, click **repeat** and specify the frequency, such as **Every Week**.

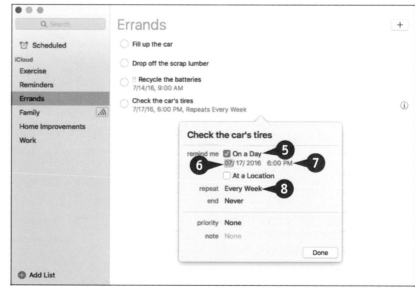

TIP

How do I link a reminder to a location?

In the pop-up panel containing the reminder's details, click **At a Location** (☐ changes to ☑). A new section appears under At a Location. In the text box, type a contact's name or an address, and then click the correct location in the Suggestions list that appears. Click either **Arriving** (○ changes to ◉) or **Leaving** (○ changes to ◉).

continued ▶

To find the reminders you need to work with, you can either browse through your reminders or search through them.

When you have completed the task for a reminder, you select the reminder's check box to mark it as complete. The reminder then disappears from your reminder lists, but you can view your completed reminders at any time by displaying the Completed list.

Track Your Commitments with Reminders (continued)

9 Click **priority** ( ) and then click the priority: **None**, **Low**, **Medium**, or **High**.

10 Click **note** and type any notes needed for the reminder.

11 Click **Done**.

The Info panel closes.

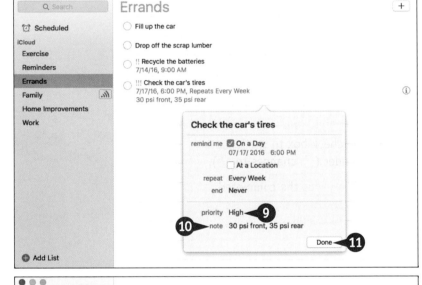

Search for a Reminder

1 Click in the Search box.

Note: You do not need to select a particular list before searching, because Reminders searches across all your reminder lists.

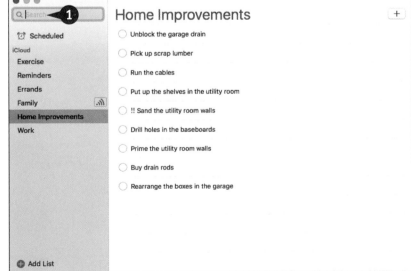

2 Start typing your search term or terms.

D A list of matches appears.

E You can click **Clear** (⊗) to clear the search, restoring the view to the reminders list you were viewing before.

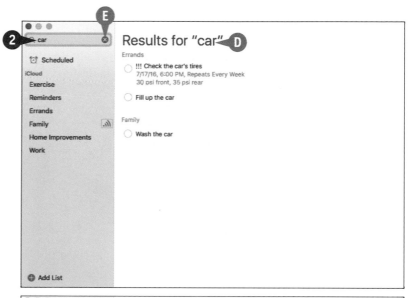

Mark a Reminder as Completed

1 Click the check box to the left of the reminder (◯ changes to ✓).

Reminders slides the completed reminder to the top of the list and then removes it.

Note: To see the reminders you have completed, scroll to the top of the reminder list. The Completed line appears, showing the number of items you have completed. Click **Show** to display the completed items.

Note: To delete a reminder, press Control +click it, and then click **Delete** on the contextual menu.

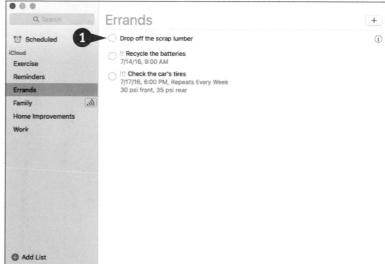

TIPS

How can I look at multiple reminder lists at the same time?

Press Control +click a list and then click **Open List in New Window** on the contextual menu to open a new window showing that list.

How do I change the color of a reminder list?

Press Control +click the list to display the contextual menu, and then click the desired color at the bottom of the menu.

Get Directions

OS X's Maps app enables you to pinpoint your MacBook's location by using known wireless networks. You can view your location on a road map, display a satellite picture, or view transit information for some areas. You can easily switch among map types to find the most useful one for your current needs, and you can use Maps to get directions to where you want to go.

Get Directions

Open Maps and Find Your Location

1 Click **Maps** (🗺️) on the Dock.

Note: If Maps (🗺️) does not appear on the Dock, click **Launchpad** (🚀) on the Dock and then click **Maps** (🗺️) on the Launchpad screen.

The Maps window opens.

2 Click **Show Your Current Location** (➤).

Ⓐ A blue dot shows your current location. The blue circle indicates that Maps is determining your location.

Change the Map Type and Zoom In or Out

3 Click **Satellite**.

The map switches to Satellite view, showing satellite images with place names.

4 Click **Zoom Out** (−) one or more times.

The map zooms out.

Note: Click **Zoom In** (+) to zoom in.

Note: You can rotate the map by placing two fingers on the trackpad and turning them. To return the map to its default northward orientation, click the orange triangle on the 3D icon (🧭).

Ⓑ You can click **Show** and then click **Show Traffic** to show traffic, or click **Show 3D Map** to switch to a 3D map.

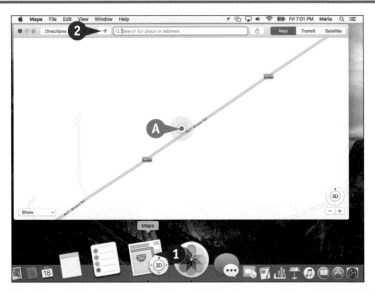

Get Directions

1 Click **Directions**.

The Directions pane opens, suggesting Current Location as your starting point.

2 Click **Start** and type your start point.

The Suggestions panel appears.

3 Click the best suggestion.

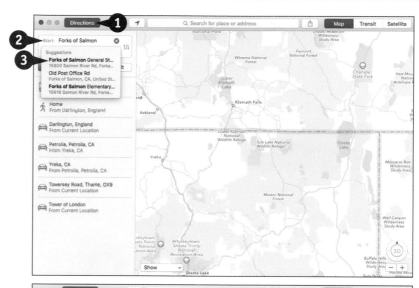

4 Click **End** and type your end point.

Maps displays suggested routes.

C The green pin marks the start.

D The red pin marks the end.

E The current route appears in darker blue.

F The current route's details appear in the Directions pane.

G You can click another route or its time box to display its details.

5 Click a direction to display that part of the route.

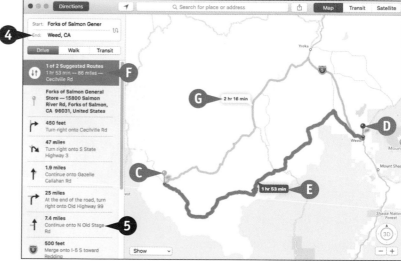

How do I get directions for walking?

Tap **Walk** in the Directions panel to display the distance and time for walking the route. Be aware that walking directions may be inaccurate or optimistic. Before walking the route, verify that it does not send you across pedestrian-free bridges or through rail tunnels.

How can I send directions to my iPhone?

Click **Share** (⬆) to display the Share pop-up menu, and then click **AirDrop** to display the AirDrop dialog. Unlock your iPhone if it is locked. Then, on your MacBook, click the iPhone's icon in the AirDrop dialog. On the iPhone, click **Accept**. The Maps app on the iPhone displays the directions.

Explore with 3D Flyovers in Maps

The Maps app enables you not only to find out where you are and get directions to places, but also to explore with 3D flyovers of the places on the map.

To use 3D flyovers, you navigate to the place you want to explore, and then switch on the 3D feature. You can then zoom in and out on the map, pan around, and move backward to forward.

Explore with Maps

1 Click **Maps** (🗺) on the Dock.

Note: If Maps (🗺) does not appear on the Dock, click **Launchpad** (🚀) on the Dock and then click **Maps** (🗺) on the Launchpad screen.

The Maps window opens.

2 Display the area of interest in the middle of the screen by browsing or searching.

3 Click **3D** (🌐).

The map switches to Flyover view.

4 Click **Zoom In** (+) to zoom in.

5 Click and drag to scroll the map.

Note: You can also scroll the map by placing two fingers on the trackpad and dragging.

6 Place two fingers on the trackpad and turn them clockwise or counterclockwise.

Note: You can also rotate the view by pressing Option +clicking and dragging clockwise or counterclockwise.

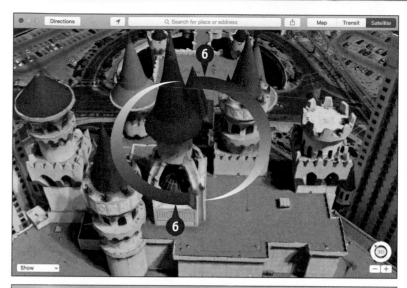

The view rotates, and you can explore.

Note: Pan and zoom as needed to explore the area.

Ⓐ The red arrow on the 3D icon (⊚) indicates north. You can click this icon to restore the direction to north.

7 Click **3D** (⊚).

The map returns to normal view.

TIP

What does 3D do with the Standard map?

When you tap **3D** (⊚) to switch on Flyover with the Standard map displayed, Maps tilts the map at an angle, as you might do with a paper map, and displays outlines of buildings if they are available. For most purposes, Flyover is most useful with the Satellite map.

CHAPTER 10

Enjoying Music, Video, and Books

Your MacBook comes equipped with apps for enjoying music, video, and books. iTunes enables you to copy songs from CDs, play them back, and watch videos, movies, and podcasts. iBooks enables you to build an e-book library on your MacBook and read books anywhere.

Add Your Music to iTunes

Tunes enables you to build your music library quickly by adding your existing songs to it. You can copy songs from your CDs by using a SuperDrive or other optical drive connected to your MacBook. You can also import songs that you already have as digital files on your MacBook.

When importing songs from CDs, you can choose among different settings to create files using different formats and higher or lower audio quality. The highest-quality files give the best sound but require the most space on your MacBook's disk.

Add Your Music to iTunes

1 Click **iTunes** (♫) on the Dock.

iTunes opens.

2 Insert a CD in the optical drive.

iTunes looks up the CD's details online and opens a dialog asking if you want to import the CD.

Note: If you want to prevent iTunes from prompting you to import each audio CD you insert, click **Do not ask me again** (☐ changes to ☑) before clicking **No**.

3 Click **No**.

The dialog closes.

4 Click **CD Info**.

The CD Info dialog opens.

5 Verify that the information is correct. If it is not, correct it.

Note: Many entries for CDs in the online database that iTunes uses contain misspelled or inaccurate information.

6 Click **Album is a compilation of songs by various artists** (☐ changes to ☑) if the CD is a compilation by various artists.

7 Click **OK**.

The CD Info dialog closes.

8 Click **Import CD**.

The Import Settings dialog opens.

9 Click **Import Using** (⬍) and select the encoder to use.

10 Click **Setting** (⬍) and select the setting.

11 Click **Use error correction when reading Audio CDs** (☐ changes to ☑).

12 Click **OK**.

The Import Settings dialog closes.

iTunes imports the songs.

13 When iTunes finishes importing, click **Eject** (⏏).

The optical drive ejects the CD.

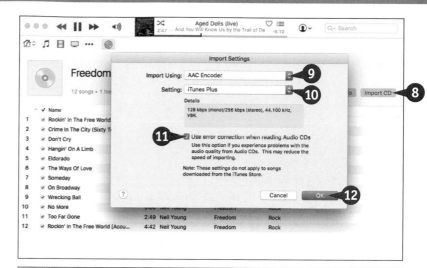

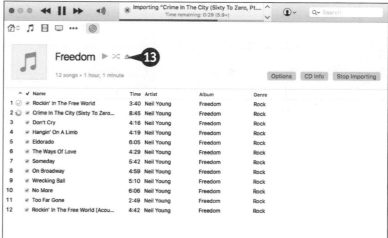

TIPS

How can I create MP3 files rather than AAC files?
In the Import Settings dialog, click **Import Using** (⬍) and select **MP3 Encoder**. Click **Setting** (⬍) and select the quality you want: **Higher Quality** gives reasonable quality, but for top quality, select **Custom**, click **Stereo Bit Rate** (⬍), and then click the **320 kbps** bit rate.

Should I use error correction?
Using error correction for reading CDs is almost always a good idea. Importing may be a little slower, but not enough to matter.

Set Up Home Sharing

iTunes includes a feature called Home Sharing that enables you to share songs and videos among your and your family's Macs, PCs, and iOS devices. Home Sharing saves time and effort over copying song files manually between computers. Each family member who uses Home Sharing must have an Apple ID, such as the one created when setting up an account on Apple's iTunes Store. Anyone without an Apple ID can create one in a couple of minutes.

Set Up Home Sharing

1 Click **iTunes** (🎵) on the Dock.

iTunes opens.

2 Click **File**.

The File menu opens.

3 Highlight **Home Sharing**.

The Home Sharing submenu opens.

4 Click **Turn On Home Sharing**.

The Enter the Apple ID Used to Create Your Home Share dialog opens.

5 Type your Apple ID.

6 Type your password.

7 Click **Turn On Home Sharing**.

Note: If iTunes prompts you to authorize your computer in order to activate Home Sharing, click **Authorize** and follow the prompts for authorizing the computer.

The Home Sharing screen appears.

8 Click **Done**.

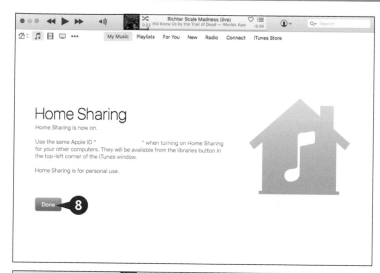

Your library appears again.

9 Click **Source** (⌂).

10 Click the appropriate shared library in the Home Shares list on the menu.

The shared content appears.

11 Select the items you want to import.

12 Click **Import**.

iTunes imports the items.

TIPS

How do I set up Family Sharing?

Press `Control`+click **System Preferences** (⚙) on the Dock and click **iCloud** to open iCloud preferences. Click **Set Up Family** to display the Family Sharing pane. You can then click **Add** (✚) to start adding a family member. To share items you purchase, click **Share my purchases** (☐ changes to ☑). Click **Done**.

How can I share music without using Home Sharing?

Click **iTunes** and then click **Preferences**. Click **Sharing** (🔲) to display the Sharing pane. Click **Share my library on my local network** (☐ changes to ☑) and then click **Share entire library** (○ changes to ◉) or **Share selected playlists** (○ changes to ◉). Others can then play your shared content but not copy it.

Buy Songs Online

iTunes enables you to buy songs and other content from the iTunes Store, Apple's online store for music and media. To buy items from the iTunes Store, you must set up an account including either your credit card details or another means of payment, such as an iTunes Gift Card, PayPal, or an allowance account. If you do not already have an account, iTunes prompts you to set one up when you first attempt to buy an item.

Buy Songs Online

1 Click **iTunes** (🎵) on the Dock.

iTunes opens.

2 Click **iTunes Store**.

iTunes displays the home page of the iTunes store.

3 Click **Music** (♫).

4 Click **Genres** (▼).

The Genres pop-up menu opens.

5 Click the type of music you want to browse.

iTunes displays the kind of music you clicked.

6 Click an item to display information on it.

7 Highlight a song and click **Play** () to play a sample.

8 Click the price button.

A You can click **Buy** to buy the whole album.

Note: If the Sign In to the iTunes Store dialog opens, type your password, and then click **Buy**.

iTunes downloads the song.

Note: To locate the song, click **My Music**, click **Playlists**, and then click the **Purchased** playlist. This playlist shows songs you have purchased from the iTunes Store.

TIPS

What other online stores sell songs I can play in iTunes?
Many online stores sell songs in the widely used MP3 format, which you can play in iTunes and on iOS devices. Explore stores such as Amazon.com (www.amazon.com), eMusic (www.emusic.com), and 7digital (www.7digital.com). To add the songs to iTunes, click **File** on the menu bar, click **Add Library**, select the file or files, and then click **Open**.

How can I restart a download that fails?
Click **Store** and select **Check for Available Downloads**. Sign in if iTunes prompts you to do so. iTunes then automatically restarts any downloads that were not completed.

Play Videos

iTunes enables you to play videos, including video podcasts. You can buy music videos, TV shows, and movies from the iTunes Store or export files of your own movies from iMovie or other applications. After adding videos to iTunes, you access them by selecting **Movies** or **TV Shows**, as appropriate, in the Source pop-up menu.

You can watch video content either within the iTunes window or full screen. You can also play videos from your MacBook to a TV connected to an Apple TV.

Play Videos

1 Click **iTunes** (🎵) on the Dock.

iTunes opens.

2 Click **Movies** (▤).

Note: To watch a TV show, click **TV Shows** (▭).

The Movies screen appears.

3 On the navigation bar, click the view to use: **My Movies**, **Unwatched**, **Home Videos**, **Playlists**, or **iTunes Store**.

iTunes displays the movies in the view you click.

4 Position the pointer over the movie you want to play.

The Play button appears.

5 Click **Play** (▶).

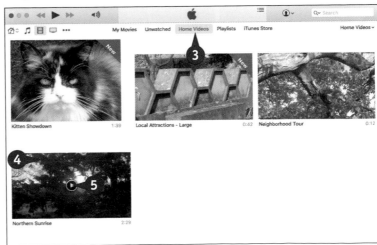

iTunes starts playing the movie.

6 Move the pointer over the video.

The pop-up control bar appears.

7 Use the controls on the pop-up bar to control playback.

A You can click **Full Screen** (⬚) to switch to full-screen viewing.

8 Click **Close** (⊗) to stop viewing the video.

TIP

How do I play a video from iTunes on the TV connected to my Apple TV?

First, make sure your MacBook is connected to the same network as the Apple TV via either a wireless network or a wired network. You can then click **AirPlay** (▭) to the right of the volume control in iTunes to display the AirPlay menu. Click the Apple TV's name on the menu. iTunes sends the video output to the Apple TV, which displays it on the TV's screen.

Create Playlists

iTunes enables you to create playlists that contain the songs you want in your preferred order. Playlists are a great way of getting more enjoyment out of your music. You can listen to a playlist, share it with others, or burn it to a CD for listening on a CD player.

To create a playlist, you drag items to the Playlists pane. In Songs, Albums, Artists, or Genres view, the Playlists pane automatically appears on the right side of the window when you start dragging songs.

Create Playlists

1 Click **iTunes** (♫) on the Dock.

iTunes opens.

2 Select one or more songs you want to put into a new playlist.

Note: Click the first song you want to select, and then press ⌘+click each other song.

3 Click **File**.

The File menu opens.

4 Highlight **New**.

The New submenu opens.

5 Click **Playlist from Selection**.

The Playlists screen appears, showing the playlist with a default name, Playlist, which is selected so you can type over it.

6 Type the name for the playlist and press Return.

7 Click **Edit Playlist**.

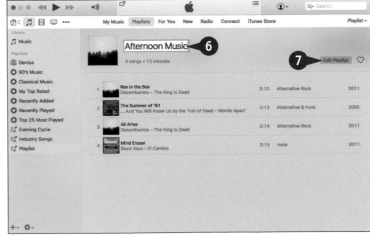

The Playlist pane appears on the right side of the iTunes window, showing the playlist you created.

8 Click and drag other songs, artists, albums, or genres to the playlist. The blue line shows where the songs will land in the playlist.

Note: You can click and drag songs to the playlist from other views, such as Albums view or Genres view.

9 Click **Add description**.

10 Type a description for the playlist to help you identify it.

A You can click **Sort By** (⌄) and then click a different sort order, such as **Name** or **Plays**.

11 Click and drag the songs in the playlist into the order you want.

12 Click **Done**.

You can now play the playlist by clicking **Playlists** and then double-clicking the playlist.

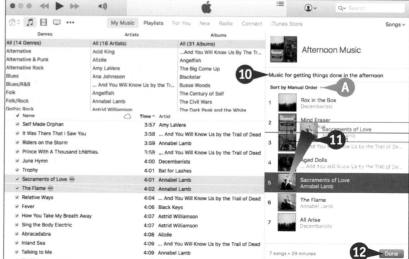

TIP

How can I keep my playlists organized?

You can organize your playlists into playlist folders. Click **File**, highlight **New**, and then select **Playlist Folder**. iTunes creates a folder and displays an edit box around the name. Type the name for the folder and press Return to apply it. You can then click and drag playlists to the folder. Click **Expand** (▶) to expand a folder and reveal its playlists; click **Collapse** (▼) to collapse the folder and hide its playlists.

Create Smart Playlists

Instead of creating playlists manually by adding songs to them, you can have iTunes' Smart Playlists feature create playlists automatically for you. A *Smart Playlist* is a playlist iTunes builds based on criteria you specify. You can set iTunes to update a Smart Playlist automatically as well.

To create a Smart Playlist, you set up the criteria, also called *rules*, and name the playlist. iTunes then adds content to the playlist for you.

Create Smart Playlists

1 Click **iTunes** (♫) on the Dock.

iTunes opens.

2 Click **File**.

The File menu opens.

3 Highlight **New**.

The New submenu opens.

4 Click **Smart Playlist**.

Note: You can also start a Smart Playlist by pressing ⌘+ Option + N .

The Smart Playlist dialog opens.

5 Click the first ⬍ and select the item for the first condition — for example, **Genre**.

6 Click the second ⬍ and select the comparison for the first condition — for example, **contains**.

7 Click the text field and type the text for the comparison — for example, **Alternative** — making the condition "Genre contains Alternative."

8 To add another condition, click **Add** (⊕).

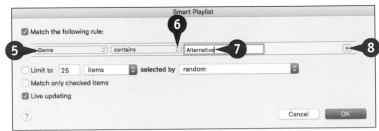

9 Click **Match** (⬍) and select **any** to match any of the rules or **all** to match all the rules.

10 Set up the second condition by repeating steps **4** to **6**.

Note: You can add as many conditions as you need to define the playlist.

Ⓐ You can limit the playlist by clicking **Limit to** (☐ changes to ☑) and specifying the limit.

11 Click **Live updating** (☐ changes to ☑).

12 Click **OK**.

iTunes creates the Smart Playlist and adds it to the Playlists section of the Source list.

Ⓑ An edit box appears around the suggested name.

13 Type the name for the Smart Playlist and press [Return].

iTunes applies the name to the playlist.

TIPS

How do I produce a Smart Playlist the right length for a CD?

In the Smart Playlist dialog, first click **Limit to** (☐ changes to ☑). Click the left pop-up menu (⬍) and select **minutes**, and then set the number before it to **74** or **80**, depending on the capacity of the CD.

What does Match Only Checked Items do?

Click **Match only checked items** (☐ changes to ☑) to restrict your Smart Playlist to songs whose check boxes are selected. This means you can uncheck the check box for a song to prevent it from appearing in your Smart Playlists.

Listen to iTunes Radio and Internet Radio

iTunes enables you to listen to online radio stations. The iTunes Radio feature comes set to access a selection of stations on demand, which means you can pause the radio stream and resume it from the same place. You can skip some songs if you do not want to listen to them, and you can create custom stations. To listen to iTunes Radio, you must sign in to the Apple Music service.

You can also use iTunes to access radio stations that broadcast across the Internet in real time. When listening to such stations, you cannot pause the content or skip songs.

Listen to iTunes Radio and Internet Radio

Listen to a Radio Station

1 Click **iTunes** (♫) on the Dock.

iTunes opens.

2 Click **Radio**.

The Radio screen appears.

A The Beats 1 station appears at the top of the screen. You can click **Listen Now** to start listening to it.

3 Position the pointer over the station you want to listen to.

The Play button (▶) appears.

4 Click **Play** (▶).

The station starts playing.

B Details of the current song appear.

C You can click **Skip** (▶▶) to skip to the next track.

D You can click **More** (•••) to display a menu of other actions, such as starting a new station from the artist or sharing the song.

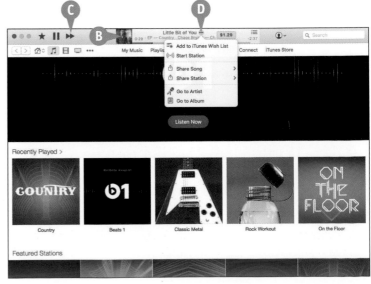

5 To explore other stations, scroll down.

The Featured Stations list appears.

E To play a featured station, move the pointer over it, and then click **Play** (▶).

F You can search by clicking **Search** and typing an artist's name, a keyword, or a genre.

6 Scroll down farther.

The Genre list appears, showing genres such as Pop, Country, and Hip-Hop/R&B.

G To play a station, move the pointer over it, and then click **Play** (▶).

TIPS

How can I listen to Internet radio stations?
Click **View** on the menu bar, highlight **More**, and then click **Internet Radio**; alternatively, press ⌘+9. The Internet Radio screen appears, showing a list of categories. Expand the category you want and then double-click a radio station to start it playing.

How can I listen to an Internet radio station that does not appear on iTunes' list?
Find out the URL of the station's audio stream by consulting the station's website. In iTunes, click **File** and select **Open Stream** to display the Open Stream dialog. Type or paste the URL into the dialog and click **OK**. iTunes starts playing the radio station's audio stream.

Enjoy Podcasts

A *podcast* is an audio or video file that you can download from the Internet and play on your MacBook or a digital player like the iPhone, iPad, or iPod. iTunes enables you to access a wide variety of podcasts on the iTunes Store. The iTunes Store makes a wide variety of podcasts available. You can either download a single podcast episode or subscribe to a podcast so that iTunes automatically downloads new episodes for you.

Enjoy Podcasts

1 Click **iTunes** (⌥) on the Dock.

iTunes opens.

2 Click **iTunes Store**.

iTunes displays the home page of the iTunes Store.

3 Click **More** (•••).

The More pop-up panel appears.

4 Click **Podcasts**.

The Podcasts page on the iTunes Store appears.

5 Click **All Genres** (⌄).

The pop-up menu opens.

6 Click the category of podcasts you want to browse.

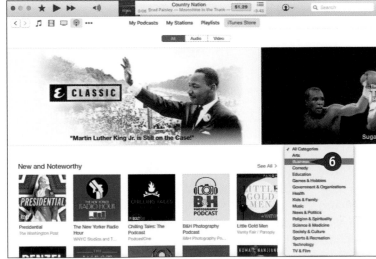

iTunes shows the category you clicked.

7 Click the podcast you want to view.

8 Click **Subscribe** if you want to subscribe to the podcast.

A confirmation dialog opens.

Ⓐ You can click the **Get** button or the price button to download a single episode.

9 Click **Subscribe**.

iTunes subscribes you to the podcast and downloads the available episodes.

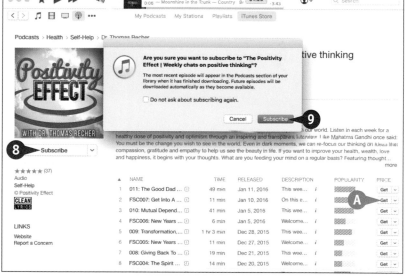

TIP

How do I watch the podcasts I have downloaded?

In iTunes, click **More** (•••) to display the More pop-up panel, and then click **Podcasts**. The Podcasts screen appears. Click **My Podcasts** to display your podcasts. You can then click a podcast in the left pane to display the available episodes in the right pane, and then double-click the episode you want to listen to or watch. iTunes starts playing the podcast and displays a bar of pop-up controls for managing playback.

Read Books

OS X includes the iBooks app, which enables you to enjoy electronic books, or *e-books*, on your MacBook. Using iBooks, you can read e-books that you already have on your MacBook, download free or paid-for e-books from online stores, or read PDF files stored on your MacBook.

Before you can read e-books that you have on your MacBook, you must add them to iBooks. You can then open a book and start reading it.

Read Books

Add Your E-Books to iBooks

Note: This method shows you how to add e-books not purchased from Apple. Any books you have bought via iBooks appear automatically in the iBooks app when you sign in using your Apple ID.

1. Click **iBooks** (⬜) on the Dock.

Note: If iBooks (⬜) does not appear on the Dock, click **Launchpad** (⬜) on the Dock and then click **iBooks** (⬜) on the Launchpad screen.

   The iBooks window opens.

2. Click **File**.

   The File menu opens.

3. Click **Add to Library**.

   The Add to Library dialog opens.

4. Navigate to the folder that contains the books.

5. Select the books you want to add to iBooks.

6. Click **Add**.

   The Add to Library dialog closes.

   The books appear in iBooks.

Read E-Books

1 Click **iBooks** (◯) on the Dock.

The iBooks window opens.

2 Click the button for the view by which you want to browse. For example, click **All Books** to view all your books.

Ⓐ You can search for a book by clicking in the search box and typing keywords.

3 Double-click the book you want to open.

The book opens.

4 Press ▶ to display the next page or ◀ to display the previous page.

Note: You can also swipe left or right on the trackpad to change pages.

Ⓑ You can click **Appearance** (ₐA) to adjust the appearance of the page and the text.

Ⓒ You can click **Library** (◣) to display your library, leaving the book open.

5 When you finish reading, click **Close** (⬤).

The book closes, and your library appears.

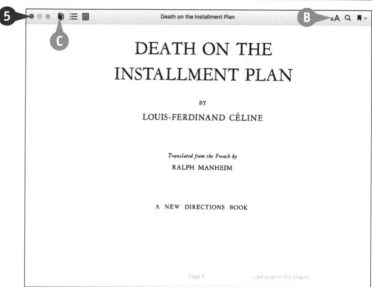

TIP

How can I add my Kindle e-books to iBooks?
As of this writing, iBooks cannot display books in Amazon's proprietary Kindle format. To read Kindle books on your Mac, download the free Kindle app from the App Store and log in to the Kindle service using the e-mail address and password you have registered with Amazon.

CHAPTER 11

Making the Most of Your Photos

Each new MacBook comes with Photos, a powerful but easy-to-use application for managing, improving, and enjoying your photos. You can import photos from your digital camera, phone, or tablet; crop them, straighten them, and improve their colors; and turn them into albums, slide shows, or e-mail messages.

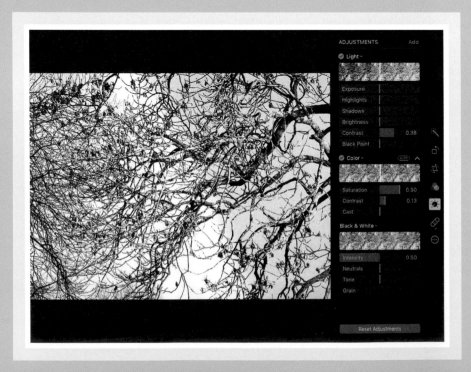

Import Photos

Photos enables you to import photos directly from a wide range of digital cameras, phones, and tablets, including the iPhone, iPad, and iPod touch. Photos normally recognizes a camera automatically when you connect it to your MacBook and switch it on.

If you do not have a suitable cable to connect your digital camera directly to your MacBook, you can remove the digital camera's memory card and insert it in a memory card reader connected to the MacBook or in the SDXC slot of a MacBook that has one.

Import Photos

1 Connect your digital camera or device to your MacBook via USB.

2 Turn on the digital camera or device.

Note: Some digital cameras turn on automatically when you connect them to a powered USB port, but most cameras need to be turned on manually. Phones and tablets usually remain on and wake from sleep.

Photos opens and displays the Import tab.

Ⓐ If Photos does not open automatically, click **Photos** (✿) on the Dock, click **Import**, and then click **Open Photos for this device** (☐ changes to ✅).

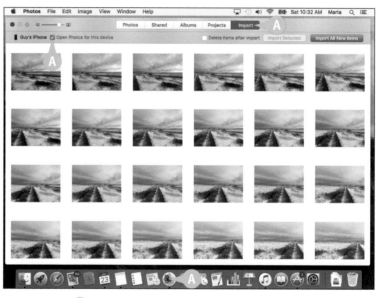

Ⓑ You can click and drag the **Zoom** slider to enlarge the thumbnails.

Note: Scroll up and down as needed by swiping or dragging two fingers on the trackpad.

3 Click each photo you want to import, placing a check mark (✅) on it.

Note: To select a range of photos, click the first photo, and then press **Shift**+click the last photo.

Note: If you want to import all the new photos, you need not select any.

4 Click **Delete items after import**
(☐ changes to ☑) if you want
Photos to delete the photos from
your camera or device after importing
them.

5 Click **Import Selected** to import the
photos you selected. Click **Import All
New Items** to import all the photos.

Photos copies the photos from the
digital camera to your MacBook.

Ⓒ Photos displays the Albums tab,
showing the Last Import album. This
album contains the photos you have
just imported.

Ⓓ An individual photo appears as a
thumbnail.

Ⓔ Photos in a burst appear as a stack.

Ⓕ OS X briefly displays a notification
confirming the photos have been
imported.

Note: For a digital camera, click **Eject** (⏏)
next to the camera's name in the Source
list to eject the camera before you
disconnect it.

6 Disconnect the camera from your
MacBook.

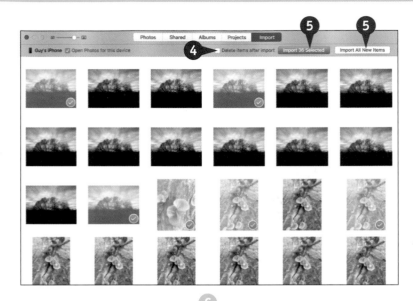

TIP

Should I use the Delete Items After Import feature?

The Delete Items After Import feature is useful if you need to remove items from your camera or device
automatically after importing them into Photos on your MacBook — to free up storage space on that camera
or device, for example. Before using Delete Items After Import, verify that Photos is importing photos from
your camera or device without problems.

If you prefer to keep the photos on your camera or device so that you can enjoy them there, do not use Delete
Items After Import.

Browse Your Photos

To locate the photos you want to view and work with, you browse your photos. Photos enables you to browse your photos easily: You first select a category in the tab bar at the top of the Photos window, and then use the main part of the window to view the photos in the source.

If you have just imported photos, the best way to begin browsing is by viewing the Last Import album, which contains the photos you most recently imported.

Browse Your Photos

Open the Photos App and Browse by Albums

1 Click **Photos** (🌸) on the Dock.

Photos opens.

2 Click **Albums**.

Note: If the Photos window is too narrow for the tab bar to fit, a pop-up menu replaces the tabs. Click 🔽 and then click **Albums** on the pop-up menu.

Note: The Import tab appears only when Photos detects a camera or device connected.

The Albums pane appears.

3 Double-click **Last Import**.

The Last Import album appears, showing the last batch of photos you imported into Photos.

Note: Scroll up and down as needed by swiping or dragging two fingers on the trackpad.

Ⓐ You can move the pointer over a photo and click **Add to Favorites** (🖤 changes to 🤍) to add the photo to your Favorites.

4 Double-click the photo you want to view.

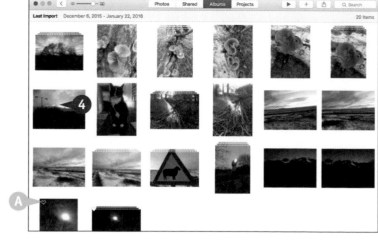

Photos displays the photo.

Ⓑ You can press **Control**+click the photo to display the contextual menu.

Ⓒ You can click **Share** to display options for sharing the photo.

Ⓓ You can click **Delete 1 Photo** to delete this photo.

⑤ Swipe left with two fingers on the trackpad to display the next photo, or swipe right with two fingers to display the previous photo.

The next photo or the previous photo appears, depending on which way you swiped.

Note: You can also press ⬅ to display the previous photo or ➡ to display the next photo. Alternatively, move the pointer to the white space to the left or right of the current photo and click **Previous** (**<**) or **Next** (**>**).

⑥ Click and drag the **Zoom** slider to zoom in.

continued ▶

TIP

Is there another way to navigate the Photos app?

You can click **View** on the menu bar and click **Show Sidebar** to display the sidebar on the left side of the Photos window and to hide the navigation bar at the top of the window. The sidebar contains categories, such as Shared and Albums, that you can click to navigate the Photos interface.

You may find the sidebar handy if you are used to iPhoto, the predecessor to the Photos app. Various versions of iPhoto used the sidebar as the default means of navigation.

The Photos app organizes your photos into groups called Years, Collections, and Moments. A Moment contains the photos taken in a short period of time and in a small geographical area. A Collection contains a group of related Moments. A Year is either a literal calendar year or a group of calendar years, depending on how many photos your library contains.

Browse Your Photos (continued)

Photos zooms in on the middle of the photo.

Note: You can also zoom in by placing two fingers, or your finger and thumb, together on the trackpad and then moving them apart. To zoom out, place two fingers, or your finger and thumb, apart and then pinch inward.

7 Drag with two fingers as needed to pan around the photo after zooming in.

8 Click **Back** (<).

The Photos pane appears, showing the Years groups.

Browse Photos by Years, Collections, and Moments

Note: You may see only one Year group in the Years pane, even if the photos span multiple calendar years.

1 In the Years pane, click the photo thumbnails for the Year you want to view.

Note: You can double-click a thumbnail to open that photo.

The Collections pane for the Year appears, showing larger thumbnails that represent the Moments.

② Click the thumbnail for the Moment you want to view.

Note: You can double-click a thumbnail to open that photo.

Ⓔ You can move the pointer over a Moment to display pop-up controls. You can then click **Play a Slideshow** (▶) to play a slide show of the Moment or click **Add** (✚) to display options for adding the Moment to an album, a slide show, or a print project.

The photos in the Moment appear.

Ⓕ You can double-click a photo to open it.

③ Click **Back** (❮).

The Collections pane appears again.

④ Click **Back** (❮) again.

The Years pane appears again.

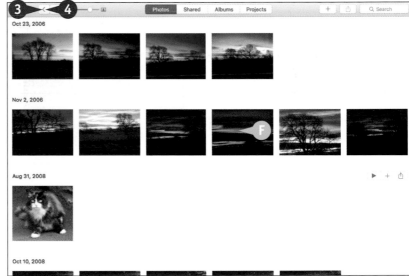

TIP

What is the Faces album?
The Faces album, which you can access by clicking **Albums** on the tab bar at the top of the Photos window and then double-clicking **Faces**, contains faces that you have identified to Photos. See the section "Identify Faces in Photos," later in this chapter, for more information on using the Faces album.

continued ▶

281

The Photos app enables you to browse your photos by the locations in which you took them or the locations with which you tagged them. Browsing by locations is helpful when you need to find photos taken at a particular place without having to search by dates. Photos shows only the main locations when the map is zoomed out, but displays more location detail the further you zoom in.

Browse Your Photos (continued)

Browse Your Photos by Locations

1 In the Years pane, click the heading for the Year you want to browse.

The Photos app displays a map showing the locations in which the photos in the Year were taken.

2 Click **Zoom In** (✛) one or more times to zoom in.

G You can click **Zoom Out** (—) to zoom out.

Note: You can also zoom in by pinching apart on the trackpad or zoom out by pinching together.

H You can click **Satellite** to switch to the photographic Satellite View or click **Hybrid** to switch to Hybrid View. Hybrid View adds text labels to Satellite View.

3 Click the thumbnail for the photo or group of photos you want to see.

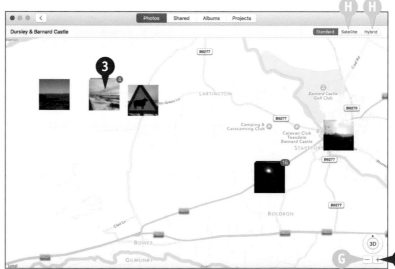

The photos taken in that location appear.

4 Double-click the photo you want to view.

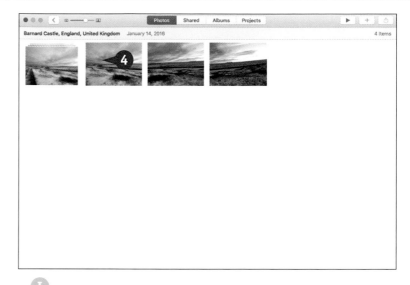

The photo opens.

Ⓘ You can click **Zoom** (⬤) to expand the Photos window to full screen so that you can examine the photo more closely.

5 Click **Back** (‹).

The photos in the location appear.

6 Click **Back** (‹) again.

The Years pane appears.

TIP

How do I add location information to a photo that lacks it?
Open the photo and click **Info** (ⓘ) to display the Info pane. Click **Assign a Location** and start typing the address or other identifying information. In the pop-up menu of results, click the correct information. A map appears with a pin showing the location. If necessary, press Shift +drag the pin to adjust the location. Click **Close** (⬤) to close the Info pane.

Select Photos from Bursts

Many digital cameras and devices, including recent models of iPhone, can take bursts of photos. Bursts are great when you are trying to capture facial expressions, live action, or other unrepeatable moments.

The Photos app enables you to browse the photos you have taken in bursts. From a burst, you can choose which photos to keep as individual photos; you can also choose whether to keep the rest of the burst photos or delete them.

Select Photos from Bursts

1 In Photos, click **Albums**.

The Albums pane appears.

2 Double-click the album you want to open. This example uses **Last Import**.

The album opens.

Note: Scroll up and down as needed by swiping or dragging two fingers on the trackpad.

Ⓐ Each burst appears as a stack of photos.

3 Double-click the burst you want to open.

Photos displays the burst.

4 Click **Make a Selection**.

Note: The Make a Selection prompt appears on a burst of photos, not on individual photos.

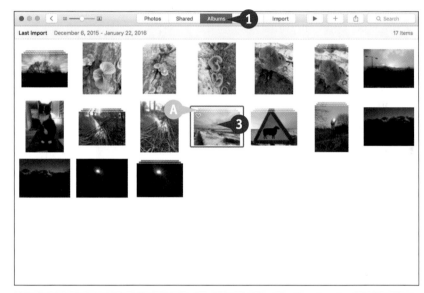

The Make a Selection pane appears.

B The Burst indicator shows you how many photos the burst contains.

C You can click **Next** (>), swipe left with two fingers, or press ➡ to display the next photo.

D The inverted triangle indicates the thumbnail for the current photo.

E The gray circle indicates the photo that currently appears at the top of the stack in the burst.

5 Click the thumbnail for the photo you want to view.

The photo appears.

6 Click the selection circle (⬤ changes to ✅) if you want to keep the photo.

F A check mark appears on the thumbnail for each photo you select.

G The readout shows how many photos you have selected.

7 When you finish selecting photos from the burst, click **Done**.

The Would You Like to Keep the Other Photos in This Burst? dialog opens.

8 Click **Keep Only Selection** or **Keep Everything**, as needed.

TIP

How can I quickly access and review the bursts in my Photos library?
Click **Albums** on the tab bar to display the Albums pane, and then double-click **Bursts** to open the Bursts album. You can then either browse the bursts or double-click the burst you want to open.

Crop a Photo

To improve a photo's composition and emphasize its subject, you can crop off the parts you do not want to keep. Photos enables you to crop to any rectangular area within a photo, so you can choose exactly the part of the photo that you need. You can either constrain the crop area to a specific aspect ratio or crop freely. Constraining an area to specific dimensions is useful for producing an image with a specific aspect ratio, such as 3 × 5 or the ratio of your MacBook's display.

Crop a Photo

1 In Photos, open the photo you want to edit.

2 Click **Edit**.

Photos opens the photo for editing and displays the editing tools.

3 Click **Crop** (⊡).

Ⓐ You can click **Revert to Original** at any point to undo all the changes you have made to the photo.

Photos displays the cropping tools.

④ If you want to crop to specific proportions or dimensions, click **Aspect** (▥ changes to ▥).

The Aspect pop-up menu opens.

⑤ For non-square aspects, click **Crop as Landscape** (▦ changes to ✓) or **Crop as Portrait** (▦ changes to ✓) to set the orientation.

⑥ Click the aspect ratio you want to use, such as **4:3**.

The crop box changes to show the aspect ratio you chose.

Ⓑ You can click **Flip Horizontally** (▲) to flip the photo horizontally. Hold Option (▲ changes to ▶) and then click **Flip Vertically** (▶) to flip the photo vertically.

⑦ Click and drag the corner handles to crop to the area you want.

⑧ If necessary, click inside the cropping rectangle and drag the picture to change the part shown.

⑨ Click **Done**.

Photos crops the picture to the area you chose.

Photos hides the editing tools again.

TIPS

I cropped off the wrong part of the photo. How can I get back the missing part?
Open the photo, click **Edit**, and then click **Revert to Original**.

How can I crop a photo evenly around its center?
Hold Option as you drag the cropping handles. Holding Option makes Photos adjust the crop box around the center of the photo.

Rotate or Straighten a Photo

With digital cameras, and especially with phones and tablets, you can easily take photos with the device sideways or the wrong way up. Photos enables you to rotate a photo easily by 90 or 180 degrees to the correct orientation.

Photos also enables you to straighten a photo by rotating it a few degrees clockwise or counterclockwise. To keep the straightened picture in its current aspect ratio, Photos automatically crops off the parts that no longer fit.

Rotate or Straighten a Photo

Rotate a Photo

1 In Photos, press `Control`+click the photo you want to rotate.

The contextual menu opens.

2 Click **Rotate Clockwise**.

Note: Press `Option` and then click **Rotate Counterclockwise** to rotate the photo counterclockwise.

Photos rotates the photo 90 degrees clockwise.

Note: If you need to rotate the photo further, repeat the move.

Straighten a Photo

1 In Photos, open the photo you want to straighten.

2 Click **Edit**.

Photos opens the photo for editing and displays the editing tools.

③ Click **Crop** (⬚).

Ⓐ You can click **Rotate** (⬛) to rotate the photo 90 degrees counterclockwise. To rotate the photo 90 degrees clockwise, press `Option` (⬛ changes to ⬛) and then click **Rotate** (⬛).

Photos displays the cropping and straightening tools.

④ Click and drag the **Angle** dial to straighten the photo.

Note: Use the major and minor gridlines in the straightening grid to judge when lines in the picture have reached the horizontal position or the vertical position.

⑤ Click **Done**.

Photos applies the straightening.

Photos hides the editing tools again.

TIP

What does the Auto button in the Crop pane do?

Click the Auto button to apply automatic straightening to the photo you are editing. This feature analyzes the horizontal and vertical lines in the photo and attempts to apply straightening based on what it finds. For photos that have obvious orientation problems, this feature can work well. For other photos, such as those where you need to use the background rather than a foreground object to determine what should be horizontal and what should be vertical, you may do better to apply straightening manually.

Remove Red-Eye

A camera's flash can make all the difference when you are taking photos in dark or dull conditions, but flash often gives people *red-eye* — glaring red spots in the eyes. Photos' Fix Red-Eye tool enables you to remove red-eye from your photos, making your subjects look normal again.

To use Fix Red-Eye, you open the photo and switch to Edit mode. You can then either have Photos detect and fix the red-eye automatically or fix it manually by clicking the eyes.

Remove Red-Eye

1 In Photos, open the photo from which you want to remove red-eye.

2 Click **Edit**.

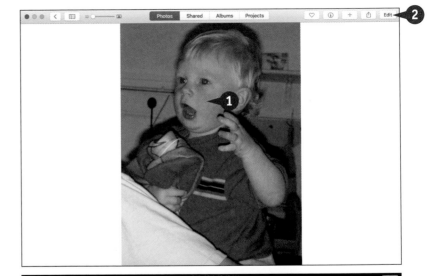

Photos opens the photo for editing and displays the editing tools.

3 Click **Red-eye** (⊘).

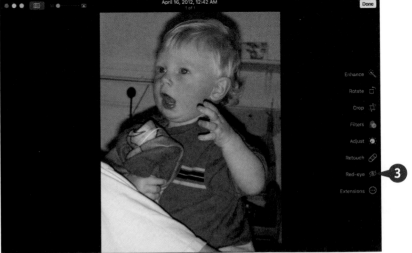

Photos displays the red-eye tools.

4 Click and drag the **Zoom** slider to zoom in.

Ⓐ You can click **Auto** to have Photos attempt to remove any red-eye in the photo automatically. See the tip in this section.

5 Click and drag the **Size** slider to set the size of the circle for removing red-eye.

6 Click the first eye afflicted with red-eye.

Ⓑ Photos removes the red-eye from the eye.

7 Click the other afflicted eye.

8 Click **Done**.

Photos applies the changes to the photo.

Photos hides the editing tools again.

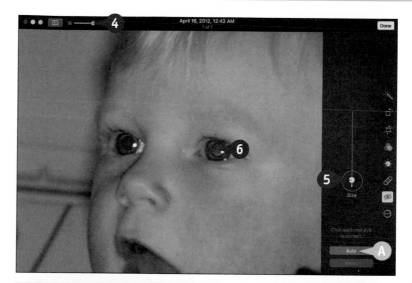

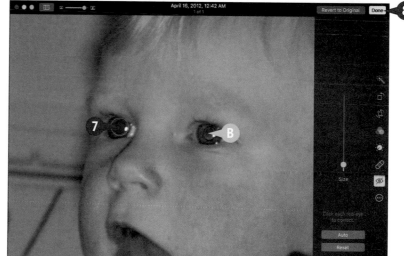

TIP

Should I use the Auto button or fix red-eye manually?
This is up to you. The Auto button should be the quickest way to remove red-eye from a photo, and in many photos it successfully identifies and removes red-eye. But where the tool cannot remove red-eye automatically, drag the **Size** slider to the right size for the red-eye you need to remove, and then click each affected eye in turn.

Improve a Photo's Colors

Photos includes powerful tools for improving the colors in your photos. If a photo is too light, too dark, or the colors look wrong, you can use these tools to make it look better.

Usually, the best way to start is to use the Enhance tool, which boosts flat colors while muting overly bright ones. If Enhance does not give you the results you need, you can use the Adjust tools to edit settings such as exposure, contrast, and saturation.

Improve a Photo's Colors

Quickly Enhance the Colors in a Photo

1 In Photos, open the photo you want to enhance.

2 Click **Edit**.

Photos opens the photo for editing and displays the editing tools.

3 Click **Enhance** (■).

Photos adjusts the exposure and enhances the colors.

Note: If the Enhance tool does not improve the photo, click **Revert to Original** and use the Adjust tools instead.

4 Click **Done**.

Photos applies the changes to the photo.

Use the Adjust Tools

1 Open the photo you want to adjust.

2 Click **Edit**.

Photos opens the photo for editing and displays the editing tools.

3 Click **Adjust** (■).

The Adjustments tools appear.

Note: If the set of tools you want to appear is collapsed, move the pointer over its heading and click **Expand** (▼) to expand it.

Ⓐ You can click **Auto** to have Photos adjust the group of settings automatically.

④ Drag the group's slider to adjust all the settings using preset balances.

⑤ Drag an individual slider to adjust that setting alone.

Ⓑ You can click **Reset Adjustments** to undo your adjustments.

Note: If you need to make the same adjustments to other photos, press `Control`+click the photo and click **Copy Adjustments**. You can then open each other photo for editing, press `Control`+click the photo, and click **Paste Adjustments** to apply the copied adjustments.

⑥ When you finish working on the colors, click **Done**.

Photos applies the changes to the photo.

Photos hides the editing tools again.

TIP

How do I control which Adjustments tools appear?

Click **Add** at the top of the Adjustments pane to display the pop-up menu of tools. Click each tool you want to display, placing a check mark next to it; click to remove the check mark from each tool you want to remove. There are three categories of tools. The Basic category contains Histogram, Light, Color, and Black & White. The Details category contains Sharpen, Definition, Noise Reduction, and Vignette. The Advanced category contains White Balance and Levels.

Add Filters to Photos

Photos includes eight preset filters that you can quickly apply to change a photo's look and add life and interest to it. For example, you can change a color photo to black-and-white, boost or fade the color, or apply an instant-camera filter.

To add filters, you open the photo for editing and display the Filters panel. You can then experiment with the available filters to get the combination that works best.

Add Filters to Photos

1. In Photos, open the photo to which you want to apply a filter.

2. Click **Edit**.

Photos opens the photo for editing and displays the editing tools.

3. Click **Filters** ().

The Filters pane appears.

④ Click the filter you want to apply. This example uses the Process filter.

Note: The Photo Booth app provides a similar but more extensive collection of filters.

The photo takes on the filter.

⑤ When you are satisfied with the filter, click **Done**.

Photos applies the filter to the photo.

Photos hides the editing tools again.

Create Photo Albums

W hen you want to assemble a custom collection of photos, you create a new album. You can then add to it exactly the photos you want from any of the sources available in Photos. After assembling the collection of photos, you can arrange them in your preferred order.

Photos can also create *Smart Albums* that automatically include all photos that meet the criteria you choose. Photos updates Smart Albums automatically when you download photos that match the criteria.

Create Photo Albums

1 In Photos, click **Albums**.

The Albums pane appears.

2 Click **Create** (**+**).

The Create pop-up menu opens.

3 Click **Album**.

Note: To add photos to an existing album, select the photos, click **Create** (**+**), and click **Album**. In the Add Photos to Album dialog, click **Album** (⬍), click the album, and then click **OK**.

The Create New Album dialog opens.

4 Type the album name in the Album Name box.

5 Click **OK**.

The pane for adding items to the album appears.

Ⓐ You can click **Favorites** to see the photos you have marked as favorites.

⑥ Click each photo you want to add. A selection circle (✓) appears on each photo you click.

Ⓑ You can click **Selected** to see photos you have already selected. This is useful when your selections in the All Items pane do not fit in the Photos window.

⑦ Click **Add**.

The photos in the album appear.

⑧ To change the order of the photos, click a photo and drag it to where you want it.

Photos arranges the photos.

⑨ Click **Back** (‹) when you want to return to the Albums pane.

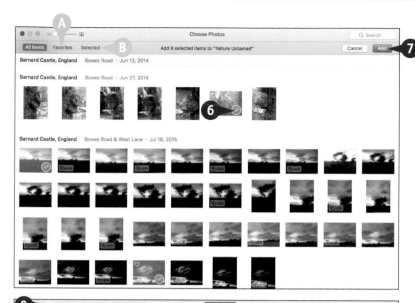

TIP

What is a Smart Album, and how do I create one?

A Smart Album is an album based on criteria you choose. For example, you can create a Smart Album of photos with the keyword "family" and a rating of four stars or better. Photos then automatically adds each photo that matches those criteria to the Smart Album. To create a new Smart Album, click **File** and select **New Smart Album**, and then set your criteria in the New Smart Album dialog. Click **Add** (⊕) to add another row of criteria to the Smart Album.

Create and Play Slide Shows

ne of the best ways to enjoy your photos and share them with others is to play a slide show. Photos enables you to create two types of slide shows: instant slide shows and saved slide shows. For an instant slide show, you simply select the collection of photos you want to view and then start the slide show playing, as explained in the tip in this section. For a saved slide show, you select the photos for the slide show, arrange them into your preferred order, and save the show so that you can run it when needed.

Create and Play Slide Shows

1 In Photos, click **File**.

The File menu opens.

2 Click **Create Slideshow**.

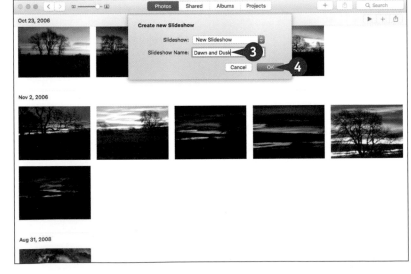

The Create New Slideshow dialog opens.

3 Type the slide show name in the Slideshow Name box.

4 Click **OK**.

The pane for adding items to the slide show appears.

Ⓐ You can click **Favorites** to see the photos you have marked as favorites.

5 Click each photo you want to add. A selection circle (Ⓐ) appears on each photo you click.

Ⓑ You can click **Selected** to see photos you have already selected. This is useful when you have selected photos spread widely in the All Items pane.

6 Click **Add**.

The photos in the slide show appear.

Ⓒ The Projects tab becomes active, because the slide show is a project.

Ⓓ The slide show's first slide and title appear.

Ⓔ You can click **Preview** to preview the slide show with its current settings.

Ⓕ You can click **Add** (⊕) to add other slides to the slide show.

Ⓖ You can click **Loop Slideshow** (🔁 changes to 🔁) to turn off looping.

TIP

How do I play an instant slide show?
Click **Photos** to display the Years pane, and then click the Year that contains the photos you want to view as a slide show; if you want to view a Collection or a Moment instead, display the pane in which that Collection or that Moment appears. Move the pointer over the Year, Collection, or Moment so that the pop-up controls appear, and then click **Play Slideshow** (▶). In the Slideshow pop-up panel that opens, click **Themes** and then click the theme; then click **Music** and click the music. Click **Play Slideshow** (▶) when you are ready to start the slide show.

continued ▶

To make a slide show look the way you want it to, you can give the slide show one of Photos' themes. The themes include animated transitions between slides that give your slide show a particular look.

During the slide show, you can play a particular song or an existing playlist, or you can create a custom playlist to accompany the slide show. You can also choose whether to play each slide for a minimum length of time or to fit the slide show to the music you provide for it.

Create and Play Slide Shows (continued)

7 Click and drag the photos into the order in which you want them to appear in the slide show.

8 Click **Themes** (▢).

The Themes pane appears.

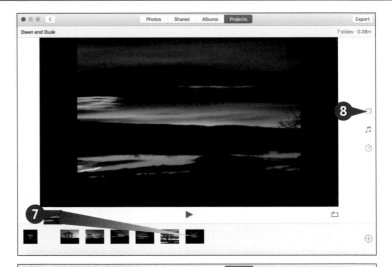

9 Click the theme you want to use. This example uses **Ken Burns**, an effect that gradually pans and zooms over a photo.

The preview pane shows a preview of the theme.

H For Ken Burns, click **Ken Burns Effect** (▢) in the lower-left corner of the preview. Click **Ken Burns In-Point** (◀) to display the In-Point controls, drag the slider to zoom the photo, and then drag the photo to display the area at which to start the effect. Click **Ken Burns Out-Point** (▶) to display the Out-Point controls, and then zoom and drag to set the out-point.

10 Click **Music** (♫).

The Music pane appears.

🄸 The Selected Music section shows the default music for the theme at first.

⑪ Click **Music** (◉) and then click **Theme Songs** or **iTunes** to specify the source of the music.

⑫ In the list of music that appears, click the song or playlist to use.

⑬ Click **Duration Settings** (◌).

The Duration panel appears.

⑭ Click **Fit to Music** (◯ changes to ◉) or **Custom** (◯ changes to ◉), as needed.

Note: If you click **Custom**, drag the slider to set the time.

⑮ Click **Scale photos to fit screen** (☐ changes to ☑) to scale the photos to fit the screen size.

Note: Scale Photos to Fit Screen appears only for some themes.

⑯ Click **Play** (▶).

Photos starts playing the slide show.

TIP

How do I delete the text from the title slide?
Press `Control`+click the title slide in the thumbnail bar at the bottom of the screen, and then click **Delete Text** on the contextual menu.

Identify Faces in Photos

The Faces feature in the Photos app enables you to use facial recognition to automatically identify the people in your photos. First, you identify a face and teach Photos the name for it. Second, Photos scans your other photos for other instances of the same face. Third, you review the suggested faces that Photos has found, confirm the matches, and reject the misses.

After identifying faces, you can browse your photos by them, or use them to create albums, slide shows, or other collections.

Identify Faces in Photos

Identify a Face

1 In Photos, open the photo that contains the face.

2 Click **Info** (ⓘ).

The Info pane appears.

3 Click **Add Faces**.

A white outline appears around the face.

Note: If the white outline is not around the face, click and drag the outline to the middle of the face. You can click and drag to resize the outline as needed.

Ⓐ If Photos has identified a bogus face, click **Close** (ⓧ).

4 Click **unnamed** or **Click to Name**, depending on which appears.

5 Start typing the name.

Photos displays matching names from your contacts.

6 Either click the appropriate contact or finish typing the name and press **Return**.

Photos adds the face.

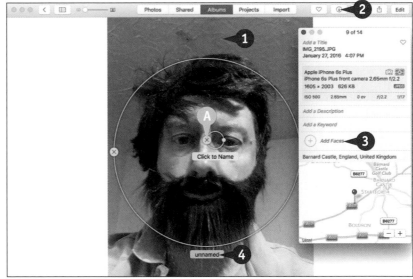

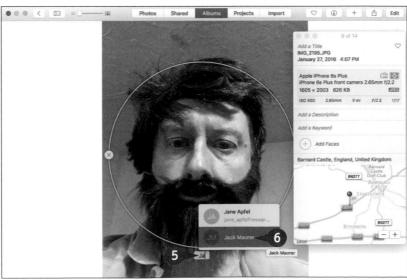

Add Faces from the Suggested Faces List

1 Click **Albums**.

The Albums pane appears.

2 Double-click **Faces**.

The Faces album opens, showing the faces you have identified so far.

3 In the Suggested Faces list, double-click the face you want to identify.

Ⓑ If there are multiple suggestions for the same person, click the first suggestion, press ⌘+click each other suggestion, and then press `Return`.

A dialog opens.

4 Type the person's name.

5 Click **Continue**.

Photos displays a pane stating how many photos of the person you have added.

Note: Photos may automatically add photos that are similar to a photo you have identified.

6 Click **Done**.

The Faces album appears again, and you can work with other faces as needed.

TIP

How accurate is the Faces feature?

Faces in an enjoyable feature in the Photos app and can deliver reasonable results, especially if you take clear and close-up portraits of modest numbers of people. As of this writing, Faces tends to produce false positives, identifying faces where there are none, but you can quickly and easily dismiss any suggested face.

E-Mail a Photo

From Photos, you can quickly create an e-mail message containing one or more photos you want to send to a contact or multiple contacts. You can choose among various graphical designs, add any text message needed to explain what you are sending, and choose between including the full version of the photo and creating a smaller version of it that will transfer more quickly.

E-Mail a Photo

1 In Photos, click the photo you want to send via e-mail.

2 Click **Share** (⬆) on the toolbar.

The Share pop-up menu opens.

3 Click **Mail** (📧).

Note: The first time you give the Mail command, you may need to follow through a procedure to set up Photos with your e-mail account.

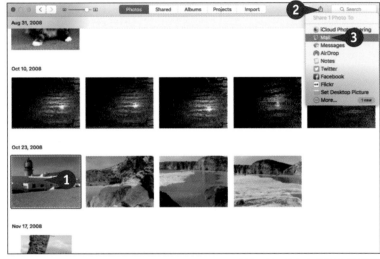

Photos creates a message containing the photo.

4 Type the recipient's address.

Ⓐ If Photos displays a pop-up menu of matching contacts, click the correct address.

5 Click **Subject** and type the subject for the message.

6 Click in the message box and type any message text needed to explain why you are sending the photo.

7 Click **Image Size** (⬍).

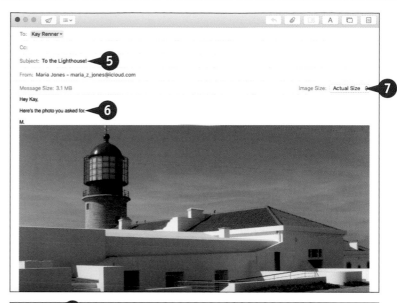

The Image Size pop-up menu opens.

8 Click the size of photo to send — for example, **Large**. See the tip for recommendations.

9 Click **Send** (✒).

Photos sends the message.

TIP

Which size should I use for sending a photo?
In the Image Size pop-up menu, choose **Small** if the recipient needs only to view the photos at a small size in the message. Choose **Medium** to let the recipient view more detail in the photos in the message. Choose **Large** to send versions of the photos that the recipient can save and use in albums or web pages. Choose **Actual Size** to send the photos unchanged, so that the recipient can enjoy, edit, and use them at full resolution.

Take Photos or Movies of Yourself

Your MacBook includes a built-in FaceTime HD camera that is great not only for video chats with Messages and FaceTime but also for taking photos and movies of yourself using the Photo Booth application. You can use Photo Booth's special effects to enliven the photos or movies. The special effects include distorted views, color changes such as Thermal Camera and X-Ray, and preset backgrounds that you can use to replace your real-world background.

Take Photos or Movies of Yourself

1 Click **Launchpad** ( ) on the Dock.

The Launchpad screen appears.

2 Click **Photo Booth** ( ).

Photo Booth opens.

3 If your face appears off center, either rotate or tilt your MacBook's screen or move yourself so that your face is correctly positioned.

4 Choose the type of picture to take:

Ⓐ For four pictures, click **Take four quick pictures** ( ).

Ⓑ For a single still, click **Take a still picture** ( ).

Ⓒ For a movie, click **Record a movie clip** ( ).

5 To add effects to the photo or movie, click **Effects**.

The Photo Booth window shows various effects applied to the preview.

Note: To see more effects, click **Previous** (◀) or **Next** (▶) or click a different dot in the bar. The center effect on each screen is Normal. Use this effect to remove any other effect.

6 Click the effect you want to use. This example uses **Thermal Camera**.

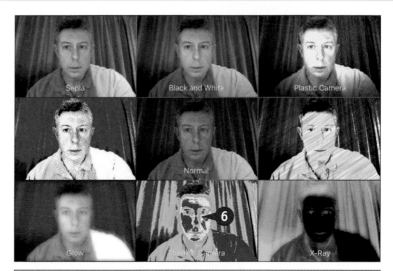

7 Click **Take Photo** (◉) or **Take Movie** (◻).

Photo Booth counts down from three and then takes the photo or photos, or starts recording the movie.

If you are taking a movie, click **Stop Recording** (◼) when you are ready to stop.

Photo Booth adds the photo or movie to the photo well, a bar that appears below the preview window.

TIP

How can I use the photos and movies I take in Photo Booth?

After taking a photo or movie, click it in the photo well, and then click **Share** (⬆). Photo Booth displays a panel with buttons for sharing the photo or movie. Click **Mail** to send it in a message. Click **Add to Photos** to add it to Photos. Click **Change Profile Picture** to use it as your account picture. Click **Messages** to make it your picture in Messages.

CHAPTER 12

Networking and Protecting Your MacBook

OS X enables you to share files, printers, scanners, and optical drives across networks. OS X includes many security features for protecting your MacBook against network and Internet threats.

Transfer Files Using AirDrop

OS X's AirDrop feature enables you to transfer files easily via wireless between your MacBook and nearby Macs or iOS devices via drag and drop. Activating AirDrop in a Finder window shows you available Macs and iOS devices, and you can drag a file to the Mac or iOS device to which you want to send it. Similarly, nearby Macs and iOS devices can send files to your MacBook via AirDrop, and you can decide whether to accept or reject each file.

Transfer Files Using AirDrop

Send a File via AirDrop

1 Click **Finder** (🙂) on the Dock.

A Finder window opens.

Note: If AirDrop does not appear in the sidebar, click **Go** on the menu bar and then click **AirDrop**. If AirDrop does not appear on the Go menu either, your Mac is not compatible with AirDrop.

2 Click **AirDrop** (◉).

The AirDrop screen appears.

3 Click **Allow me to be discovered by**.

The pop-up menu opens.

4 Click **No One**, **Contacts Only**, or **Everyone** to specify which people's Macs and iOS devices can see your MacBook via AirDrop.

5 Press ⌘+N.

A second Finder window opens.

6 Arrange the Finder windows so you can see both.

7 Click and drag the file to the icon for the Mac or iOS device you want to send it to.

The Mac or iOS device prompts the user to accept the file.

If the user accepts the file, the Finder sends the file to the recipient.

Note: If the Mac or iOS device declines the file, the Finder displays a dialog telling you so.

Receive a File via AirDrop

When someone sends you a file via AirDrop, a dialog appears on-screen.

1 Click the appropriate button:

Ⓐ Click **Accept & Open** to save the file and open it for viewing.

Ⓑ Click **Decline** to decline the transfer.

Ⓒ Click **Accept** to save the file so you can use it later.

If you accept the file, your MacBook receives the file.

If you click **Accept & Open**, your MacBook opens the file in the default application for that file type, if it has a default application. You can then work with the file.

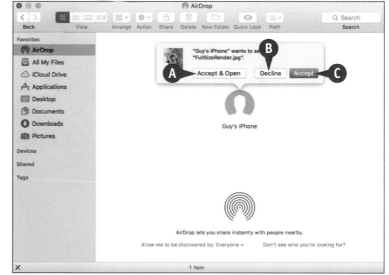

TIP

Should I use AirDrop or a shared folder on the network to transfer files?
If your MacBook connects to a network with shared folders, use those folders instead of AirDrop. By storing a file in a shared folder, you and your colleagues can work on it directly without transferring copies back and forth. AirDrop is useful for sharing on networks that do not have shared folders or for sharing files with Macs to which your MacBook does not normally connect. As an alternative, you can use Messages to transfer files.

Connect to a Shared Folder

O S X enables each Mac to share folders with other computers on the same network. You can connect your MacBook to other Macs and work with the files in their shared folders.

The user who sets up the sharing can assign other users different levels of access to the folder. Depending on the permissions set for the folder, you may be able to view files in the folder but not alter them, or you may be able to create, change, and delete files in the folder.

Connect to a Shared Folder

1 Click **Finder** (icon) on the Dock.

A Finder window opens.

2 If the Shared category is collapsed, position the pointer over it, and then click **Show** to expand it.

3 Click the computer that is sharing the folder.

4 Click **Connect As**.

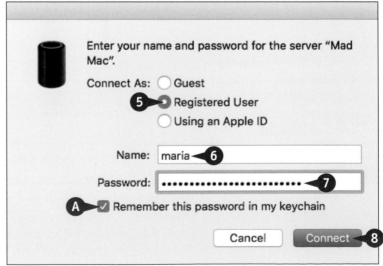

The Connect As dialog opens.

5 Click **Registered User** (○ changes to ●) if you have a user account on the Mac. Click **Using an Apple ID** (○ changes to ●) to log in via your Apple ID. Otherwise, click **Guest** (○ changes to ●) and go to step **8**.

6 Type your username or Apple ID.

7 Type your password.

A You can click **Remember this password in my keychain** (☐ changes to ☑) if you want to store your password for future use.

8 Click **Connect**.

312

The Connect As dialog closes.

B The shared folders appear.

Note: The shared folders you see are the folders you have permission to access. Other users may be able to access different folders.

9 Click the folder whose contents you want to see.

10 Work with files as usual. For example, open a file to work on it, or copy it to your MacBook.

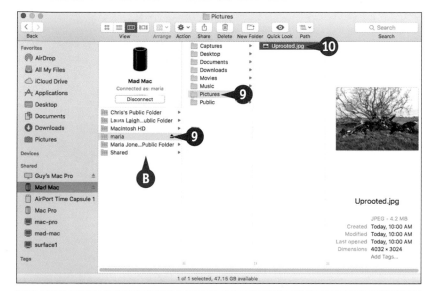

11 When you finish using the shared folder, click **Eject** (⏏) next to the computer's name in the Shared list.

Your MacBook disconnects from the computer sharing the files.

C You can also click **Disconnect** to disconnect from the sharing computer.

TIP

How can I connect to a shared folder that does not appear in the Shared list in the Finder window?
If the shared folder does not appear in the Shared list, find out the name or IP address of the computer sharing the folder. Click **Go** on the menu bar and click **Connect to Server**. The Connect to Server dialog opens. In the Server Address field, type or paste the computer's name or IP address; for a Windows computer, type **smb://** and then the IP address. Click **Connect**, and then provide your username and password if prompted. To reconnect to a server you have used before, click **Choose a Recent Server** (⊙˅) in the Connect to Server dialog and then click **Connect**.

Share a Folder

OS X enables you to share folders on your MacBook with other users on the network. When you share a folder, you control what other users can access it. You can set different levels of permission for different users, such as allowing some users to change files while allowing other users to view files but not change them.

To share a folder, you configure the File Sharing service in Sharing preferences. System Preferences sets up sharing for Macs automatically. You can configure sharing for Windows users manually.

Share a Folder

1 Press **Control** + click **System Preferences** (⚙) on the Dock.

The contextual menu opens.

2 Click **Sharing**.

System Preferences opens and displays the Sharing pane.

3 Click **File Sharing** (☐ changes to ☑).

System Preferences turns on file sharing.

4 Click **Add** (➕) under the Shared Folders box.

A dialog for choosing a folder opens.

5 Click the folder you want to share.

6 Click **Add**.

Note: Each user account includes a Drop Box folder into which other people can place files and folders but whose contents only you can see. To access this folder, click **Finder** (😀) on the Dock, click **Go** on the menu bar, and then click **Home**. Click or double-click **Public**, depending on the Finder view, and then click or double-click **Drop Box**.

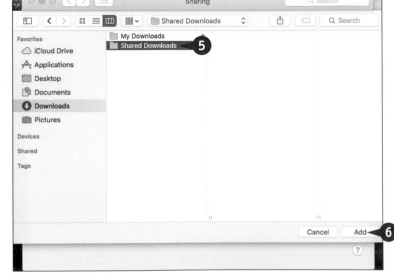

The dialog closes, and the folder appears in the Shared Folders list.

7 Click the folder.

8 Click **Everyone**.

9 Click **Permissions** (⬍) and select the appropriate permission. See the tip for details.

10 If you need to configure sharing for Windows users, click **Options**. Otherwise, go to step **16**.

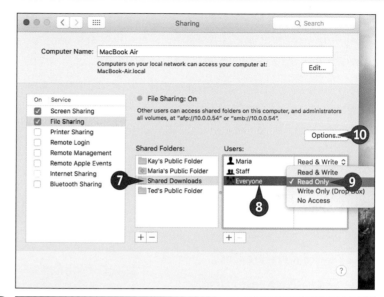

The Options dialog opens.

11 Click **Share files and folders using SMB** (☐ changes to ☑).

12 Click **On** for a user (☐ changes to ☑).

The Authenticate dialog opens.

13 Type the user's password.

14 Click **OK**.

The Authenticate dialog closes.

15 Click **Done**.

The Options dialog closes.

16 Click **Close** (⬤).

System Preferences closes.

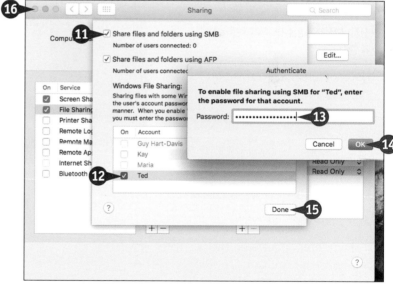

TIP

What permissions should I assign to a folder I share?

Assign **Read Only** permission if you want other people to be able only to open or copy files in the folder. If you want other people to be able to create and change files in the folder, including renaming and deleting them, click **Read & Write**. If you need to create a drop box folder that people cannot view but can add files to, click **Write Only (Drop Box)**.

Connect to a Shared Printer

OS X enables you to connect to shared printers on the network and print documents to them. By sharing printers, you can not only enable each computer to print different types of documents as needed but also reduce the costs of printing.

To use a shared printer, you first set it up on your MacBook using Printers & Scanners preferences. After you set up the printer, you can access it from the Print dialog just like a printer connected directly to your MacBook.

Connect to a Shared Printer

1 Click **Apple** (🍎).

The Apple menu opens.

2 Click **System Preferences**.

The System Preferences window opens.

3 Click **Printers & Scanners** (🖨).

The Printers & Scanners pane appears.

4 Click **Add** (✚).

Ⓐ If the printer appears on the pop-up menu, you can click the printer and go to step **9**.

Note: If no printer or scanner is available on the network, the pop-up menu does not appear. Instead, the Add dialog appears. Go to step **6**.

5 Click **Add Printer or Scanner**.

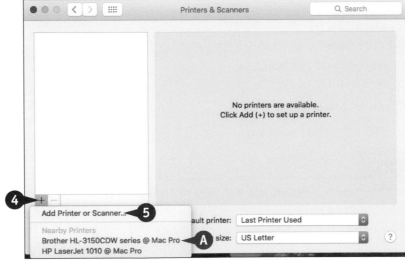

The Add dialog opens.

6 Click **Default** (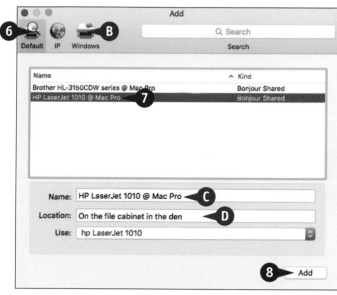).

B Click **Windows** ( ) to see printers shared by Windows PCs on the network.

The Default pane appears.

7 Click the printer.

C You can change the name shown in the Name box.

D You can change the location shown in the Location box.

8 Click **Add**.

The Add dialog closes.

Note: If System Preferences prompts you to download and install software for the printer, click **Download & Install**.

The printer appears in the Printers & Scanners pane.

9 Click **Default printer** ( ) and click the printer to use as the default. Your options are Last Printer Used or one of the printers you have added.

10 Click **Default paper size** ( ) and click the default paper size, such as US Letter.

11 Click **Close** ( ).

System Preferences closes.

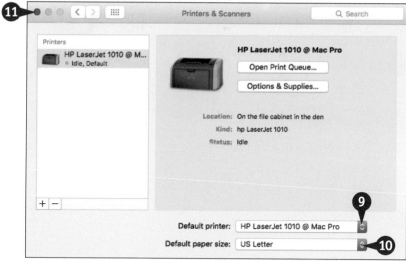

TIP

What should I do when the Use pop-up menu says "Choose a Driver or Printer Model"?
This message appears when OS X cannot identify the driver software needed for the printer. Click **Use** ( ) and then click **Select Software**. The Printer Software dialog opens. Type a distinctive part of the name in the search box to see a list of matching items, and then click the driver for the printer model. Click **OK**.

Share Your MacBook's Printer

OS X's Printer Sharing feature enables you to share a printer connected to your MacBook with other computers on your network. You can choose what users can print on the printer and block other users from accessing the printer.

To share the printer, you turn on the Printer Sharing feature in Sharing preferences, specify the printer, and set permissions for using it. Permitted users can access the printer from the Print dialog on their computers any time your MacBook is running.

Share Your MacBook's Printer

1 Click **System Preferences** (⚙) on the Dock.

Note: If System Preferences (⚙) does not appear on the Dock, click **Apple** (🍎) to open the Apple menu and then click **System Preferences**.

The System Preferences window opens.

2 Click **Sharing** (🔲).

The Sharing pane opens.

3 Click **Printer Sharing** (☐ changes to ☑).

OS X turns on Printer Sharing and displays the Printer Sharing preferences.

4 Click each printer you want to share (☐ changes to ☑).

A OS X makes the printer available to everyone by default.

5 To control who can use the printer, click **Add** (➕).

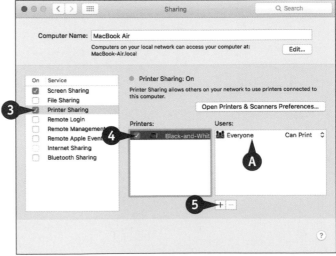

A dialog for selecting users opens.

6 Click the user you want to add.

Note: To select multiple users, click the first, and then press ⌘+click each of the others.

7 Click **Select**.

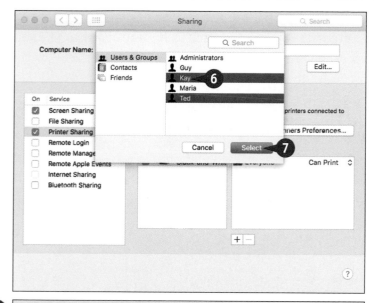

B Each user appears in the Users list.

C OS X automatically changes the Everyone item from Can Print to No Access.

8 Click **Close** (●).

System Preferences closes.

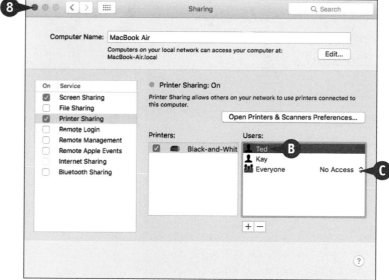

TIPS

How can Windows users share my MacBook's printer?

Users of PCs running Windows need to install Apple's Bonjour Print Services for Windows to access shared printers. Bonjour Print Services for Windows is available free from https://support.apple.com/kb/DL999.

How can I print from my iPad or iPhone to my MacBook's printer?

First, see whether the printer is AirPrint-capable. If so, you can print by selecting the printer on your iOS device, usually from an app's Share menu. If not, either add Printer Pro to your iOS device or install handyPrint (www.netputing.com/handyprint/) on your MacBook.

Connect Remotely via Back to My Mac

OS X's Back to My Mac feature enables you to connect one Mac remotely to another Mac across the Internet. You can use Back to My Mac either to use your MacBook to control another Mac remotely or to use another Mac to control your MacBook. Back to My Mac lets you view the remote Mac's screen and control the Mac.

Back to My MacBook requires you to have set up iCloud on both the remote Mac and the Mac you use to connect.

Connect Remotely via Back to My Mac

Turn On Screen Sharing and File Sharing

1 Click **Apple** ( ).

The Apple menu opens.

2 Click **System Preferences**.

System Preferences opens.

3 Click **iCloud** ( ).

The iCloud pane opens.

4 Click **Back to My Mac**
(changes to).

5 Click **Details**.

Note: The Details button does not appear if file sharing and screen sharing are already turned on. If you need to configure sharing, click **Show All** and then click **Sharing** to display the Sharing pane.

The Details dialog opens.

6 Click **Open Sharing**.

The Sharing pane opens.

7 Click **Screen Sharing** (□ changes to ✓).

The Screen Sharing controls appear.

8 Click **Only these users** (○ changes to ◉).

9 Verify that the list shows the users who will need to connect. You can click **Add** (✛) to add a user or **Remove** (—) to remove a user.

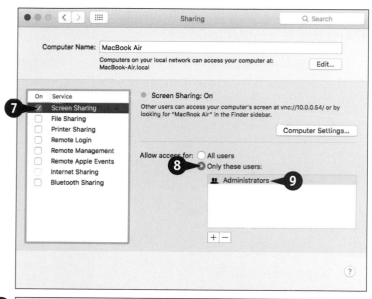

10 Click **File Sharing** (□ changes to ✓).

The File Sharing controls appear.

11 Verify that the Shared Folders list shows the folders you want to share.

12 Verify that the Users list shows the users who will need to connect. You can click **Add** (✛) to add a user or **Remove** (—) to remove a user.

13 Click **Close** (●).

System Preferences closes.

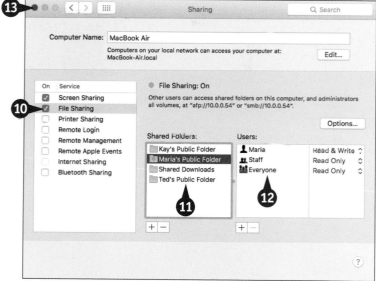

TIP

Why does Back to My Mac fail to connect and instead gives me a message about NAT-PMP?

Back to My Mac establishes a two-way path through your Internet router to the iCloud servers using either the Network Address Translation Port Mapping Protocol, NAT-PMP, or Universal Plug and Play, UPnP. If Back to My Mac cannot connect, turn on NAT-PMP or UPnP on your router. Most routers support one, the other, or both. Consult your router's documentation to find out how to turn on NAT-PMP or UPnP.

continued ▶

Connect Remotely via Back to My Mac (continued)

After enabling Back to My Mac on both the remote Mac and the local Mac, you can use Back to My Mac to connect remotely across the Internet.

You use the Sharing section of a Finder window to establish the connection. The remote Mac's desktop appears in a Screen Sharing window on the Mac you are using. You can control the remote Mac using the mouse and keyboard, enabling you to work much as if you were sitting at it, although screen updates appear more slowly.

Connect Remotely via Back to My Mac (continued)

Use Screen Sharing via Back to My Mac

1 Click **Finder** (🙂) on the Dock.

A Finder window opens.

2 If the Shared category is collapsed, position the pointer over it and click **Show** to expand it.

3 Click the Mac to which you want to connect.

A Finder establishes the connection.

B The remote Mac's shared folders appear.

4 Click **Share Screen**.

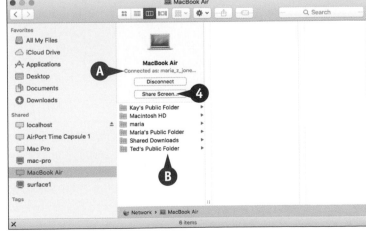

A Screen Sharing window opens, showing the remote Mac's desktop.

5 Work on the remote Mac using normal techniques.

C Click **Scaling** (⌘ changes to 🔲) to scale the remote screen to the window.

D To transfer data via the clipboard, click **Clipboard** (📋▾) and click **Get Clipboard** or **Send Clipboard**.

Note: Click **View** on the menu bar and then click **Enter Full Screen** to view the remote Mac full screen.

End Your Screen Sharing Session

1 Click **Screen Sharing**.

The Screen Sharing menu opens.

2 Click **Quit Screen Sharing**.

The Screen Sharing window closes.

TIP

What may be preventing Back to My Mac from connecting to the iCloud servers?
If you use the OS X firewall to protect your MacBook from dangerous Internet traffic, you must allow File Sharing (AFP, SMB) connections and Screen Sharing connections for Back to My Mac to work. If you use the Block All Incoming Connections feature of the firewall, Back to My Mac cannot work.

Turn Off Automatic Login

OS X enables you to set your MacBook to log in one user account automatically, bypassing the login screen. Automatic login is convenient if you are the only person who can access your MacBook, but it is more secure to disable automatic login so each user must log in.

To enable or disable automatic login, you use the Login Options pane in Users & Groups preferences. You must have an administrator account or provide administrator credentials to change these options.

Turn Off Automatic Login

1 Press **Control** + click **System Preferences** (⚙) on the Dock.

The contextual menu opens.

2 Click **Security & Privacy**.

System Preferences opens and displays the Security & Privacy pane.

3 Click **General**.

The General pane appears.

4 Click the **lock** icon (🔒).

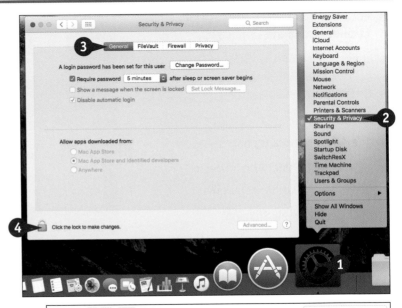

The authentication dialog opens.

5 Type your password.

6 Click **Unlock**.

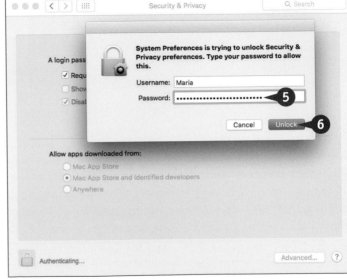

System Preferences unlocks the preferences (🔒 changes to 🔓).

7 Click **Disable automatic login** (☐ changes to ☑).

8 For greater security, click **Require password *N* seconds after sleep or screen saver begins** (☐ changes to ☑).

9 Click the pop-up menu (◉) and click **immediately** or a short time: 5 seconds, 1 minute, or 5 minutes.

10 Click **Advanced**.

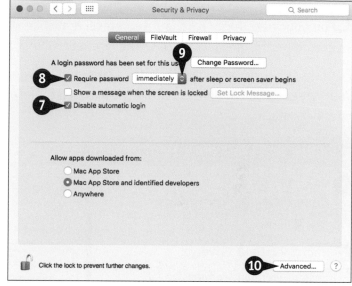

The Advanced dialog opens.

11 Click **Log out after *N* minutes of inactivity** (☐ changes to ☑).

12 Click the text box and enter the period of inactivity.

13 Click **OK**.

The Advanced dialog closes.

14 Click **Close** (⬤).

System Preferences closes.

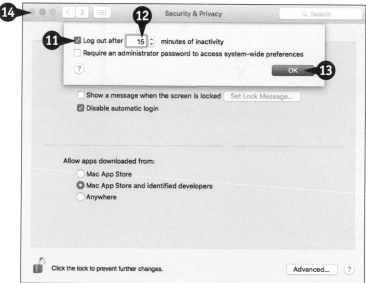

TIP

What other options can I set to tighten my MacBook's security?
In Users & Groups preferences, click **Login Options**. You can then click **Name and password** (◯ changes to ◉) to hide the list of usernames so that anyone logging on must type a username as well as a password. Click **Show the Sleep, Restart, and Shut Down buttons** (☑ changes to ☐) to remove these buttons from the login screen, so that nobody can shut down the MacBook without logging in unless he turns off the MacBook's power. Click **Show password hints** (☑ changes to ☐) if you want to prevent password hints from appearing.

Enable and Configure the Firewall

OS X includes a firewall that protects your MacBook from unauthorized access by other computers on your network or on the Internet. OS X enables you to configure the firewall to suit your needs. To configure the firewall, you use the Firewall pane in Security & Privacy preferences.

Even if your Internet router includes a firewall configured to prevent Internet threats from reaching your network, you should use the OS X firewall to protect against threats from other computers on your network.

Enable and Configure the Firewall

① Press **Control** + click **System Preferences** (⚙) on the Dock.

The contextual menu opens.

② Click **Security & Privacy**.

System Preferences opens and displays the Security & Privacy pane.

③ Click **Firewall**.

The Firewall pane appears.

④ Click the **lock** icon (🔒).

The authentication dialog opens.

⑤ Type your password.

⑥ Click **Unlock**.

System Preferences unlocks the preferences (🔒 changes to 🔓).

⑦ If "Firewall: Off" appears, click **Turn On Firewall**.

The firewall starts, and "Firewall: On" appears.

⑧ Click **Firewall Options**.

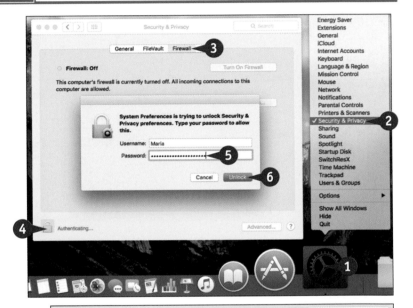

The Firewall Options dialog opens.

9 Click **Automatically allow signed software to receive incoming connections** (☑ changes to ☐) if you want to prevent your MacBook from accepting connections automatically across the network.

10 Click **Enable stealth mode** (☐ changes to ☑) if you want to prevent your MacBook from responding to network test applications.

11 To allow incoming connections to a particular application, click **Add** (**+**).

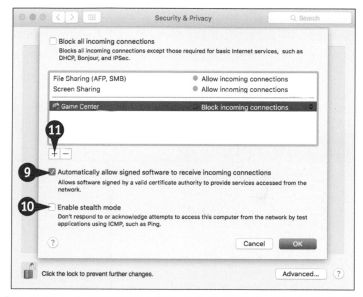

The Add dialog opens.

12 Click the app.

13 Click **Add**.

System Preferences adds the app to the list.

14 Click **OK**.

The Firewall Options dialog closes.

15 Click **Close** (●).

System Preferences closes.

TIPS

When should I use the Block All Incoming Connections option?

Click **Block all incoming connections** when you need to tighten security as much as possible. The usual reason for blocking all connections is when connecting your MacBook to a network that you cannot trust, such as a public wireless network.

How do I block incoming connections only to a specific application?

Add that application to the list in the Advanced dialog. Then click the application's **Allow incoming connections** button in the list and click **Block incoming connections**.

Choose Privacy Settings

The settings in the Privacy pane in Security & Privacy preferences enable you to control which apps can request access to potentially sensitive information, such as the MacBook's location, and files, such as contacts and photos. You can also specify whether to send diagnostic data and usage data to Apple, to help it improve OS X and its apps, and whether to share app crash data with the developers of the apps in question.

Choose Privacy Settings

1 Press **Control**+click **System Preferences** (⚙) on the Dock.

The contextual menu opens.

2 Click **Security & Privacy**.

System Preferences opens and displays the Security & Privacy pane.

3 Click **Privacy**.

The Privacy pane appears.

4 Click the **lock** icon (🔒).

The authentication dialog opens.

5 Type your password.

6 Click **Unlock**.

The controls in the Privacy pane become enabled.

7 Click **Location Services**.

The Location Services preferences appear.

8 Click **Enable Location Services** to enable (☑) or disable (☐) the feature.

9 If you enable Location Services, click each app in the list to enable (☑) or disable (☐) its use of Location Services.

10 Click **Details**.

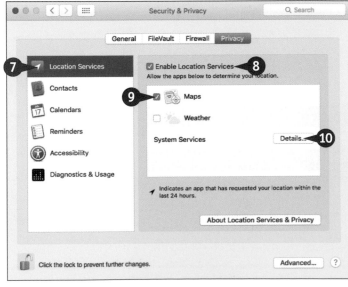

The Allow System Services to Determine Your Location dialog opens.

11 Click **Safari & Spotlight Suggestions** to enable (☑) or disable (☐) Safari and Spotlight Suggestions determining your location.

12 Click **Show location icon in menu bar when System Services request your location** to enable (☑) or disable (☐) the icon appearing in the menu bar.

13 Click **Done**.

14 Click **Contacts** and choose which apps can access contacts.

15 Click **Calendars** and choose which apps can access calendars.

16 Click **Reminders** and choose which apps can access reminders.

17 Click **Accessibility** and choose which apps can control your MacBook.

18 Click **Diagnostics & Usage**.

19 Click **Send diagnostic & usage data to Apple** to enable (☑) or disable (☐) sharing diagnostic and usage data.

20 Click **Share crash data with app developers** to enable (☑) or disable (☐) sharing apps' crash data with their developers.

21 Click **Close** (●).

System Preferences closes.

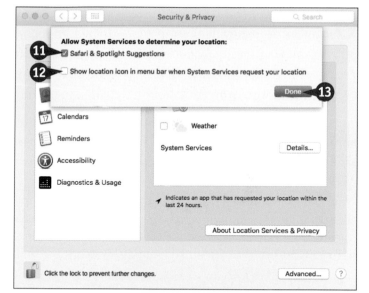

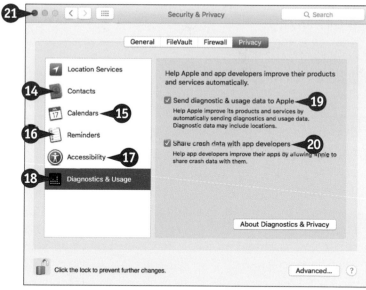

TIP

What does the Advanced button in Privacy preferences do?

The Advanced button is shared among all four Security & Privacy preferences panes — the General pane, the FileVault pane, the Firewall pane, and the Privacy pane — rather than being specific to any pane. See the section "Turn Off Automatic Login," earlier in this chapter, for coverage of the options in the Advanced dialog, which appears when you click this button.

Install and Use Antivirus Software

OS X includes a built-in antimalware app called XProtect that helps protect your MacBook against *malware* — malevolent software — hidden in incoming files, such as files you download or that others send you. It is a good idea to augment this protection by installing and running antivirus software. You can buy and download antivirus software from the App Store, buy it on a disc from a physical store or by mail order, or download it from a website. Some antivirus apps are free; others are pay software.

You install the antivirus software in a similar way to other apps. However, after installing the antivirus software, you may need to restart your MacBook.

Choose Antivirus Software

You can choose from a wide range of antivirus apps to protect your MacBook. Some apps provide only features for scanning files for viruses, whereas other apps are complete security suites. You will likely want protection against *malware*, malevolent software, which includes viruses; Trojan-horse programs that hide harm in a program that seems helpful; and rootkits, which try to build secret entry points into your computer.

Protection against spyware programs, adware programs, and infected websites is useful, too. Features designed to detect phishing messages may also be helpful, but you may find that Mail's Junk Mail feature and your own evaluation give you more consistent results.

When choosing an antivirus software package, assess your needs and decide whether you need a full-blown security app or simply an antivirus app. Bear in mind that the larger the antivirus or security app, the more likely it is to cause your MacBook to run more slowly, because most antivirus and security apps need to run all the time to keep your MacBook safe.

Download and Install an Antivirus App

The App Store enables you to browse a wide range of antivirus apps. You can examine detailed descriptions of each app's features, see user ratings, and read user reviews.

To download and install an antivirus app from the App Store, first click **App Store** (🅐) on the Dock. If the App Store icon does not appear on the Dock, click **Launchpad** (🚀) on the Dock and then click **App Store** (🅐) on the Launchpad screen.

Click in the Search box in the upper-right corner of the screen, type **antivirus**, and press Return. The App Store app displays a list of results. You can click a result to display the details screen for the app.

To buy an app, click **Get** for a free app or the price button for a pay app. For either type of item, click **Install App**. If the App Store app prompts you to sign in, type your password and click **Sign In**. The App Store app then downloads the app. When the download finishes, OS X installs the app automatically.

You can buy antivirus apps in stores or download them from the websites of antivirus companies. Before downloading any app from a website, verify that the app is genuine and that it gets good reviews — if not, it may be dangerous.

Run Your Antivirus App and Update It If Necessary

After installing your antivirus app, run it by clicking **Launchpad** (🚀) on the Dock and then clicking the app's icon on the Launchpad screen.

When you first run an antivirus app, it may prompt you to update its virus signatures or malware signatures. If this happens, give the command for proceeding with the update. For example, in Bitdefender Virus Scanner, select (☑) the **Let Bitdefender update its signatures for improved malware detection** and then click **Finish**.

Scan Your MacBook with Your Antivirus App

Many antivirus apps run continuously in the background, automatically monitoring what happens on your MacBook. Other apps you run as needed; for example, if you suspect that your MacBook has contracted malware, you can run a scan to detect and remove it.

Most antivirus apps enable you to choose which areas of your MacBook to scan and how deeply to scan them. For example, in Bitdefender Virus Scanner, you can click **Scan Critical Locations** to scan important locations and folders such as the main Library folder and the main Applications folder; click **Deep System Scan** to scan your MacBook in depth; or click **Scan a Custom Location** to specify the location you want to scan.

What effect running a deep scan has on your MacBook's performance depends on the antivirus app and on your MacBook's configuration. But in general, it is best not to use your MacBook for intensive computing tasks while running a deep scan. Instead, set a deep scan running when you are planning to leave your MacBook for a while.

Recognize and Avoid Phishing Attacks

Phishing is an attack in which someone tries to make you provide valuable information such as bank account numbers, login names, passwords, or credit card numbers. After acquiring this information, the phisher either uses it directly — for example, withdrawing money from your bank account — or sells it to criminals.

Mail and Safari help protect you against phishing. Mail scans your incoming messages and marks any that may be phishing. Safari enables you to check a website's digital certificate to make sure it is valid.

Recognize and Avoid Phishing Attacks

Recognize a Phishing E-Mail Message

1 In Mail, open the message.

2 Look for signs of phishing:

A Mail has detected suspicious signs in the message.

B The message does not show your name as the recipient.

C The message has a generic greeting, such as Dear Customer, or no greeting at all.

D The message claims you need to take action, such as clearing a security lockout or reenabling your account.

E The message contains links it encourages you to click.

3 Position the pointer over a link but do not click.

F A ScreenTip appears showing the address to which the link leads.

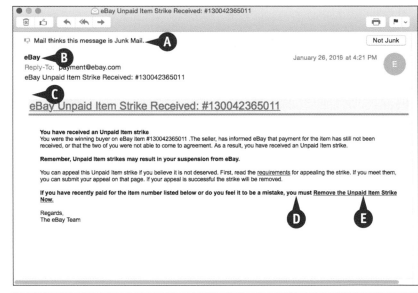

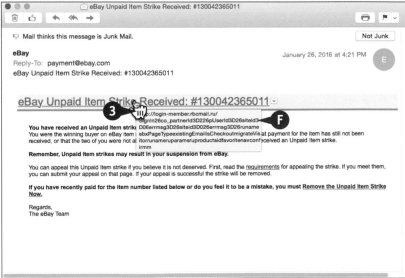

Connect Securely to a Website

1. Click **Safari** () on the Dock.

2. Click the address box.

3. Type the address of the website and press **Return**.

4. Click the **padlock** icon (🔒).

Note: Safari displays the padlock icon when you have connected securely to a website. The address of a secure connection starts with https:// instead of http://. You can view the full address by clicking the address box.

A dialog opens.

5. Click **Show Certificate**.

The dialog expands, showing the details of the digital certificate that identifies the website.

6. Verify that the certificate is valid.

7. Click **OK**.

The dialog closes.

8. If you are convinced that the website is genuine, log in to it.

TIPS

Is it possible to make a secure connection to a dangerous website?

Yes. The padlock icon means only that the connection between your MacBook and the website server is secure and cannot be read in transmission. The website may be safe or it may be dangerous; it is up to you to establish which.

Is a message definitely genuine if it includes my name?

Even if a message includes your name, be alert for other signs of phishing. Some phishers send customized phishing messages in the hope of ensnaring particular high-value victims. This technique is called *spear-phishing*. Evaluate the message's content for sense and likelihood, and remember that anything too good to be true is usually not true.

CHAPTER 13

Troubleshooting Your MacBook

To keep your MacBook running well, you need to perform basic maintenance, such as emptying the Trash, updating OS X and your apps with the latest fixes, and backing up your files. You may also need to troubleshoot your MacBook, solving problems such as corrupt preferences files, disk permission errors, or drive failure.

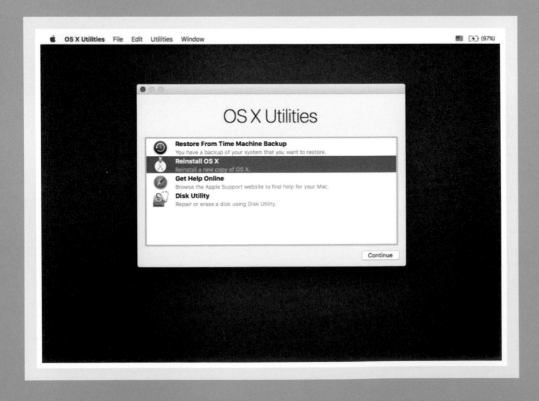

Using OS X's Help System

OS X has a built-in help system that enables you to solve problems that you encounter when using your MacBook and its software. You can launch the help system from the menu bar of the Finder. You can then either browse or search to find the information you need.

Most apps that run on OS X include help files. In such apps, you can use the Help menu at the right end of the menu bar to browse or search the help files.

Using OS X's Help System

1 Click anywhere on the desktop.

The Finder becomes active.

2 Click **Help**.

The Help menu opens.

3 Click **Mac Help**.

The Mac Help window opens.

A You can click **OS X overview** to display an overview of OS X.

B You can click **Show topics** to display a sidebar on the left of the window containing a navigable hierarchy of help topics.

4 Click the search box.

5 Start typing a question or some keywords.

C Search results appear as you type.

6 Click the appropriate search result.

The Mac Help window shows a list of topics related to your search terms.

7 Click the topic you want to view.

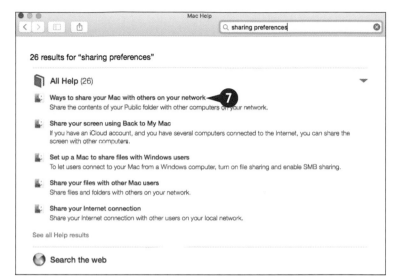

Mac Help displays the topic.

D Click a link to open another topic, an app or utility, or a web page.

E Click **Back** (◁) to return to the previous screen you viewed.

F Click **Home** (▭) to return to the Help Center screen.

8 When you finish using Help, click **Close** (●).

The Mac Help window closes.

Can I print out a help topic for reference?

To print the current topic, click **Share** (⬆), and then click **Print** on the pop-up menu. This menu also includes commands for adding a help topic to your Reading List in Safari, saving it to Notes or Reminders, or sharing it with other people or other apps.

How do I get help for other apps?

Each app has its own Help menu. Activate the app, click **Help** to open the Help menu, and then either click the help topic for the app or type your search terms and press **Return**.

Reclaim Space by Emptying the Trash

I n OS X, the Trash is a receptacle for files you delete from your MacBook's drives. Any file you place in the Trash remains there until you empty the Trash, or until the Trash runs out of space for files and automatically deletes the earliest files it contains; until then, you can recover the file from the Trash. You can reclaim drive space by emptying the Trash manually.

Reclaim Space by Emptying the Trash

Empty the Trash

1 Click **Trash** (🗑) on the Dock.

Note: If the Trash icon on the Dock is the empty Trash can (🗑), the Trash is already empty.

2 Look through the files and folders in the Trash to make sure it contains nothing you want to keep.

To quickly view the contents of a file, use Quick Look. Click the file, and then press `Spacebar`.

Note: You cannot open a file while it is in the Trash. If you want to open a file, you must remove it from the Trash.

3 Click **Empty**.

A dialog opens to confirm that you want to permanently erase the items in the Trash.

Note: You can turn off the confirmation of deleting files. Click **Finder** and then click **Preferences.** Click **Advanced** and then click **Show warning before emptying the Trash** (☑ changes to ☐).

④ Click **Empty Trash.**

OS X empties the Trash and then closes the Finder window.

Restore a File or Folder to Its Previous Location

① In the Trash folder, click the file or folder.

② Click **Action** (✿ ⌄).

③ Click **Put Back.**

Note: You can also press Control + click an item and click **Put Back** on the contextual menu.

OS X restores the file or folder to its previous location.

Note: To move a file from the Trash to another folder, drag the file to that folder. For example, you can drag a file to the desktop.

TIPS

Is there a quicker way to empty the Trash?

If you are sure that the Trash contains no files or folders you need, press Control + click **Trash** (🗑) on the Dock. The Dock menu opens. Click **Empty Trash.** A confirmation dialog opens. Click **Empty Trash.**

Why does the Put Back command not appear on the Action menu?

If the Put Back command is missing, it means that the folder from which you moved the item to the Trash is no longer there. If the folder is in the Trash, click the folder, click **Action** (✿ ⌄), and then click **Put Back**; you can then put back in it the file you want to recover. Alternatively, drag the file to another folder.

Keep Your MacBook Current with Updates

The App Store app built into OS X includes a feature for keeping your MacBook, its operating system, and your App Store apps up to date. You can use the App Store app to check for updates and to install them. You can choose which updates to install.

Your MacBook must be connected to the Internet when you check for updates and download them. You can install most updates when your MacBook is either online or offline. Some updates require restarting your MacBook.

Keep Your MacBook Current with Updates

Ⓐ A badge on the App Store icon indicates the number of updates available.

① Click **App Store** (🔵) on the Dock.

Note: If App Store (🔵) does not appear on the Dock, click **Launchpad** (🚀) on the Dock and then click **App Store** (🔵) on the Launchpad screen.

Note: You can also open the App Store app by clicking **Apple** (🍎) and then clicking **App Store**.

The App Store app opens.

② Click **Updates**.

The Updates pane appears.

App Store automatically checks for updates.

If updates are available, the Updates Available list shows the details.

Note: If the message No Updates Available appears, go to step **5**.

Ⓑ You can install an individual update by clicking **Update**. If the update requires a restart, click **Restart**.

Ⓒ You can click **More** to display full details of the update.

③ To install all the updates, click **Update All**.

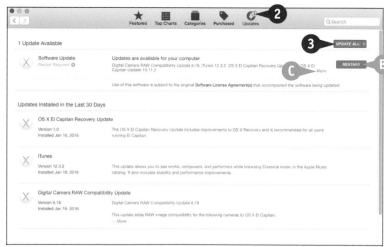

Note: You can set the App Store app to install updates or remind you later. Click ![icon] next to Update All and then click **Try in an Hour**, **Try Tonight**, or **Remind Me Tomorrow**, as needed.

> If installing the updates requires a restart, App Store displays a dialog.

4 Click **Restart**.

D You can click **Later** and then click **Install in an Hour**, **Install Tonight**, or **Remind Me Tomorrow**.

> OS X installs the updates, restarting your MacBook if necessary.

E App Store appears and checks for updates.

Note: If App Store finds further updates, click **Update All** to install them.

5 Click **Close** (●).

> The App Store app closes.

TIPS

Why does the App Store app sometimes prompt me to install updates?

In OS X, App Store comes set to check for updates automatically; when it finds updates, it prompts you to install them. You can change the frequency of these checks, choose whether to download important updates automatically, or turn off automatic checks. See the next section, "Control Checking for Software Updates," for instructions.

Which updates should I install?

Normally, it is best to install all available system updates unless you hear that a specific update may cause problems with your MacBook. In that case, wait until Apple fixes the update. For app updates, it is wise to wait for user feedback, because some updates create incompatibilities for documents created in earlier versions.

Control Checking for Software Updates

OS X's App Store app enables you to check easily for software updates available through the App Store. These include updates for OS X itself, the apps that Apple releases, and third-party apps sold through the App Store. To keep your MacBook running smoothly and protect it from both online and offline threats, you should apply software updates when they become available.

You can configure the App Store app to check automatically for updates on a schedule. You can also check for updates manually.

Control Checking for Software Updates

1 Click **System Preferences** (⚙) on the Dock.

Note: You can also open System Preferences by clicking **Apple** () on the menu bar and then clicking **System Preferences**.

The System Preferences window opens.

2 Click **App Store** (Ⓐ).

The App Store preferences pane appears.

3 Click **Automatically check for updates** (☐ changes to ☑).

4 Click **Download newly available updates in the background** (☐ changes to ☑) if you want to download updates.

Note: Downloading updates in the background is usually helpful, because you can then install the updates quickly.

5 Click **Install app updates** (☐ changes to ☑) if you want to install app updates automatically.

6 Click **Install OS X updates** (☐ changes to ✅) if you want to install operating system updates automatically.

7 Click **Install system data files and security updates** (☐ changes to ✅).

8 Click **Automatically download apps purchased on other Macs** (☐ changes to ✅) if you want to automatically add apps you buy on other Macs using the same Apple ID to your MacBook.

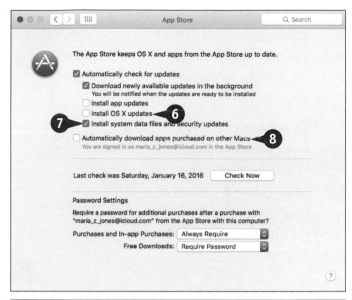

A You can click **Check Now** to check for updates.

9 Click **Purchases and In-app Purchases** (⬍) and then click **Always Require** or **Require After 15 Minutes**, as needed.

Note: For security, choose **Always Require** for both Purchases and In-app Purchases and Free Downloads.

10 Click **Free Downloads** (⬍) and then click **Require Password** or **Save Password**, as needed.

11 Click **Close** (⬤).

System Preferences closes.

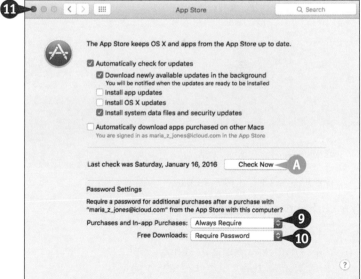

TIP

Which updates should I install?

It is normally a good idea to install all updates to keep your MacBook protected against threats and to make sure you have the latest fixes and upgrades for OS X and your apps. For security, click **Install system data files and security updates** (☐ changes to ✅) to make App Store install these items automatically. You may prefer to install the app updates manually at a time of your choosing.

Back Up Your Files

To enable you to keep your valuable files safe, OS X includes an automatic backup application called Time Machine. Time Machine automatically saves copies of your files to an external drive or an AirPort Time Capsule. You can choose what drive to use, how frequently to back up your files, and what folders to include.

To protect your data, you must back up your files. Time Machine is the most convenient choice because it takes only a few minutes to set up and thereafter runs automatically.

Back Up Your Files

1 If you will use an external drive for Time Machine, connect the drive to your MacBook.

2 Press ⌘+click **System Preferences** (⚙) on the Dock.

The contextual menu appears.

3 Click **Time Machine**.

The System Preferences window opens, showing the Time Machine preferences pane.

4 Click the switch to move it to On.

The Select Disk dialog opens.

5 Click the drive or AirPort Time Capsule you want to use for backup.

A You can click **Encrypt backups** (☐ changes to ☑) to encrypt your backups.

6 Click **Use Disk**.

The Select Disk dialog closes.

B You can click **Show Time Machine in menu bar** (☐ changes to ☑) to give yourself easy access to Time Machine.

7 Click **Options**.

The Options dialog opens.

8 Click **Back up while on battery power** (☐ changes to ☑) if you want your MacBook to perform backups even when it is running on battery power.

9 Click **Notify after old backups are deleted** (☐ changes to ☑) if you want notifications of deletions.

10 Click **Add** (➕).

A dialog opens.

11 Select each drive or folder you want to exclude from backup.

12 Click **Exclude**.

The dialog closes, and Time Machine adds the items to the Exclude These Items from Backups dialog.

13 Click **Save** to close the Options dialog.

14 Click the **System Preferences** menu and click **Quit System Preferences** to close System Preferences.

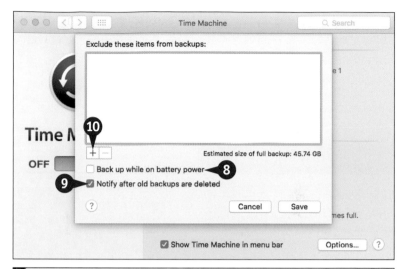

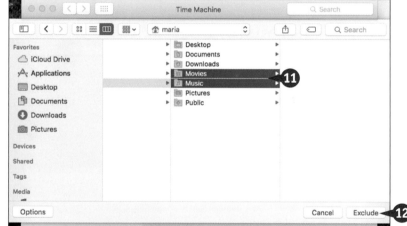

TIPS

What kind of drive should I use for Time Machine?
Depending on your MacBook model, you can connect an external drive to your MacBook by using USB or Thunderbolt. Thunderbolt is faster than USB but is usually expensive. Buy a drive that has at least twice as much storage as your MacBook has, and preferably much more, to ensure that you have plenty of space for backups.

How often does Time Machine back up my files?
Time Machine starts to back up all your files 2 minutes after you set it up. After that, it creates an hourly backup of files that have changed since the last backup. Time Machine consolidates the hourly backups into daily backups, and then consolidates those into weekly backups.

Recover Files from Backup

OS X's Time Machine feature enables you to recover files easily from your backups. So when you delete a file by accident, or discover that a file has become corrupted, you can recover the file from backup by opening Time Machine. You can recover either the latest copy of the file or an earlier copy.

If you still have the current copy of the file that you recover, you can choose whether to overwrite that copy or keep it. Time Machine refers to this copy as the "original" file.

Recover Files from Backup

Note: This section shows you how to recover files using the Finder. To recover old data within Contacts, Calendar, or Mail, open the appropriate app and make it active before giving the Enter Time Machine command.

1 Click **Time Machine** (🕐) on the menu bar.

The Time Machine menu opens.

2 Click **Enter Time Machine**.

Note: If the Time Machine status icon does not appear on the menu bar, click **Launchpad** (🚀) on the Dock, and then click **Time Machine** (⚙) on the Launchpad screen.

Time Machine opens.

A The front window shows your MacBook's drive or drives in their current state.

B Backups of the selected drive or folder appear in the windows behind it, newest at the front.

C The timeline on the right shows how far back in time the available backups go.

3 Click the date or time from which you want to recover the files or folders.

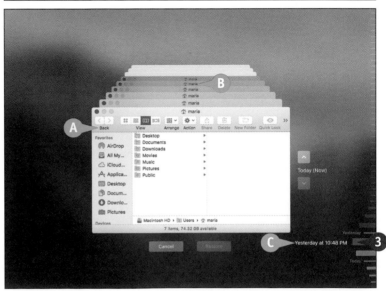

Time Machine brings the backup you chose to the front.

④ Select the item or items you want to restore.

⑤ Click **Restore**.

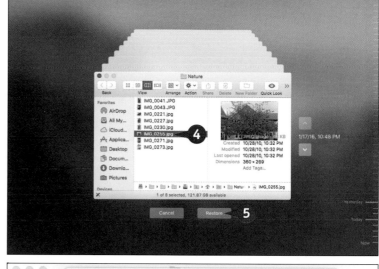

Time Machine disappears.

If restoring a file will overwrite the current version, the Copy dialog opens.

Choose how to handle the file conflict:

Ⓓ Click **Replace** to replace the current file with the older file.

Ⓔ Click **Keep Original** to keep the current file.

Ⓕ Click **Keep Both** to keep both versions of the file. Time Machine adds "(Original)" to the name of the current version.

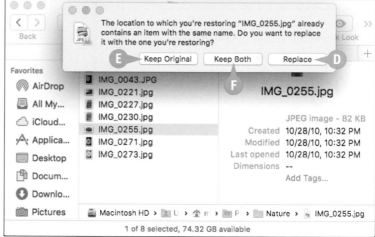

TIPS

What do the arrow buttons to the right of the Finder window in Time Machine do?

The two arrow buttons enable you to navigate among the available backups. Click the upward arrow to move to the previous backup, further in the past. Click the downward arrow to move to the next backup, nearer to the present.

How do I create Time Machine backups manually?

Click **Time Machine** (🕙) on the menu bar and select **Back Up Now**. The menu also enables you to enter Time Machine and open Time Machine preferences.

Recover When OS X Crashes

Normally, OS X runs stably and smoothly, but sometimes the operating system may suffer a crash. Crashes can occur for various reasons, including power fluctuations, bad memory modules, an app having become corrupted, or problems with disk permissions.

Your MacBook may detect that the crash has occurred and display an informational message, but in other cases the MacBook's screen may simply freeze and continue displaying the same information. Normally, you can recover from a crash by turning off your MacBook's power and then turning it on again.

Recover When OS X Crashes

Recover from the Screen Freezing

1 If the pointer shows the "wait" cursor that looks like a spinning beach ball, wait a couple of minutes to see if OS X can recover from the problem. If the pointer has disappeared, go straight to step **2**.

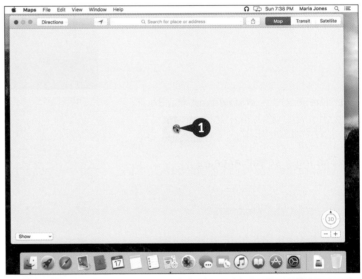

2 To verify that your MacBook is not responding, press keys on the keyboard or move your fingers on the trackpad.

3 Press and hold ⌘+Control and press the MacBook's power button.

4 If the MacBook does not respond to that key combination, press and hold the MacBook's power button for about 4 seconds.

The MacBook turns off.

5 Wait at least 8 seconds, and then press the power button once to restart the MacBook.

Recover from a Detected Crash

When your MacBook detects an OS X crash, it dims the screen and displays a message in the center.

1 Read the message for information.

2 Press and hold the MacBook's power button for about 4 seconds.

The MacBook turns off.

3 Wait at least 8 seconds, and then press the power button once to restart the MacBook.

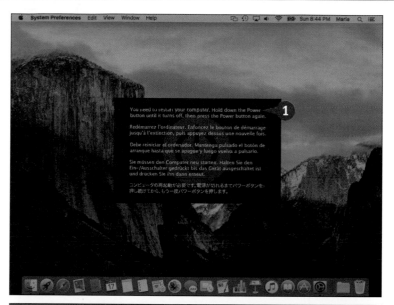

Note: Depending on how your MacBook is configured, OS X may log you in automatically or display the Login dialog.

The login screen appears.

4 Click your username, and then log in to your account as normal.

TIP

How can I avoid crashes?

- Limit the number of apps you run at the same time. When you finish using an app, quit it.
- Keep at least 15 percent of your MacBook's drive free. Click the desktop, click **Go** on the menu bar, and then click **Computer** to open a Finder window showing the Computer folder. Press `Control`+click **Macintosh HD** and click **Get Info**. In the General section, look at the Capacity readout and the Available readout.
- If running a particular app causes your MacBook to crash, uninstall and reinstall that app.

Troubleshoot Corrupt Preference Files

OS X and many apps enable you to set preferences to customize the way they run. Each app stores its configuration in a special file called a *preference file*. Sometimes a preference file becomes corrupted, which may prevent the app from running properly or cause it to crash.

To fix the problem, you delete the preference file. This forces the app to create a new preference file from scratch with default settings. When the app is running properly again, you can choose your custom settings again.

Troubleshoot Corrupt Preference Files

1 Quit the problem app if it is running. Click the app's menu, such as the **Contacts** menu for the Contacts app, and then click the Quit command, such as **Quit Contacts**.

Note: If you cannot quit the app by using its Quit command, force quit it. Press `Option`+click the app's Dock icon and click **Force Quit** on the contextual menu.

2 Click an open space on the desktop.

The Finder becomes active.

3 Click **Go**.

The Go menu opens.

4 Press and hold `Option`.

The Library item appears on the Go menu.

Note: OS X hides the Library item on the Go menu until you press `Option`.

5 Click **Library**.

The contents of the Library folder appear.

6 Click **Preferences**.

The contents of the Preferences folder appear.

7 Click the preference file for the problem application. See the tip in this section for help on identifying the file.

Note: If the application has two or more preference files, move them all to the Trash.

8 Click **Action** (✿ ⌄).

The Action menu opens.

9 Click **Move to Trash**.

OS X moves the file to the Trash.

10 Start the application.

The application creates a new preference file containing default settings.

11 Set preferences in the application. In most applications, click the application's menu and click **Preferences** to open the Preferences window.

The application saves your preferences in the new preference file.

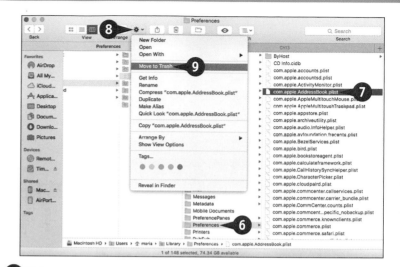

TIP

How do I find the right preference file to delete?

The names of most preference files use the format com.*company*.*application*.plist, where *company* is the manufacturer's name, *application* is the application's name, and .plist is the file extension for a property list file. For example, com.apple.mail.plist is the preference file for the Mail app, and com.microsoft.Excel.plist is the Excel preference file. If you cannot locate the preference file by browsing the Preferences folder, search online to learn the exact name.

Run First Aid from Within OS X

OS X includes automatic tools for fixing minor problems that may occur as your MacBook runs. Normally, the operating system resolves these problems in the background without your involvement.

However, sometimes your MacBook may exhibit disk problems that these automatic tools cannot fix. In such cases, you can run the First Aid tool from within OS X to try to resolve the issue.

Run First Aid from Within OS X

1 Click **Launchpad** (🚀) on the Dock.

The Launchpad screen appears.

2 Press **D**.

Launchpad displays only those items that include a word starting with *D*.

3 Click **Disk Utility**.

Disk Utility opens.

4 Click your MacBook's drive.

The controls for manipulating the drive appear.

5 Click **First Aid**.

The Would You Like to Run First Aid dialog opens.

6 Click **Run**.

Ⓐ Disk Utility searches for problems and resolves any that it can resolve. The process may take several minutes.

7 Click **Show Details** if you want to see details of the repairs.

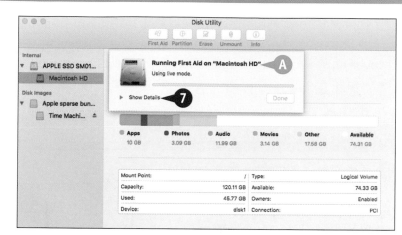

Disk Utility informs you when the First Aid process is complete.

8 Click **Done**.

The dialog closes.

9 Click **Close** (●).

Disk Utility closes.

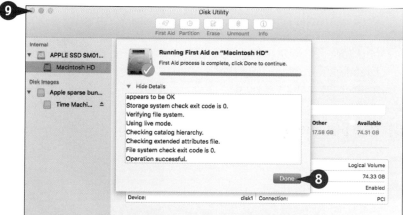

TIPS

For what types of problems would I run First Aid?

Here are three examples. First, your MacBook may not be able to access an external device that worked previously; second, a file you need to open may have become corrupted; and third, you find that apps freeze or quit spontaneously.

What should I do if Disk Utility says my MacBook's disk is about to fail?

Back up all your data immediately using Time Machine, as explained earlier in this chapter. You will then need to replace the disk. Replacing the disk on most MacBook models is a task for trained technicians, but it is worth researching whether your MacBook has a user-replaceable disk.

Run First Aid from OS X Utilities

If your MacBook will not start, you may be able to fix the problem by running First Aid. To do so, you start your MacBook from the recovery partition, which contains tools called OS X Utilities for recovering from problems. OS X Utilities enables you to launch the Disk Utility tool from outside OS X when the operating system is not working.

Run First Aid from OS X Utilities

1 Start your MacBook by pressing the power button.

Note: If your MacBook is running, restart it by clicking **Apple** (🍎) and then pressing Option+clicking **Restart**.

2 At the startup chime, press and hold ⌘+R until the Apple logo appears.

Your MacBook starts from the recovery partition.

The Welcome screen appears.

3 Click the language you want to use.

4 Click **Continue** (→).

The OS X Utilities screen appears.

5 Click **Disk Utility**.

6 Click **Continue**.

The Disk Utility window opens.

7 Click your MacBook's internal drive.

The controls for manipulating the drive appear.

8 Click **First Aid**.

The Would You Like to Run First Aid dialog opens.

9 Click **Run**.

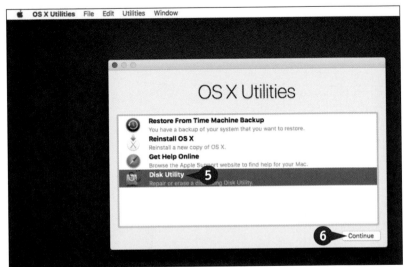

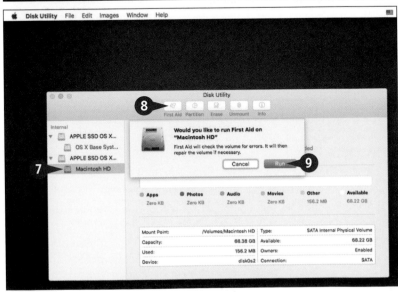

354

Disk Utility analyzes the drive and repairs problems, displaying its progress as it does so.

Disk Utility informs you when the First Aid process is complete.

10 Click **Done**.

The dialog closes.

11 Click **Disk Utility**.

The Disk Utility menu opens.

12 Click **Quit Disk Utility**.

Disk Utility closes, and the Install OS X dialog opens.

13 Click **OS X Utilities**.

The OS X Utilities menu opens.

14 Click **Quit OS X Utilities**.

A confirmation dialog opens.

15 Click **Restart**.

Your MacBook restarts into OS X from the internal drive.

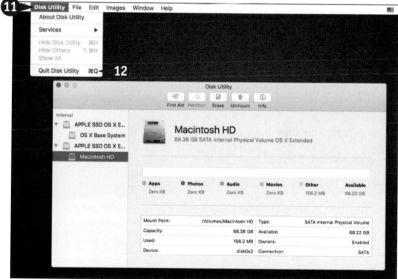

TIP

What do I do if my MacBook cannot start after repairing the drive?
If your MacBook cannot start after repairing the drive, try using a different startup volume. At the startup chime, press and hold ⌘+R. In OS X Utilities, click **Restore From Time Machine Backup** and then click **Continue**. Click **OS X Installer** and click **Quit OS X Installer**. In the Time Machine System Restore dialog that opens, click **Choose Startup Disk**. In the Choose Startup Disk dialog that opens, click the startup volume, and then click **Restart**. Your MacBook starts from the volume you selected.

Reinstall OS X to Solve Severe Problems

If your MacBook suffers severe software damage, OS X may not be able to run. When this happens, you can fix the problem by reinstalling OS X. You may also need to reinstall OS X if your MacBook runs but crashes frequently and you are not able to restore stability by repairing the permissions or repairing the disk.

OS X includes a recovery partition that enables you to begin reinstalling the operating system. Once connected to the Internet, your MacBook can then download the files it needs from Apple's servers and complete the reinstallation.

Reinstall OS X to Solve Severe Problems

1 Press the power button.

2 At the startup chime, press and hold ⌘+R until the Apple logo appears.

Your MacBook starts from the recovery partition.

The Welcome screen appears.

3 Click the language you want to use.

4 Click **Continue** (→).

The OS X Utilities screen appears.

5 Click **Reinstall OS X**.

6 Click **Continue**.

The Install OS X screen appears.

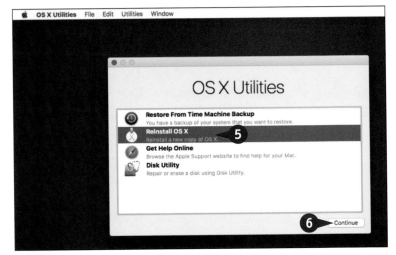

7 Click **Continue**.

A dialog opens telling you your computer's eligibility will be verified with Apple.

8 Click **Continue**.

The Software License Agreement screen appears.

9 Click **Continue**.

A confirmation dialog opens.

10 Click **Agree**.

The screen for selecting the installation disk appears.

11 Click the disk.

12 Click **Install**.

Note: If the Sign In to Download from the App Store dialog opens, type your Apple ID and your password, and then click **Sign In**.

Install OS X begins downloading the components it needs to install OS X.

13 After the reinstallation finishes and your MacBook restarts, log in. You can then access your files as before.

TIP

How do I start the reinstallation if my MacBook is powered on?

If your MacBook is powered on and OS X is responding normally, restart your MacBook by clicking **Apple** (), clicking **Restart**, and then clicking **Restart** in the Are You Sure You Want to Restart Your Computer Now? dialog.

If your MacBook is powered on but OS X is not responding normally, press and hold the power button until the MacBook shuts down. Wait for about 8 seconds, and then press the power button to start your MacBook.

Index

Index